# Contemporary States and Societies

This new series, conceived and designed to meet the needs of today's students, provides lively and accessible introductions to key countries and regions of the world. The authors are all experts with specialist knowledge of the country or region concerned but have been chosen also for their ability to communicate clearly to a non-specialist readership. Each text has been specially commissioned for the series and is structured according to a common format.

*Published:*

Contemporary America
RUSSELL DUNCAN and JOSEPH GODDARD

Contemporary Britain
JOHN McCORMICK

Contemporary China
ALAN HUNTER and JOHN SEXTON

Contemporary Japan
DUNCAN McCARGO

Contemporary Latin America
RONALDO MUNCK

*Forthcoming:*

Contemporary Europe
B. GUY PETERS

Contemporary France
HELEN DRAKE

Contemporary Russia
MATTHEW WYMAN and EDWIN BACON

Contemporary South Africa
ANTHONY BUTLER

*In preparation:*

Contemporary Asia
Contemporary Germany
Contemporary Italy
Contemporary Spain

# Contemporary Britain

# Contemporary Britain

John McCormick

palgrave
macmillan

First published 2003 by
PALGRAVE MACMILLAN
Houndmills, Basingstoke, Hampshire RG21 6XS and
175 Fifth Avenue, New York, N.Y. 10010
Companies and representatives throughout the world

PALGRAVE MACMILLAN is the global academic imprint of the Palgrave Macmillan division of St. Martin's Press, LLC and of Palgrave Macmillan Ltd. Macmillan® is a registered trademark in the United States, United Kingdom and other countries. Palgrave is a registered trademark in the European Union and other countries.

ISBN-13: 978-0-3339-6419-4    hardback
ISBN-10: 0-333-96419-5    hardback
ISBN-13: 978-0-3339-6420-0    paperback
ISBN-10: 0-333-96420-9    paperback

This book is printed on paper suitable for recycling and made from fully managed and sustained forest sources. Logging, pulping and manufacturing processes are expected to conform to the environmental regulations of the country of origin.

A catalogue record for this book is available from the British Library.

Library of Congress Cataloging-in-Publication Data
McCormick, John, 1954–
    Contemporary Britain / John McCormick.
        p. cm. – (Contemporary states and societies)
    Includes bibliographical references (p.) and index.
    ISBN 0-333–96419–5 — ISBN 0–333–96420–9 (pbk.)
    1. Great Britain–Description and travel. I. Title. II. Series.
DA632 .M38 2003
914.1–dc21                                      2003040519

Printed and bound in Great Britain by
4edge Ltd, Hockley. www.4edge.co.uk

# Contents

# List of Illustrations, Maps, Figures, Tables and Boxes

**Illustrations**

## Maps

## Figures

## Tables

## Boxes

# Preface and Acknowledgements

This is a book about Britain, written for anyone looking for a brief and accessible guide to this remarkable country. I am a political scientist, but I have tried to make sure that there is a good balance of coverage on the key dimensions of life in Britain, ranging from its history to its geography, economy, society, culture, and political system. I have tried not to assume any prior knowledge on the part of potential readers, so all the key terms, concepts, names and events are explained.

I was born in Britain, and am still a British citizen, but I have spent most of my life living elsewhere. I was brought up in Kenya, went to boarding school in Britain, attended university in South Africa, and then lived in London from the winter of discontent in early 1979 to the height of Thatcherism in 1986. Since then I have lived in the United States, although I return to Britain at least once every year, spent part of 1999 as a visiting professor at the University of Exeter, and I still follow developments in Britain very closely. All this travelling, and all this observation from afar, has given me an unusual perspective on my home country. This book is particularly coloured by my experiences in the United States, and by the fact that I specialize in comparative politics. Consciously and subconsciously, I see Britain increasingly from the American perspective, which is why the book often makes comparisons with the American experience.

Like others in the *Contemporary States and Societies* series, *Contemporary Britain* is designed to be an introduction. It provides the key facts and figures that are needed to place Britain in its quantitative context with other countries – notably its European neighbours – but it also ties the facts together with explanatory analysis. It is deliberately short and concise, and does not claim to be comprehensive. If it can help its readers better appreciate the key themes and concepts in British political, social and economic life, dispel some of the myths that too often detract from an understanding of the country and its people, and provide some direction for further research, it will have achieved its objectives.

It was my publisher Steven Kennedy who first suggested that I write the book, and he has helped guide its development with his usual good humour and excellent judgement, so it is to him that I owe my primary gratitude. I would also like to thank the anonymous reviewers who made a number of useful suggestions, that either encouraged me to make changes or further to explain my rationale. My thanks and love also to my wife Leanne for taking care of more than her fair share of domestic duties while I was tapping away at the PC, and to our eldest son Ian for providing plenty of diversions. Our second son Stuart was born about half-way through the writing of the book, so I dedicate it to him. By the time he is old enough to read it, Britain will be a different place, but it will give him a snapshot of what his semi-homeland looked like when he was born.

JOHN MCCORMICK

*Note*:  For convenience, the terms 'Britain' and 'British' are used throughout, even though the book is about the United Kingdom.

The author and publishers are grateful to the following for permission to use copyright material: Topham Picturepoint for Illustrations 1.2, 1.3, 2.3, 2.4, 2.5, 3.1, 3.2, 3.3, 4.1, 4.2, 5.1, 5.2, 5.3, 6.1, 6.3, 7.1, 8.1 and 8.2; Hayley Madden for Illustration 7.3; Steven Kennedy for Illustrations 4.3 and 7.2. Illustrations 1.1, 2.1, 2.2 and 6.2 are by the author. Every effort has been made to trace all copyright-holders of third-party materials included in this work, but if any have been inadvertently over-looked the publishers will be pleased to make the necessary arrangement at the first opportunity.

# List of Abbreviations

BBC     British Broadcasting Corporation
EEC     European Economic Community
EFTA     European Free Trade Association
EU     European Union
GDP     gross domestic product
IRA     Irish Republican Army
MP     Member of Parliament
NATO     North Atlantic Treaty Organization
PR     proportional representation
RUC     Royal Ulster Constabulary
SNP     Scottish National Party
UK     United Kingdom

*Note*: Figures in pounds sterling in the text have been given equivalents in euros and US dollars, based on an exchange rate of £1 = €1.50 and $1.50.

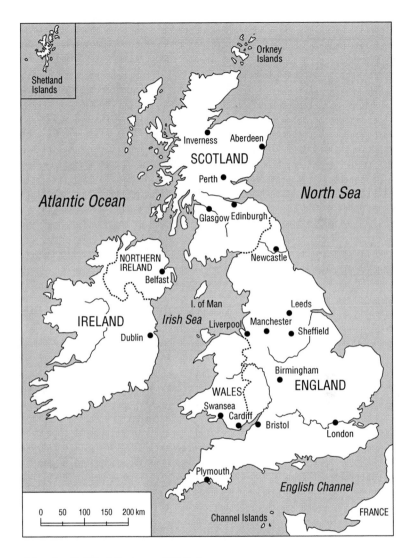

**Map 1  Political features of Britain**

# Introduction

Britain is one of the most influential countries in world history. Out of that small cluster of islands off the northwest coast of the European continent came three movements that quite literally changed the world: the industrial revolution, the parliamentary system of government, and the English language. It is no exaggeration to say that everyone in the world has been affected, directly or indirectly, by the impact of these contributions to global development. It is impossible to talk of economic change without referring back to the inventions that spawned the industrial revolution, and the impact of the writings of Adam Smith and John Maynard Keynes on our ideas about capitalism. It is impossible to talk of political change without referring back to the development of the British democratic model, and the impact of the writings of Thomas Hobbes, John Locke, John Stuart Mill, and others. And it would be difficult for the citizens of different countries to exchange their views without the help of English, which is the global language of business, communications, diplomacy and – increasingly – everyday conversation.

For these reasons alone, Britain is an important subject of study. But the motives for trying to understand Britain go further. Life is all about change, and few societies have seen such dramatic changes in the last 200 years. It has one of the oldest continuously functioning political systems in the world, yet the character of that system has been altered in response to philosophical and popular pressures. It once had the world's biggest economy, yet has found itself having to adapt to a post-imperial economic environment coloured by increased competition from the United States, Japan and its bigger European neighbours. It has a long history and strong sense of national identity, yet today finds itself being squeezed between two important pressures that are redefining the meaning of the term 'British': a rebirth of Scottish, Welsh, Irish and even English nationalism, and pressures for greater integration within the European Union.

If there is a single identifying theme that runs through this book,

1

and that defines the nature of contemporary Britain, then it is change and the implications of that change. The new realities that face the British in the twenty-first century can be found everywhere:

- in the growing racial, religious, national and cultural diversity of British society
- in the redefinition of the class system that for so long determined how Britons related to one another, but which has been diluted by improved education, the rise of the middle class, the growth of the consumer society, and a new level of affluence that has allowed greater social mobility
- in demographic shifts as the British live longer, in changes to the definition of the family, and in the move away from the old assumptions of the welfare state towards a stakeholder society in which benefits are determined by the extent to which individuals have played by the rules
- in growing demands for a written constitution, in the changing balance of power among government institutions as the executive becomes more powerful and Europe becomes more influential, in the pressures for civil service reform, and in the changing relationship between local and national government
- in the changing attitudes of voters towards government, in the questions raised about the nature of the electoral system and the balance among the major political parties, and in the rise of alternative channels by which citizens can express their views on politics
- in the dramatic technological developments taking place in the mass media, particularly television (where the three old terrestrial channels have been joined by dozens of satellite and cable options) and the internet (which has revolutionized the way that people communicate)
- in shifts in the direction of economic policy, from the interventionist approaches of the postwar years to the free-market approaches introduced in the 1980s by the Thatcher government
- in the redefinition of Britain's place in the world as it has moved from being a global and imperial power to a regional and European power, and as it asks itself questions about the meaning of 'Britishness' and how it should relate to its partners in the European Union.

In the chapters that follow, the causes and effects of these changes will be examined, and an attempt made to understand how and why contemporary Britain is different. Particular attention will be paid to the debate over the decline of Britain. Most notably in the 1960s and 1970s, academics, journalists, political leaders and citizens bemoaned the loss of Britain's preeminent economic position in the world, argued that the British political system was failing to meet the needs of the citizens of a modern democracy, and saw growing social problems in everything from lowered educational standards to decaying public services, reductions in the quality of law and order, environmental problems, and even the failure of British national sports teams to win competitions. Studies of postwar Britain were peppered with words such as 'angst', 'melancholy' and 'discontent'.

One of the arguments made in this book is that the issue of the decline of Britain is overstated. Adjustments were certainly needed after the war and the end of empire, and it was inevitable that a country which had been a dominant military and imperial power, the richest country in the world, the biggest creditor nation in the world, and the self-appointed standard-bearer for Western culture and civilization should undergo some reflection as its global status changed. However, the doomsayers failed to notice that much of the change was relative, and that in absolute terms the British - in the phrase of Prime Minister Harold Macmillan - had never had it so good. Its economy has continued to grow and is today one of the freest in the world, and the biggest in Western Europe in per capita terms. Its political system has been reformed in response to the changing needs of a post-industrial society. And in social terms, the British live longer and healthier lives, they have more access to education – particularly higher education – than ever before, they are on average much wealthier, their environment is cleaner, and their individual rights are better protected than at any time in their history.

Another of the arguments made in this book is that Britain has finally begun to realize that it is a European country, and that its future lies in greater cooperation with its neighbours on the continent. There are still many Britons who argue – like Winston Churchill – that Britain is with Europe but not of it, but this view is changing as the generations change. Britain was slow to wake up to the possibilities of European integration, and since becoming part of what is now the European Union in 1973 it has developed an unfortunate – but not always deserved – reputation as a reluctant European. But it has benefited significantly from the single European market, Thatcherite economic policies have had a dramatic impact on the policies of other EU states, and – along with France – it is the dominating actor in any attempts made by the Europeans to develop a common foreign and defence policy. Britain cannot ignore the EU, and the EU cannot ignore Britain. The next big step in the continuing relationship is when – rather than if – Britain will adopt the single European currency, the euro. These and other critical issues are addressed in the eight chapters that follow.

*Table* 0.1   Quick Facts about Britain

| | |
|---|---|
| Official name: | United Kingdom of Great Britain and Northern Ireland |
| Capital: | London |
| Area: | 244,103 sq km (94,249 square miles) |
| Population: | 59.76 million |
| Population density: | 246 per sq. km (650 per square mile) |
| Population growth rate: | 0.3% |
| Languages: | Overwhelmingly English, with some regional languages (Welsh, Gaelic) |
| Religions: | Predominantly Anglican, with Catholic and Presbyterian minorities |
| GDP (2001): | $1406 billion |
| Per capita GNP: | $24,230 |
| Distribution of GNP: | 70% services, 29% industry, 1% agriculture |
| Urban population: | 89% |
| Literacy: | 99% |
| Infant mortality: | 6 per 1000 live births |
| Life expectancy: | 77.3 years |
| Government type: | Parliamentary democracy with a constitutional monarchy |
| Administration: | Unitary |
| Executive: | Prime minister and cabinet |
| Legislature: | Bicameral Houses of Parliament; House of Lords (currently undergoing structural reform) and House of Commons (659 members). Lords are appointed; MPs are elected to renewable five-year terms |
| Party structure: | Multiparty, with two dominant parties (Labour and Conservatives) and several smaller parties |
| Judiciary: | No separate judiciary. House of Lords is highest court of appeal |
| Head of state: | Queen Elizabeth II (1952–   ) |
| Head of government: | Tony Blair (1997–   ) |

Chapter 1 provides the historical background. Beginning with the early invasions from the continent, it covers the rise and fall of feudalism, the rise of the United Kingdom, political and economic changes, and the rise and fall of the Empire. It focuses in particular on postwar history, looking at key political, economic and cultural developments, notably the impact of Thatcherism and membership of the European Union.

Chapter 2 deals with the geography and resources of Britain – both natural and human. The first half covers such issues as climate and the environment, and the second half looks at the people of Britain, at recent demographic changes, and at two important divisions: nationalism and race.

Chapter 3 focuses on British society, beginning with the class system, then looking at the changing structure of the family. It examines the welfare system, the structure and state of British education, and ends with a discussion of the performance of the criminal justice system in maintaining law and order.

Chapter 4 examines the British system of government and its major institutions: the monarchy, the prime minister and cabinet, Parliament, the judiciary, the bureaucracy, and local government. It explains how they relate to each other and their relative influence over the political process, and provides a critical assessment of the nature of British democracy.

Chapter 5 looks at civil society in Britain, beginning with a discussion of political culture, then looking at how Britons relate to government and politics through elections, political parties, interest groups and the media.

Chapter 6 turns to the structure and performance of the British economy. It assesses economic developments since 1945, contrasting the boom years of the 1950s with the crises of the 1970s, examining the changes wrought by Thatcherism, and assessing the return of the the renewed economic successes of the 1990s. It looks also at the place of Britain in the global trading system and in the European Union.

Chapter 7 provides a survey of British culture, beginning with a general outline and an analysis of the meaning of 'Britishness'. It then examines the state of the arts in Britain, with an emphasis on the theatre, film, television and popular music. It looks at how the British spend their spare time, and ends with an examination of the role of sports and religion in national life.

Chapter 8 looks at Britain's place in the world. It examines key relationships, including those with the Commonwealth, within the

Atlantic alliance, and with the United States. It then looks at Britain's troubled relationship with the rest of the European Union, and finishes with an assessment of the changing status of the British military.

# 1

# The Historical Context

Britain is a European country, and yet the British have long considered themselves somehow different from their neighbours on the European mainland. Their thinking is driven mainly by the physical isolation of the British Isles from the continent. The English Channel – 35 km (22 miles) at its narrowest – has not only helped protect Britain from many of the wars and invasions that have regularly changed the balance of power in continental Europe, but has also ensured that Britain's historical development has been different in many important respects.

Despite the pressures of integration that have come since 1973 with membership of the European Union, many Britons – especially older ones – still talk of Europe and Europeans as 'over there', and as being something quite separate from the British experience. Indeed, many know more about the history and culture of other English-speaking countries – such as the United States and Australia – than they do about their closest neighbours. Of course, the idea that Britain is somehow exclusive or unique is a fallacy; Britain may not have been invaded since 1066, but events on the continent have had a profound effect on British politics, economics and society, and vice versa. Britain is just as much a part of the European experience as France or Germany.

This chapter provides a brief survey of British history. Beginning with the Roman era, it works through the Saxon, Viking and Norman invasions; the rise and fall of feudalism; the break with the Catholic church; the changing relationship among England, Scotland, Wales and Ireland; the emergence of the parliamentary system; the rise of the British Empire; the agricultural and industrial revolutions; and the pressures leading up to two world wars. The chapter then looks in

7

more detail at developments since 1945, assessing the construction of the welfare state, the end of empire, the cultural changes of the 1960s, the economic problems of the 1970s, the advent and effects of Thatcherism, the impact of membership of the European Union, Britain's changing view of itself, and its changing relationship with the world.

The picture it paints is one of constant change. Firstly, the relationship between members of the United Kingdom – England, Scotland, Wales and Northern Ireland – has ebbed and flowed, and is today ebbing once again as powers are devolved from London to regional assemblies. Secondly, the nature of the British system of government has changed as the balance of power among the major institutions has evolved. The adjustments continue today as the powers of the prime minister are redefined, as the role of Parliament changes, and as the electoral system is restructured. Thirdly, Britain's economic fortunes have waxed and waned, from a time when it stood astride the world, to postwar decline and crisis, to reinvigoration as the state has retreated from the marketplace. Finally, Britain's place in the world has changed, from being a European to a global power, and now a leading actor in the European Union.

## The Emergence of the British state

When the Romans under Julius Caesar first arrived in Britain in 55-54 BC, they found it peopled by Celts, who had themselves arrived there between 800 and 200 BC, the latest in a long line of immigrants from Northern Europe and the Iberian peninsula. The Celts – ancestors of the Irish, Scots and Welsh of today – were not so much a race as a disparate group of peoples who shared a language, religious patterns, and social ideals. When the Romans came again in AD 43 (this time to stay), they occupied most of what is now England, Wales and southern Scotland, and the Celts were pushed west and north. England developed a social and political system significantly different from that of the rest of the British Isles – it had roads, planned towns, a centralized economy, a thriving commercial system, and for 300 years was mainly at peace. Signs of the Roman occupation are still evident, from the stretches of straight road that can be found in parts of England, to many place names, including London and any of the cities with the Latin termination for camp (*castra*), such as Winchester, Lancaster and Worcester.

The departure of the Romans at the beginning of the fifth century left behind a political vacuum into which later moved several more waves of invaders, notably Germanic tribes such as the Angles and the Saxons, who arrived in about 500–700. The Irish Celts were converted to Christianity in the early fifth century by St Patrick, but the arrival in 597 of the monk Augustine – on a mission from the Pope in Rome – brought a different form of Christianity to England; at a conference of bishops in 664 (the Synod of Whitby), it was decided to adopt the Roman rather than the Celtic form.

In the eighth century the first Viking and Danish raids took place, turning into a full-scale invasion by the mid-ninth century. By the time of the last successful invasion of Britain – by William, Duke of Normandy, in 1066 – the British Isles had become divided into two zones, one predominantly Celtic and the other predominantly Anglo-Saxon. Although England was now united under the Normans, the cultural and religious divisions persisted, England being distinguished from the Celtic regions by the development of a more stable and centralized system of government.

Like the rest of Europe, England was a feudal society. Sovereign power lay in the hands of the monarch, who owned the land on which aristocrats lived, buying access to that land with military service and using landless peasants to do the work. Monarchs also ruled by divine right, arguing that they were answerable only to God, exercised religious power on earth, and might even have been gods themselves. The position of the monarch began to change in 1215 when the despotic King John was forced by his barons – with the support of the Church – to sign the contract known as Magna Carta. Under its terms he was obliged to consult with his aristocrats before levying taxes, and to agree that he could not arbitrarily arrest or seize property from his subjects. Magna Carta did little more than confirm the privileges of the Church and the barons, but it was the first step in the reduction of monarchical power.

A second step was taken in 1265 when the Norman baron Simon de Montfort – exploiting the political weaknesses of King Henry III (1216–72) – convened the first British Parliament. It was unelected, and met only sporadically, but it included both commoners and aristocrats, monarchs came to rely on it for political support, and it was an alternative focus of political power. Magna Carta and the creation of Parliament by no means moved power into the hands of the ordinary person, but these were the first steps in the long and complex process by which democracy came to Britain.

Meanwhile, the supremacy of England over the British Isles was established as wars and attrition led slowly to the incorporation of its Celtic neighbours, and as nationalism superseded feudalism as the driving force in politics. The Normans conquered Wales in 1285 but did not fare so well in Scotland – they invaded in 1296, meeting resistance first from William Wallace, and then from Robert Bruce who routed the invaders at the Battle of Bannockburn in 1314. The Normans now looked to expand outside the British Isles, setting off the Hundred Years War against France in 1337. Revenue from estates was not enough to pay for the war, so the king – Edward III – looked to Parliament for help. It began meeting more regularly and the House of Commons began sitting separately from the barons. The war started well, with notable victories at Crecy and Poitiers, but then the Black Death in 1348–49 halved the population of England. Another victory over the French at Agincourt in 1415 marked the end of the war for the English, who now became diverted by their own War of the Roses (1455–85), in which two factions – the Lancastrians and the Yorkists – fought for control of the throne. The Lancastrians prevailed at the Battle of Bosworth in 1485, and King Henry VII became the first member of the Tudor dynasty.

To the ethnic, cultural and linguistic divisions of Britain, religious differences were added when King Henry VIII – aiming to curb the power of the church – dissolved England's ties with the Roman Catholic church in 1534 and created the Church of England. (This is why the Scots and the Irish today are mainly Catholic and Presbyterian, while the English are mainly Protestant.)

The break with the Catholic church was followed by a series of acts of Parliament in 1536–42 by which Wales was formally integrated with England. The reign of Elizabeth I (1558–1603) saw England developing new power, prosperity and cultural wealth. Sir Francis Drake set off on his voyages of discovery around the world, William Shakespeare and Christopher Marlowe wrote their plays, Ben Jonson and John Donne wrote their poems, and Thomas Morley and William Byrd wrote their music. When Elizabeth's successor James I came to the throne, Scotland and England shared a common monarch, and in 1707 a political union took place, creating Great Britain. Meanwhile, Ireland was being steadily and violently subjugated, beginning with attacks in the thirteenth century and eventually making it to all intents and purposes part of the British state by the late eighteenth century.

The dominant influence in politics continued to be the struggle for power between the monarchy and Parliament, which finally boiled

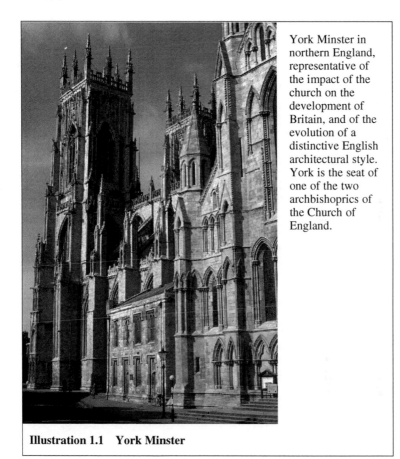

York Minster in northern England, representative of the impact of the church on the development of Britain, and of the evolution of a distinctive English architectural style. York is the seat of one of the two archbishoprics of the Church of England.

**Illustration 1.1    York Minster**

over in 1642 with the outbreak of a civil war between the two sides. This led to the execution in 1649 of King Charles I, and the declaration of a brief republic (1649–60) under the military dictatorship of Oliver Cromwell. When King James II (1685–88) tried to win back the divine right of monarchs, and to rule without Parliament, he was forced to flee the country in what was called the Glorious Revolution. His place was taken by William of Orange, who – as William III – became Britain's first constitutional monarch. In 1689 a Bill of Rights was drawn up which confirmed the supremacy of Parliament over the monarch.

The definition of 'England' was also tightened by its success in fighting off invasion, and by its critical interventions in struggles for power on the European continent, which altered the course of English, British and European history. There had been the defeat of the Spanish Armada in 1588, the defeat of an Irish-French army at the Battle of the Boyne in 1690, and then England intervened in the War of the Spanish Succession: the Duke of Marlborough waged 10 campaigns, won every battle he fought, and – at Blenheim in 1704 – ended 40 years of French military dominance on the continent. Attempted uprisings in Scotland in 1715 and 1745 failed. A century later, Britain made decisive interventions in the war against Napoleon. The French navy was defeated in 1805 at Trafalgar, and Napoleon's aspirations for European domination were finally brought to an end in 1815 at the battle of Waterloo.

With its military and political dominance under construction, Britain also underwent a social and economic revolution. In 1800, the vast majority of the population was poor and lived off the land, while barely 10 per cent lived in towns and cities. This was all to change with the rise of industry (see Box 1.1), which led to the expansion of towns and cities and the creation of factories, such that by 1900 the population had not only tripled in size – to about 38 million – but had also become more urbanized. Less than a quarter of the population lived in the rural areas, and more than 40 per cent lived in large towns and cities, usually in overcrowded and unsanitary conditions. By 1900 industrial workers outnumbered rural workers by about nine to one.

With its industry growing, Britain's priority was to find new markets and sources of raw materials, and to build on its competitive advantage over its European rivals, particularly Spain, France and the Netherlands. After centuries during which Europeans had immigrated into Britain, the British began to emigrate to Europe and further afield. England's acquisitive impulses dated back to the earliest attempts to subjugate the Scots, the Welsh and the Irish, and to the expansion of English control over parts of France during the reigns of Henry II (1154–89), Edward II (1307–27) and Henry V (1413–22). In 1583 the first English colony in the new world was established at Newfoundland, and the settlement of North America began with the foundation in 1607 of Virginia.

The defeat of the French at Quebec in 1759 preceded the Peace of Paris in 1763 by which France ceded Canada and all its territory west of the original 13 English colonies to Britain. Robert Clive's victory at the Battle of Plassey in 1759 gave Britain direct or indirect control over much of India, and in 1770 Captain James Cook landed at

**Box 1.1   The Industrial Revolution**

Alongside all the political changes taking place in Britain in the eighteenth century, there were economic developments that led to changes in the structure of British society. Organized agriculture had taken root with the Saxons, who cleared forests, introduced new methods of farming, and established the open-field system that was to remain in place until the late eighteenth century. The enclosure movement – begun in Tudor times – saw landowners gradually consolidating their property, clearing wasteland, reducing common pasture and woodland, and denying peasants access to land. The peasantry began to shrink as small landowners were squeezed out by large estates.

Meanwhile, changes began to take place in the coal mining industry, as extraction methods improved, allowing a 300 per cent increase in production during the eighteenth century alone. Manufacturing industries grew, and Britain became part of the trading system that brought together communities across Europe, and encouraged immigration, emigration, and the transfer of new technologies. New and more efficient processes for smelting iron and making steel were developed by Abraham Darby and others, which sparked the beginning of the industrial revolution. Weaving and spinning were improved by the flying shuttle (John Kay, 1733), the spinning jenny (James Hargreaves, 1765), and the water frame (Richard Arkwright, 1767). The steam engine was invented by James Watt (1769), George Stephenson developed the first railway engine (1829), industry was mechanized, and large-scale business enterprises emerged.

These technological changes brought about improvements in transport. Major roads, previously badly maintained by local parishes, were taken over by private companies, and engineers such as Robert Macadam and Thomas Telford developed new methods of building roads with harder surfaces and better drainage. The introduction of the railway made it possible to move people and goods more quickly and in greater quantities, and huge new fortunes were made by entrepreneurs. Commerce and markets grew, and Britain was forged into the world's first and most powerful industrial state. By the mid-nineteenth century it had become the 'workshop of the world', producing two-thirds of the world's coal, half its steel, half its cotton goods, and virtually all its machine tools.

Botany Bay on the newly-discovered east coast of Australia. The key to Britain's power was its navy, which won domination over its European challengers, and – in order to be maintained – demanded the development of a network of supply stations around the world. The loss of the 13 American colonies in 1781 may have dampened enthusiasm for colonialism, but the British Empire continued to widen and deepen, and it was eventually to include Canada, Australia, New Zealand, parts of West Africa, most of southern and eastern Africa, many Caribbean and Pacific islands, the Asian subcontinent, and parts of Southeast Asia.

At its height during the late Victorian era, the empire included about a quarter of the world's population. This not only meant political power for Britain, but also economic power. Britain required that all trade with its colonies was conducted using British ships, and that the colonies could buy manufactured goods only from Britain. Thus, goods imported into Britain were often reexported to the continent at a profit, and British ports began doing considerable trade with their colonial counterparts. When the Great Exhibition was held in London in 1851, it confirmed that Britain led the world in almost every field of human endeavour (for details, see Roberts and Roberts, 2002, chapter 23).

Meanwhile, changes came to the political system as the shifting balance of powers between the monarch and Parliament continued. George I (1714–27) had little interest in politics, so Parliament became more influential, and when Robert Walpole became the King's First Minister in 1721, he had so much power and independence that he was later acclaimed as Britain's first prime minister (although it was under William Pitt the Younger (1783–1801, 1804–06) that the office really took form). Parliament was still dominated by aristocrats representing the so-called 'rotten boroughs': mainly rural areas, many of which had only a handful of voters, and in some of which a seat in Parliament could be bought. The House of Lords was made up of unelected aristocrats, while the House of Commons was elected by only a small fraction of the population, in contests that were subject to bribery, fraud and intimidation. Members of Parliament were not paid, so the Commons came to be dominated by wealthy merchants and landowners.

The new middle class of industrialists and entrepreneurs found this unacceptable, and the pressure for change grew. The Great Reform Act of 1832 was followed by more changes during the later nineteenth and early twentieth centuries, which had the effect of transforming Parliament:

- Corrupt electoral districts were eliminated
- The vote was extended to the wealthy and upper middle class
- Secret voting was introduced

- Mass-membership political parties emerged
- Single-member parliamentary districts were created
- The aristocratic House of Lords lost most of its remaining powers
- The vote was extended to women.

The introduction of pensions and national insurance in 1908–11 greatly increased government spending, and thus the need to generate revenue. At first much came from duties on selected agricultural imports, but increasingly it came from direct taxes, particularly on income. Then came the First World War (1914–18), the first step in a massive transformation of government, society, the economy, and of Britain's place in the global system. The cream of a generation of young Britons died in one of the most brutal and mismanaged conflicts in the history of warfare: more than 800,000 were killed or went missing, and 1.4 million were injured. After the war, alternative political ideologies grew in the face of disillusionment with the old options (see Marwick, 2000, chapter 2), women finally won the right to vote, and labour disputes became more common, peaking with the General Strike of 1926.

Nationalist movements had meanwhile begun to emerge in Ireland, India and other parts of the empire. Events in Ireland had the most immediate impact, beginning with calls in the 1880s for home rule. These were accepted in 1914, but delayed by the outbreak of war. Impatient revolutionaries staged the Easter Rebellion of 1916, which failed, and might have had no lasting impact were it not for the aggressive British response, beginning with the execution of 15 rebel leaders. A struggle for independence broke out in 1918, leading to a peace treaty in December 1921 under which Ireland was partitioned the following year; the 26 southern (and predominantly Catholic) counties became the independent Irish Free State, while the six northern (and predominantly Protestant) counties remained part of the United Kingdom. (Ireland left the Commonwealth and became a republic in 1949.)

The economic slump that followed the Wall Street crash of October 1929 brought widespread unemployment, and emphasized the impact of growing economic competition from Japan, Germany and other rising powers. The United States and the Soviet Union began their emergence as economic and military superpowers, a transition that was confirmed by the Second World War. Britain entered the war in September 1939 as the world's biggest creditor nation, but emerged six years later as one of the world's biggest debtor nations. Its

*Table* 1.1   Some key dates in British history

| | |
|---|---|
| 1066 | Norman conquest |
| 1215 | Magna Carta signed |
| 1265 | Parliament founded |
| 1534 | Creation of the Church of England |
| 1536–42 | Union with Wales |
| 1642–49 | Civil war leads to the deposition of the monarchy |
| 1649–60 | Cromwell's republic ends with restoration of the monarchy |
| 1707 | Union with Scotland |
| 1801 | Legislative union with Ireland |
| 1832 | Great Reform Act |
| 1914–18 | First World War |
| 1918 | Women over age 30 given the right to vote |
| 1922 | Irish independence |
| 1928 | All women given the right to vote |
| 1939–45 | Second World War |
| 1947 | Independence of India and Pakistan |
| 1952 | Queen Elizabeth succeeds to the throne |
| 1957–70 | Independence of most of Britain's colonies |
| 1973 | Britain joins the European Economic Community |
| 1979 | Margaret Thatcher wins first of three elections |
| 1982 | War with Argentina over the Falklands (Malvinas) |
| 1991 | British forces take part in Gulf War |
| 1994 | Opening of Channel Tunnel connecting Britain and France |
| 1996 | Crisis over mad cow disease reaches its peak |
| 1997 | (May) Tony Blair elected prime minister; (August) death of Diana, Princess of Wales; (September) referendums in Scotland and Wales approve regional assemblies |
| 1998 | (April) peace agreement signed in Northern Ireland and approved by public referendum |
| 1999 | (March–April) Britain joins NATO attacks on Serbia; (May) first elections to Scottish and Welsh assemblies; (November) Northern Ireland government meets |
| 2001 | (February) outbreak of foot-and-mouth disease decimates cattle, sheep and pig herds; (September) more than 250 Britons killed in terrorist attacks in New York and Washington DC; (November) British troops sent to Afghanistan in support of US military attacks on Taliban |
| 2002 | (June) Queen Elizabeth celebrates golden jubilee |
| 2003 | (March) Britain takes part in US-led invasion of Iraq |

wartime record was heroic: it stood virtually alone in the fight against Nazi Germany between 1939 and 1941, fought off preparations for a German invasion during the Battle of Britain in 1940, withstood the bombing of its major cities, scored the first major defeat over German forces at El Alamein in the North African desert in October 1942, and

**Illustration 1.2    Churchill and the troops**

Prime Minister Winston Churchill meets with British troops in Normandy following the D-Day landings in 1944. Churchill symbolized Britain's resistance to Nazism, which contributed in turn to the widely held view that Britain was 'with Europe but not of it'.

then played the leading role alongside the United States in invading the continent in June 1944 and finally defeating the Germans. But its economy was devastated, its political influence diminished, its export earnings and merchant shipping fleet halved, and many of its colonies were agitating for independence.

## Postwar Adjustment, 1945–79

Within weeks of the end of the war in Europe in May 1945, voters went to the polls in a general election at which the character of postwar Britain would be decided. It was widely assumed that Winston Churchill – prime minister since 1940 in a government of national unity, and the hero of Britain's wartime resistance – would be rewarded by being elected to lead a new government in his own right. Quite the opposite happened, and the result came as a shock to many inside and outside the country: a convincing mandate for the socialist Labour Party, which was voted into power in its own right for the first time, winning 393 seats in Parliament to the 213 won by the Conservatives.

What brought the change? Many explanations were offered, including criticism of the leadership of the prewar Conservative Party – which had been the largest party in Parliament for 18 years and held a majority for 16 years – during a time of poverty, unemployment, and great social and economic inequalities. It had shown its lack of sympathy for working people by breaking strikes, fighting with trade unions, and paying too little attention to education. Furthermore, the government of Neville Chamberlain (1937–40) had tried to appease the Nazis and had waited too long to begin preparing Britain for the war. When war came, the experience had brought the British closer together, obliging them to share the sacrifices of conscription, rationing and austerity, blurring class differences, and convincing many that government intervention could be helpful and useful. Finally, Labour politicians had served the country well during the war, managing home affairs and removing doubts that socialists could govern effectively and fairly (Roberts and Roberts, 2002: 809).

The new Labour government set out to put into practice its vision of a new society and a 'land fit for heroes'. Much of its thinking was prompted by the findings of a 1942 government report authored by William Beveridge, an advisor to Winston Churchill. Warning of the dangers of want, ignorance and poverty, Beveridge had recommended the introduction after the war of a universal social security system, a national health service, and policies aimed at preventing mass unemployment. His report was followed in 1944 by an Act of Parliament providing universal free education to age 15. Now, under the leadership of Prime Minister Clement Attlee, the new Labour government embarked on a programme based on three foundations:

● Completion of the welfare state. Various welfare provisions had existed long before the war – pensions had been introduced in 1908 and national health and unemployment insurance in 1911 – but Labour greatly expanded the reach of government assistance. The National Insurance Act of 1946 provided pensions for the retired, payments to the ill and the unemployed, and grants to mothers and widows. Two years later, the National Health Service was created, providing free medical and dental care for everyone. The government also responded to the shortage in housing brought on by wartime destruction. Existing houses were repaired, new houses were built, and prefabricated temporary housing was provided to ease the shortage.

- The development of a planned economy that would prevent depressions and end unemployment. Labour became actively involved in directing economic activity using monetary and fiscal controls. It altered interest rates to control investment flows, ran budget deficits to pay for its programmes, discouraged consumption by taxing luxuries and controlling imports, and took action to deal with Britain's financial crisis, including the imposition of austerity measures.
- Public ownership of key services. The government nationalized about one-fifth of British industry, including the coal, gas, electricity, iron and steel industries, the railways, the Bank of England, civil aviation, and the road transport system.

The immediate postwar years were ones of continued austerity as the country tried to recover from the war, to stabilize its economy, and to build homes and create new jobs for its citizens. Hopes for a rapid return to a peacetime quality of living were dashed, and criticisms of Labour began to build: nationalized industries were seen as inefficient and the welfare state as too expensive. At the 1951 general election, slightly more people voted for Labour than for the Conservatives, but the structure of the electoral system (see Chapter 5) meant that the Conservatives were returned to power with a small majority, under the leadership of Winston Churchill. However, he left intact most of the changes made by Labour, and British politics in the 1950s came to be driven by a consensus that whether the Conservatives or Labour were in power, they would maintain the welfare system and a mixed economy with a view to sustaining full employment. (There are critics of the consensus thesis, however, who argue that there was much more disagreement over policy than most analysts suggest – see, for example, Kerr, 1999.)

Another of the legacies of the postwar Labour government was decolonization. Before the war, Britain had been able to maintain and justify the military commitment that was a necessary part of the maintenance of its empire. However, it had already begun redefining its relationship with India, the 'jewel in the crown' of the empire. The 1935 Government of India Act gave India a large measure of self-government, but nationalist pressures continued to grow under the leadership of Mahatma Gandhi, who demanded complete independence. Britain found the economic costs of empire increasingly difficult to bear, and there was growing pressure for decolonization from the new United Nations, from a segment of the Labour government, and from nationalist movements within many British colonies. The first and biggest step was taken in August 1947 when India became independent, opting to split itself into a predominantly Hindu republic of India and a predominantly Muslim republic of Pakistan, itself divided into two separate blocks of territory. The following year the British mandate over Palestine – which had begun in 1918 – ended with the creation of Israel, and the early 1950s saw the beginning of negotiations that would lead to the independence of most of Britain's remaining African and Asian colonies; the breakthrough for Africa came in March 1957 with the independence of the Gold Coast, now Ghana.

Meanwhile, the domestic economy was recovering, and Britain began to enjoy the same kind of economic affluence then coming to much of the industrialized world. Wartime rationing ended, worker's wages increased, agricultural production grew by 160 per cent between 1945 and 1957, Britain's share of the world export market returned to prewar levels (nearly 25 per cent of world exports), mass consumption took off as middle class Britons bought new cars and consumer goods, industrial output and gross domestic product grew, and inflation and unemployment remained low. In 1957, Conservative Prime Minister Harold Macmillan made his famous declaration that the British had 'never had it so good'.

However, while the British economy prospered and grew, it did not grow as quickly as those of many other industrialized countries, notably the United States, Japan and Germany. Britain also found its relative influence in the world beginning to decline. The change can be blamed most obviously on the end of empire, but it was also brought on by the costs of the war, handicaps posed to industrial relations by class divisions, an education system that was prejudiced against business as a career, low levels of mobility within the labour force, inadequate investments in industry and in research and development, and high levels of government involvement in production and employment (Jones and Kavanagh, 1998: 179–85). (See also Box 1.2 on the Suez crisis).

Where Britain had once been a global actor, it now began to think more about its relationship with its European neighbours. During and after the war, Winston Churchill had made a number of suggestions in favour of regional integration, noting in a speech at the University of Zurich in 1946 his belief in the need for a 'United States of

Europe'. He made clear, however, that this initiative should revolve around France and West Germany, and that Britain was 'with Europe but not of it. We are interested and associated, but not absorbed' (Zurcher, 1958: 6). This view was widely supported, so that when six continental nations led by France and West Germany created an experimental European Coal and Steel Community in 1952, Britain opted not to join. Similarly, it opted not to join the European Economic Community (EEC) launched in January 1958, instead preferring to create its own looser model of cooperation in the form of the European Free Trade Association (EFTA), founded in 1960.

Even as EFTA was under discussion, however, it was clear that the European Economic Community was working, bringing down barriers to trade among its six member states and encouraging them to cooperate in an ever-greater variety of policy areas. So it was in 1961 that the Macmillan government lodged Britain's first application to join the EEC, along with Denmark, Ireland and Norway. This was dismissed out of hand by President Charles de Gaulle of France, who saw Britain as a rival for leadership in the Community, resented Britain's early lack of enthusiasm for European integration, and felt that British membership would give the United States too much influence in Europe. Britain applied again in 1967, and was vetoed by de Gaulle for similar reasons. Following the French leader's resignation in 1969, Britain applied for a third time, was accepted, and negotiations on the terms of membership opened. On 1 January 1973 Britain finally joined the EEC, along with Denmark and Ireland (for more details, see George, 1992; Buller, 1999; McCormick, 2002, chapter 3).

Meanwhile, Britain's empire had been all but dismantled. Malaysia and Singapore became independent in 1957, Nigeria and Cyprus in 1960, Kuwait and Tanzania in 1961, Jamaica and Trinidad in 1962, Kenya in 1963, Malta and Zambia in 1964, Barbados and Guyana in 1966, Mauritius and Swaziland in 1968, Fiji in 1970, and the Bahamas in 1973. The one remaining holdout in Africa was Rhodesia, whose white minority unilaterally declared independence in November 1965. (The country eventually became legally independent in 1980 as Zimbabwe.) By the mid-1970s, little was left of the empire beyond Hong Kong, the Falklands, Gibraltar and a few Caribbean and Indian Ocean islands. Where Britain had once committed its army and navy almost all over the world, it was now a second-ranking power with limited military interests. It was a key actor in the North Atlantic Treaty Organization (NATO), to be sure, had an independent nuclear deterrent, and was one of the five

---

**Box 1.2   Watershed at Suez, 1956**

The turning point in Britain's role as a world power came in 1956 on the banks of the Suez Canal. Built in 1856–69 by the British and the French (using Egyptian labour), the canal had become a conduit for British contacts and trade with India and the Pacific. Egypt became increasingly resentful over continued British control over the canal after the Second World War, especially after the 1952 coup that brought Gamal Abdel Nasser to power. Seeking to build a dam on the Nile at Aswan, Nasser sought and was promised aid from the United States, Britain and the World Bank. When he also bought arms from the Soviet bloc, the offer of aid was withdrawn, and Nasser responded by nationalizing the canal in July 1956. Political and public opinion in Britain was outraged, and Conservative Prime Minister Anthony Eden felt that – if unanswered – the nationalization would represent an end to British influence in Asia and Africa. Thus, the British government colluded with France and Israel to win the canal back.

In October 1956, when Israel launched an attack on Egypt, Britain and France insisted that both sides withdraw to a distance of 10 miles each side of the canal. When they did not, Egyptian airfields were bombed and British and French paratroopers were dropped into the canal zone. The Eisenhower administration in the United States – just a week away from an election, and keen to criticize the Soviets for putting down a democracy movement in Hungary – led the international opposition to the attack, thereby emphasizing the differences that had emerged between the Americans and the British regarding the new international order. The United States was hostile to the idea of colonialism, and was eager to see Britain tie itself more closely to its European neighbours. The British, by contrast, still refused to see themselves as Europeans and saw their main interests lying outside Europe, notably in the white dominions: Australia, Canada and New Zealand.

A ceasefire was quickly arranged, the last British troops left the canal zone in December, and in January 1957 Eden resigned, ostensibly on medical grounds, but reputedly at the demand of President Eisenhower. Britain's international prestige suffered, public opinion began to question Britain's role in the world, the process of decolonization moved into high gear, and the focus of British interests shifted from the empire to Europe (for details, see Louis and Owens, 1989).

---

members of the UN Security Council with veto power. However, cold war tensions between the United States and the USSR dominated international relations, and the British Empire had been replaced by the Commonwealth, whose interests were more cultural and economic than political.

One of the legacies of empire was the immigration into Britain of citizens from its ex-colonies. Initially, these had been from the white dominions of Australia, New Zealand and Canada, but in the 1950s there were increasing numbers of arrivals from other parts of the empire. In 1951, there had been just 75,000 non-whites in Britain, or about 0.2 per cent of the population. A labour shortage in the 1950s encouraged an influx of immigrants, mainly from the Caribbean and from India and Pakistan. The government passed a number of Immigration Acts between 1962 and 1971 aimed at restricting immigration, but a new wave of mainly Asian immigrants from Kenya and Uganda arrived at the turn of the 1970s as they were expelled by the governments of those two countries. By the early 1980s, the number of non-whites in Britain had jumped to more than two million, or about 4 per cent of the population, and racial tensions had begun to mount (see Chapter 2).

More cultural change came in the 1960s. Reacting to what they saw as the conformist and conservative 1950s, and fed by new injections of American culture, the easy availability of birth control, and concerns about social and political problems, young people adopted new attitudes, reflected in their love of rock-and-roll, new fashions, the sexual revolution, and support for mass movements whose target were mainly the Establishment: opposition to nuclear weapons, to gender discrimination, to the war in Vietnam, and to threats to the environment. The musical revolution was led by the Beatles, the Rolling Stones, the Who, the Kinks, Cream and other musicians who took the music charts on both sides the Atlantic by storm. The fashion revolution was led by designers such as Mary Quant and Biba, the introduction of the mini-skirt, and the images associated with Carnaby Street and Swinging London. Cinema captured the spirit of the new Britain as Sean Connery's James Bond exuded panache and sophistication, Michael Caine's *Alfie* glorified anti-heroes, and Lynn Redgraves's *Georgy Girl* emphasized the new social freedom of women. England won the football World Cup in 1966 and *Sergeant Pepper's Lonely Hearts Club Band* took the music world by storm in 1967 – Britain's empire may have gone, but now it dominated global popular culture.

Domestic developments of another kind exploded in Northern Ireland in 1969. The province had governed itself since 1922, largely forgotten by national government. The Protestant majority, concerned about its place in the province, had maintained a policy of discrimination towards the Catholic minority on housing, jobs and political rights, ensured in particular by its control of the police, the Royal Ulster Constabulary (RUC). In 1968, a movement campaigning for equality for Catholics had been aggressively opposed by the RUC, which also broke up a civil rights march from Belfast to Londonderry in January 1969. Violence and rioting followed, the British Army was sent in to the province to restore order in August 1969, and from there the problems escalated. Internment without trial was introduced by the British government, terrorist groups representing the Protestant and Catholic causes fought each other, while soldiers, members of the RUC, and ordinary citizens were killed and injured in street violence and bombings. Direct rule was imposed from London in March 1972 (see Chapter 2).

Meanwhile, the economic growth of the 1950s began to falter, and Britain's economy during the 1960s and 1970s continued its relative decline. Commentators and political leaders began to talk of a 'British disease' that had come to afflict the country. The Right blamed 'creeping socialism' in the form of growing welfare, powerful and recalcitrant labour unions, high rates of taxation, and the large public sector. The Left questioned this interpretation, asking why – if welfare was to blame – other countries with extensive welfare and high tax rates (such as France and Sweden) did not have similar problems. Their explanations focused less on workers and more on management, whom they blamed for failing to adjust to the postwar world in which new competition was being posed by the United States and a resurgent Germany and Japan, and failing to break a class system that prevented management and workers from developing a constructive joint effort, and that gave more value to inherited 'old money' than to 'new money' earned by hard work and entrepreneurial innovation. Confrontation became more common than co-operation in relations between managers and workers, leading to bitterness, low productivity, and a sense of 'Us versus Them'. A famous headline in a British tabloid of the time asked the last person to leave Britain kindly to switch off the lights.

In the 1970s, large reserves of oil and natural gas were discovered in the North Sea. Oil production grew during the 1970s from 635,000 barrels per year to more than 550 million barrels, and dependence on imports declined: in 1974, Britain imported 100 times more oil than it exported, but by 1980, imports and exports were almost balanced. Before the oil began to flow, though, Britain was hit by the energy crisis of 1973. Following the Arab–Israeli war of that year, Arab oil producers imposed a boycott on several countries, causing an

The Beatles in 1967: George Harrison, Ringo Starr, John Lennon, and – in front – Paul McCartney. Their music defined the cultural style of a new generation, and they were the vanguard of a movement that carried British popular culture around the world.

**Illustration 1.3   The Beatles**

increase in the price of oil and a panic among consumers. Britain was still a major importer at the time, so its import bill quadrupled, and the oil shock contributed to a balance-of-payments deficit. By the time of the 1978 energy crisis, it was in a better position to weather cuts in imports. However, since much of the oil was found off the coast of Scotland, it contributed to a new surge of Scottish nationalism, and demands for devolution, even independence.

The rejuvenation of nationalism began in Wales, where the Welsh nationalist party Plaid Cymru won its first-ever seat in Parliament at a 1966 by-election, and saw its share of the vote grow, winning two seats at the February 1974 election. In the case of Scotland, the neglect of central government combined with declining support for the Labour Party and the development of North Sea oil to give a boost to the Scottish National Party (SNP). Founded in 1928, it had never won more than about one per cent of the vote in general elections. In 1967, it won its first seat in Parliament, and its share of the Scottish vote grew from 11.4 per cent in 1970 (when it won two seats in Parliament) to 21.0 per cent in February 1974 (when it won seven seats). The Labour government responded with plans to devolve power to Scotland and Wales, and in March 1979, referendums were held in both countries, a favourable vote of 40 per cent or more being required to proceed. Only 33 per cent were in favour in Scotland, and only 12 per cent in Wales, so devolution was temporarily shelved. A new low point in Britain's economic fortunes came at the end of the 1970s. Against a background of high unemployment, 16 per cent inflation, and a record budget deficit, the Labour government of Harold Wilson was obliged in 1976 to ask the International Monetary Fund for a loan to help offset a run on the pound and to help Britain service its debts. Then, during the 'winter of discontent' in 1978–79, public-sector workers went on strike across Britain, almost shutting the country down. Clearly it was time for a new approach both to economic policy and to government. In 1979, there was a general election, which resulted in the return to power of the Conservative Party, led since 1975 by Margaret Thatcher.

## The Thatcher Revolution, 1979–90

Alone among twentieth-century British prime ministers, Margaret Thatcher's name has been applied to a set of political ideas and a style of administration. Thatcher believed she had identified the critical elements of the 'British disease', and set out to give Britain the hard medicine that she believed must be applied if the postwar decline was to be reversed. Above all, she felt, this meant an end to consensus politics and an abandonment of compromise, bargaining and the search for policies acceptable to the majority (Clarke, 1996: 367–79). In its place, Thatcher wanted a new kind of politics, variously labelled adversarial, confrontational or conviction politics.

The philosophy of Thatcherism revolved around a belief in the guidance of one's own passionately held beliefs, in markets, monetarism and authoritative government, and in the development of a strong state and a free economy (Kavanagh, 1987: 2). Marquand argues that Thatcherism had four basic dimensions: 'a sort of British Gaullism' born out of a growing sense of despair with Britain's decline, economic liberalism, traditional Toryism (including patriotism and a pride in tradition), and a style of politics that was both populist and charismatic (Marquand, 1988: 160–4). Among other things, Thatcherism meant rolling back the state, privatizing businesses and industries owned and operated by the government, reducing trade union power, promoting family values in order to ensure a 'higher' moral level in society, and a strong British role in international affairs.

The impact of Thatcherism on Britain is debatable. Her supporters argue that she instituted the changes needed to reverse Britain's economic decline by freeing up the marketplace, cutting the power of unions, reducing dependence on welfare, and promoting a stakeholder culture in which more Britons became involved in creating their own wealth and opportunities. For her detractors, she promoted class warfare, failed to meet the needs of the underclass, and allowed too many people to slip through the safety net of welfare. She also widened the gap between the 'haves' and the 'have-nots'; the number of British millionaires grew as a result of her tenure, but so did poverty and homelessness, and many felt that Britain became a less caring society.

Thatcher was also criticized for her often confrontational views on Europe, where she was frequently at odds with other European Community leaders. Europe had come to dominate domestic politics, not least because of the signing in 1986 of the Single European Act, designed to complete the final steps in one of the early goals of European integration: the creation of a European market free of borders, within which there was free movement of people, money, goods and services. Europe was also growing, with membership bringing in three poorer countries: Greece, Spain and Portugal. Finally, in 1994, the Channel Tunnel was opened for service, removing an important psychological barrier between Britain and the continent. Despite these developments, Thatcher dragged her feet on Europe, most famously demanding (and receiving) a reduction in Britain's contributions to the Community budget.

Thatcher won three elections (1979, 1983 and 1987), but by the late 1980s had become widely unpopular, both within her party and within the broader electorate. Her insistence on seeking advice from outside the cabinet combined with differences over policy to lead to resignations by key ministers in her government, emphasizing her weakness. Her attempt in 1989–90 to replace progressive local taxes (rates) with a poll tax to which rich and poor alike would be subject proved very unpopular. Finally, a squabble between pro- and anti-European Conservatives (the latter led by Thatcher) revealed that her policies on Europe were becoming too divisive. In 1990, after a party leadership vote which she won, but not convincingly, Thatcher resigned the leadership and the prime ministership, and was replaced by John Major. He won his own mandate at the 1992 general election, but in-fighting continued within the Conservatives, mainly over Europe, and the opposition Labour Party in 1994 elected a new leader – Tony Blair – who was intent on reforming the party. Membership of the European Union combined with the effects of Thatcherism to bring great change to Britain. It was visible in the renewal of cities, in the rise of a new entrepreneurial spirit that was transforming the attitudes of business and industry, and in the growth of the middle class and the consumer society. The average Briton today is healthier, better-educated and better dressed than before, and there is a new spirit of liveliness and optimism, at least among the younger generations. Many even argue that Britain is being Americanized – not only has its economy rediscovered something of the competitive nature that made it so strong in the nineteenth century, but many aspects of politics (notably election campaigns) have taken on a more competitive American character.

**Britain under Blair**

The legacy of Thatcherism has been reflected in the policies pursued since May 1997 by the Labour government of Tony Blair. Astonishing political analysts with the scale of its victory, the rejuvenated Labour Party swept the internally divided Conservative Party out of office after 18 years in power, winning a remarkable 177-seat majority in Parliament. Under Tony Blair, 'New' Labour in opposition had abandoned many of its traditionally socialist ideas, and adopted key elements of the Thatcher programme. Blair came into office underlining the importance of the free market, and emphasizing the need to improve education, rebuild the national health-care system, invest more heavily in Britain's human capital, build a society less dependent on government, take a tough stance on crime, and work in a more constructive fashion with Britain's EU partners. Blair also made much of his opinion that Britain should be 'repackaged' as a society that had deep roots in history and culture, but which was also forward-looking and economically dynamic.

During its first term in office (1997–2001), the Blair administration made some far-reaching changes to the institutions of government:

- Sweeping reforms were made to the upper chamber of Parliament, the House of Lords, long criticized for being anachronistic and undemocratic. The right of hereditary aristocrats to sit in the House ended in 1999, and a commission was appointed to develop plans for the future of the chamber.

- Following referendums in 1997, regional assemblies were created for Wales and Scotland, completing the process of devolution first discussed in the 1970s. Elected mayors were also created for several major cities, including London.
- Proportional representation (PR) was introduced for the 1998-99 elections to the regional assemblies, and for the 1999 elections to the European Parliament, the assumption being that PR might also eventually be introduced for the general election.
- The Bank of England was given independence in 1997.

Coincidentally, the first Blair administration also saw a new and critical focus on the place of the monarchy in British national life. In an attempt to make the monarchy more open and relevant, Queen Elizabeth – starting in the late 1960s – had allowed greater media access to the life of her family. This became something of a feeding frenzy in the 1980s and 1990s as the failed marriages of her three eldest children – Charles, Anne and Andrew – attracted the attention of the tabloid press and its readers. In particular, the open, fun-loving, fashionable and socially conscious side of Princess Diana, who in 1981 had married Prince Charles, the heir to the throne, appeared very different from the rather stiff and dowdy persona of the Queen. The monarchy seemed to be increasingly out of touch, in contrast to continental monarchies that were busy making themselves more accessible. Then, in August 1997, Princess Diana – by now divorced from Charles – was killed in a car accident in Paris, and the remarkable public outpouring of grief in Britain stood in stark contrast to the reserved response of the Queen, who for several days failed to make a public statement or to sanction an official royal response. This single event seemed to represent a broader need for the monarchy to modernize and to catch up with a new set of public expectations about its status and role.

Meanwhile, there were important developments in Northern Ireland. The conflict had worsened during the 1980s, with sectarian killings, and bombings both in Northern Ireland and on the British mainland; by the mid-1990s more than 3500 people had been killed. It put a strain on government resources, incurred additional costs for the military, and tarnished Britain's reputation as a champion of civil rights and liberties: trial without jury was allowed, as was arrest for seven days without charge, and a ban was imposed on broadcasting interviews with terrorists. An attempt was made on the life of Margaret Thatcher in 1984, and a mortar attack was made on the London residence of the prime minister in 1991.

An Anglo-Irish agreement was drawn up in 1985 pledging the British and Irish governments to work towards a solution that would recognize differences between the Catholic and Protestant communities in the province. In 1993, the Downing Street Declaration committed the government to hold talks with any groups that renounced violence, and negotiations began in 1995. They continued under the Blair government, which underwrote negotiations between the warring factions chaired by former US Senator George Mitchell. These led to the Good Friday Agreement of April 1998 which brought about a ceasefire between the warring sides, set up a regional assembly for Northern Ireland in which Protestants and Catholics shared power, and created cross-border councils that would bring members of the new assembly together with members of the British and Irish parliaments. After a delay involving a dispute over whether or not the Irish Republican Army (IRA) would turn in its weapons, the new Northern Ireland regional government eventually met for the first time in November 1999, and the prospects for a lasting peace looked better than they had for more than 30 years.

One of the biggest issues facing Britain as this book went to press was its position on the single European currency, the euro (see Box 6.2). In January–February 2002, 12 of the 15 EU member states replaced their national currencies with the euro, the only holdouts being Denmark, Sweden and Britain. Majority public opinion in Britain is hostile to the abolition of the pound, but Tony Blair himself is in favour, his government has set its own series of economic tests for joining the euro (see Chapter 6), and he has promised to put the issue to a public referendum.

On foreign policy, the Blair administration has proved more willing to commit British troops to service overseas than were any of its Labour predecessors. Britain played an active role in the NATO attack on Serbia in 1999, in response to a programme of ethnic cleansing directed by the Milosevic regime against Albanians living in the province of Kosovo. Blair proved the most hawkish of NATO leaders, even expressing willingness to commit ground troops to the province before bombing had ended. Following the terrorist attacks of September 2001 on targets in New York and Washington DC, Blair was quick to come to the support of the Bush administration, and British troops played a key role in mopping-up and peacekeeping operations in Afghanistan following the US-led attacks on the Taliban regime in late 2001 and early 2002. Blair also went against public and political feeling in Britain and the EU in 2002–03 by refusing to oppose the plans of the Bush administration to remove Saddam Hussein from power in Iraq. British troops were at the forefront of the controversial invasion of Iraq that began in March 2003.

If Blair was active on the international stage, his government came in for criticism at home for its failure to stem the decline in the quality of public services. Waiting lists for patients wanting operations under the National Health Service grew, several headline-making and deadly accidents underlined the declining state of Britain's railways, and concerns were raised about the state of the British educational system. But the economy was doing well, the Conservatives did not offer a popular alternative, and Blair was returned to office in the June 2001 election with his majority barely reduced. The gloss of victory was tarnished somewhat by a fall in voter turnout (from 71 per cent in 1997 to just over 59 per cent in 2001), and the result was seen as much as a reflection of voter disillusionment with the still-divided Conservative Party as of support for Labour.

Britain in the twenty-first century is a very different place than it was even just a generation ago. It has seen fundamental changes in its system of government and in the character of its politics, its economy is much improved since the dark days of the 1970s and 1980s, both government and the public sector have become more responsive to the needs of consumers and citizens, Britain plays a more aggressive role in the international arena, and – whether the British like it or not – the definition of 'Britain' is being reviewed as the relationship between England, Scotland, Wales and Northern Ireland changes, and as its place in the European Union evolves.

# 2

# Land and People

Britain is a small, crowded, island country. Perhaps the first thing that new visitors notice is its compactness: houses are mainly small, people live in close proximity to one another, and the landscape everywhere bears the imprint of human activity. It is difficult to avoid permanent human habitation, whether in the form of sprawling cities, small villages or isolated farmhouses. Similarly, it is impossible to ignore the changes wrought by humans; the conversion of land to agriculture has combined with the removal of forests and the use of hedgerows as plot dividers to create a landscape that is almost unique and instantly recognizable: winding roads, immaculately maintained fields, patches of woodland, compact towns and villages, landscaped parks and public footpaths.

This is a society where a large population has had to make the best possible use of a small area of land. Some might argue that the British have also been moulded by the climate of their country, with its mild temperatures and often persistent rain. Climate has helped make Britons a phlegmatic people, and has driven some to leave for sunnier and drier parts of the world – it is sometimes joked that it helped drive the creation of the British Empire. Britain is also a society that has had to make use of limited natural resources, and that has depended heavily on the sea for sustenance. Britain has rich agricultural land, and meets most of its basic food needs. It has a wealth of energy resources, from the coal that drove the industrial revolution to the oil and natural gas that meet Britain's needs today. However, the changes brought first by agriculture and then by industry have taken their toll on the environment, first with the air and water pollution that once characterized Britain's cities, then with the threats posed to nature and wildlife by more 'efficient' agriculture.

The people of Britain have also been influenced by important social divisions, the most fundamental of which stem from the cultural, historical, political and linguistic differences that distinguish the English, the Scottish, the Welsh and the Irish from each other. This is still a 'united' kingdom, but nationalist movements against English domination first took Ireland out of the union, then brought violence and civil strife to Northern Ireland, and encouraged movements for greater local control – and even for independence – in Wales and Scotland. The redefinition of the term 'British' was further complicated by waves of non-white immigration after the Second World War, which pushed the issue of race up the political and social agenda.

This chapter looks at the geography, natural resources and people of Britain. The first half examines topography, climate and key natural resources, and looks at the state of the British environment, the threats it faces and the policy responses it has prompted. The second half of the chapter looks at the people of Britain, at recent demographic changes, and at two important divisions: nationalism (and its impact on regionalism), and race.

## The Geography of Britain

The most notable geographical facts about the UK are (a) it is small, (b) it is an island state, and (c) its dimensions are moderate in almost every way: there are no extremes of distance, height, length, climate, or variety of animal life and vegetation. It has no great mountain chains, no great rivers or estuaries, no large lakes, and no sweeping forests. Its highest mountain (Ben Nevis in Scotland) is less than one-sixth the height of Mt Everest, its largest lake (Lough Neagh in Northern Ireland) could fit into Lake Superior more than 215 times, and its longest river (the Severn in England) is barely one-twentieth the length of the Nile. It has just 420 animal species and 1400 flowering plant species, few of which are unique to the British Isles.

At the same time, though, Britain is notable for the variety of its landscapes, which are the product of a combination of geological and climatic change over time, and of centuries of human activity. Its geological history has seen the British landmass pushed from the southern hemisphere to the northern, and its landscape types have included tropical rain forests, deserts, freezing ice caps, high mountains and mudflats. The last great natural influence on its geology

---

**Box 2.1   Britain or the UK: what's in a name?**

Something that routinely confuses and puzzles people – even sometimes the British themselves – is the correct name of the country. The
problem stems from the fact that the United Kingdom is actually four
countries in one: a union of England, Scotland, Wales and Northern
Ireland. Each has its own separate identity, its own flags, its own
history and culture, its own 'national' sports teams, and – in the case of
Scotland – its own separate legal and educational system.

Formally, the full name of the country is the United Kingdom of Great
Britain and Northern Ireland. While Great Britain consists of England,
Scotland and Wales, Northern Ireland is physically separate, but is part
of the union with Great Britain. However, while the term United
Kingdom is used at government conferences and in diplomatic dealings, in everyday conversation most Britons use the terms 'Britain' and
'British' as shorthand, even though it is technically incorrect to refer to
all four countries together as anything but the United Kingdom. If this
is a forgivable sin, it is much more unforgivable to use the term
'England' when referring to the United Kingdom, as (for example)
many Americans persist in doing. It would be tantamount to describing
all Americans as 'Texans' or all Germans as 'Bavarians'.

The complications do not end there. The Isle of Man in the Irish Sea,
and the Channel Islands to the south of England – consisting of Jersey,
Guernsey and neighbouring smaller islands – are usually assumed to be
part of the UK. Their inhabitants speak English, and their ways of life
are almost indistinguishable from those of people on the mainland. Yet
the islands are not part of the United Kingdom, nor are they even
members of the European Union. Instead they are dependencies of the
British Crown. They each have their own legislatures and system of law
(the Tynwald on the Isle of Man is the oldest continuously functioning
legislature in the world), and the British government is responsible for
their foreign and defence policies. The free movement of services and
people that applies to the EU does not apply to the islands, making it
difficult for someone living in mainland Britain to move permanently
to one of the islands.

---

came with the Ice Age, which ended 375,000 years ago, and
during which ice sheets and glaciers covered all but what are now
the most extreme southern reaches of England. The result is that
Britain today has – for its size – one of the richest and most diverse
sets of geological features of any country in the world: examples of
most of the different kinds of rock, soils, minerals and land forms
found elsewhere in the world can be found somewhere in the British
Isles.

During the Ice Age, Britain was connected to the European mainland, but the melting of the icecaps caused the sea level to rise, creating the island of Great Britain and many of its neighbouring smaller islands, such as the Isle of Wight off the southern coast of England, Anglesey off the northern coast of Wales, the Isle of Man in the Irish Sea, and the islands of Arran, Islay, Mull, Skye and the Hebrides off the west coat of Scotland. Britain is now divided from the continent by the North Sea, and by the English Channel, which – at its narrowest point – is just 35 km (22 miles) across. Britain and Ireland for their part are divided by the North Channel, which is 21 km (13 miles) across at its narrowest point. The only land boundary that the UK has with another country is the 488-km (303-mile) border with Ireland.

The landscape continues to change even today. The long-term effects of the end of the Ice Age mean that Scotland is slowly rising, while southern England is slowly sinking and the sea is moving up its estuaries; at one of its lowest points in the Fens of East Anglia, wetlands prevail. The weather and the sea continue to exert their effects on the land, with wind and rain breaking down exposed rocks, rivers eroding the land and carrying debris downstream, and the action of wind and the oceans breaking up coastal rocks and headlands. Added to these changes have been the effects of humans on the landscape, almost every accessible square metre of which has been remodelled by human activity.

Physically (see Map 2.1), Britain can be broadly divided into highland and lowland regions. The highest land is found in the south west (Dartmoor and Exmoor), and the Pennine mountains of north central England; the Cambrian mountains of Wales; the central areas of Northern Ireland; and the southern uplands, Grampian mountains, and north-west highlands of Scotland. The statistics are modest: the highest mountain in England is Scafell Pike in the northwestern Lake District (978 metres/3209 feet), and the highest mountain in Britain is Ben Nevis in Scotland (1343 metres/4406 feet). The rest of Britain consists of plains and lowlands interspersed with moorland and the gently undulating chalk downs of the south east.

The climate of Britain is notorious, to residents and visitors alike. Climatologists describe it as moderate, a polite term for the often cool and wet summers and the mild and snowless winters, prompting the old joke that the only difference between the winter and the summer is that the rain is warmer in the summer. The most telling influences on the climate are surrounding seas (which act as a temperature buffer

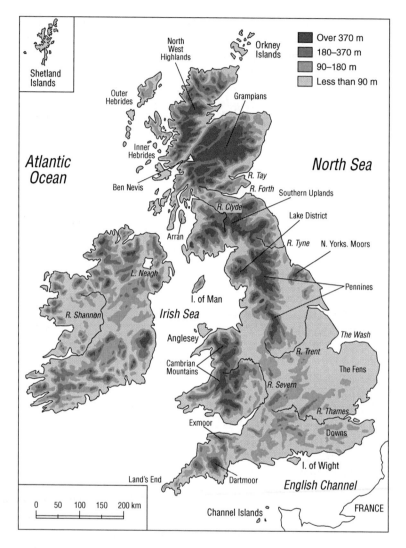

**Map 2.1   Physical features of Britain**

that keeps coastal areas cool when inland areas are warm, and vice versa), the intersection between cool air moving down from the North Pole and warm air moving up from the tropics, and the Gulf Stream, which carries warmer water from the tropics to the Arctic, and has a moderating effect on Britain's weather, making it much warmer than areas at similar latitudes in Asia or North America. January temperatures are generally in the range of 3–5°C (37–41°F) and July temperatures are in the range 11–16°C (52–61°F). Rainfall is usually well distributed throughout the year, and tends to be soft and steady rather than sharp and heavy, with few major storms, One of the effects is the characteristic lush greenery of the British landscape, throughout the summer and the winter. Another effect is that the British often do not know how to respond to extreme weather, such as very hot summers or heavy snow in winter.

**Natural Resources**

Britain may not be well-endowed in land, and may have lost most of its natural forest cover to agriculture, but it has a wealth of commercial energy resources: it is one of the most fuel-rich countries in the EU, with significant supplies of coal, natural gas and oil. It is also rich in fisheries, although a combination of quotas established by the European Union and competition from fishing boats from other EU countries has adversely impacted fishing communities in recent years. Finally, Britain has much rich and productive agricultural land, and is self-sufficient in almost every foodstuff that can be grown in its climate.

Coal was one of the foundations of the industrial revolution. It was the presence of vast coal resources in the midlands and the north of England, and the south of Wales, that offered the opportunity for the generation of steam power, which in turn allowed for the exploitation of seams of coal that had previously been out of reach. While coal is still an important source of energy, it now accounts for just 16 per cent of British energy consumption, down from 30 per cent in 1990; most is used to generate electricity at steam-powered generation plants. Coal has been superceded by two other sources of energy in which Britain is well-endowed: natural gas (supplying 41 per cent of energy needs) and oil (supplying 32 per cent of needs). Britain is the world's tenth-largest oil producer, but it does not produce enough to meet domestic needs, its reserves are fast running out, and it is still a net importer. By contrast, it meets 98 per cent of its natural gas needs with domestic production.

As an island nation, Britain is also – not surprisingly – well-endowed with fisheries. As one of the EU's largest fishing nations, it meets about half of its own domestic demand. The size of the fishing fleet has fallen by nearly one-third in the last 10 years, and employment in the fishing industry by a quarter, but total landings by quantity and value have remained steady, as has household consumption. But life has changed for fishing communities. First, fish catches dropped substantially as a result of overfishing and of changes in the breeding patterns of fish. Then fishing quotas were imposed under the EU's Common Fisheries Policy, new technology has improved the efficiency of catching fish, and access to waters outside the 20km (12-mile) limit has been opened up to fishing boats from other EU countries. The impact has been most obvious in Britain's traditional fishing communities, where fewer people work in fishing, and new jobs in other fields have not always been created to take up the slack.

Agriculture in Britain has long been among the most technologically innovative and productive in the world. Technical advances have allowed British farmers fully to exploit the limited land area of Britain to produce as much as is physically possible from a country with its climate. Farmland takes up just over three-quarters of the land area of Britain (much higher than the figure for the EU as a whole, which is just 42 per cent), and there are about 235,000 farm units, ranging in size from large industrial operations to small family farms. Barely two per cent of the workforce is employed in agriculture, and it contributes just 1 per cent of Britain's gross domestic product (figures which are similar to those in other European countries), but Britain's farmers provide two-thirds of the country's food needs, with much left over for export.

Half of Britain's farms concentrate on dairy farming, and on raising beef cattle and sheep; most of the beef and sheep farms are in the northern, western and south-western parts of the country, and they account for about one-third of Britain's agricultural output. The other half focus on poultry and egg production (in which Britain is almost self-sufficient) and on raising arable crops such as wheat, barley, oats and vegetables; crop farms are found particularly in eastern and central-southern England. The agricultural industry has benefitted from the EU's controversial Common Agricultural Policy, which sets minimum guaranteed prices for food products. While it has helped promote European agricultural production, standardized the quality of that production, and increased productivity and efficiency, it has also swallowed up about half the EU's annual budget, promoted over-production, encouraged farmers to rely more on chemical fertilizers and pesticides, and has upset the EU's major trading partners (even

**Illustration 2.1   Exmoor, England**

British agriculture is both productive and technologically innovative, and has given the British landscape its characteristic look of small fields divided by hedgerows. Even national parks – such as Exmoor in southwest England, shown here – are still farmed.

those which, like the United States, have their own system of subsidies to farmers).

British agriculture in recent years has been hit by two disasters that have brought economic hardship to farmers, many of whom have gone out of business. The first was the advent of mad cow disease (BSE, or Bovine Spongiform Encephalopathy). First identified in the mid-1980s, it led to controls on the use of cattle organs in animal feed in 1990. When the government announced a link between BSE and a human equivalent in 1996, the EU imposed a worldwide ban on exports of all British beef (finally lifted in 1998). The second was the outbreak in February 2001 of foot-and-mouth disease, which began in northern England and quickly spread to other parts of the country. Over the next seven months, in order to contain the disease, more than three million sheep, nearly 600,000 cattle, and nearly 140,000 pigs were slaughtered. The combined effects of BSE, foot-and-mouth disease, and the fall in the numbers of tourists visiting Britain brought significant hardship to Britain's rural areas.

**Illustration 2.2   Glen Docherty, Scotland**

The rugged beauty of the Scottish highlands. In contrast to its densely populated southern neighbour, Scotland is relatively lightly populated, and much of its landscape shows fewer obvious signs of the modern impact of human habitation and economic development.

## The Environment

The state of the British environment has been determined by three major forces: Britain's long history of human settlement, the density of its human population, and the long-term effects of the industrial revolution. These have combined to make sure that there is no true wilderness left in Britain, and that every part of the country has been directly or indirectly impacted by human development. In many ways, the British countryside is nothing more than a huge man-made park, interspersed with large pockets of farmland. Nature and agriculture have long had to coexist, with nature usually coming off worst. Industry and population growth have also combined to produce a society heavily impacted by the fallout from the use of fossil fuels and the growth of road vehicle traffic. Britain was once notorious for its urban smogs, and indeed the term 'smog' was coined to describe the combination of smoke and fog that once polluted the air over major cities, notably London. Air and water in Britain is cleaner today than at any time since the rise of industry, but most of Britain's major environmental problems – like those of all post-industrial societies – still stem from the use of fossil fuels.

The natural vegetation of the British Isles is deciduous woodland, but there is very little left. Except for heaths and moors, most of Britain was once covered by forests made up largely of species of trees typical of temperate woodland, such as oak, ash, beech, elm and – along the banks of rivers – water-loving species such as alder and willow. The first forest clearances were carried out by Neolithic man beginning about 6000 years ago, since when there has been an almost continuous process of change. In the Middle Ages, forests still occupied about one-third of the land area, but today only about seven per cent of land is covered by forest, and less than one-third of what remains consists of ancient woodlands and broadleaf forests. Visitors to Sherwood Forest, the New Forest and Forest of Dean will find only the vestiges of once great natural forests. Changes since the Second World War have been driven by government policies that have allowed landowners to make more money from converting woodland to cornfields or to commercial conifer plantations. The result is that Britain today has less forest cover per square kilometre than any other country in Europe except Ireland. It has only been during the last 20–30 years that there has been real public awareness and concern about the loss of forests, and campaigns have developed to stop the losses.

Wildlife and natural habitat in Britain is severely limited by human settlement, and is now found only in those areas not immediately impacted by human activity, or in isolated pockets surrounded by farmland or in the heart of cities. Agricultural intensification during and after the Second World War combined with the spread of cities and the creation of new towns to bring marked changes to the landscape. Wetland, moorland, heathland and downland were 'reclaimed', hedgerows and woodland were cleared to make way for bigger fields that were easier to plough and to crop, and increasing quantities of chemical fertilizer were applied to the land (Shoard, 1980). The resulting increase in agricultural yields has been remarkable, but the natural environment has suffered proportionately:

● While the population and size of Britain's major urban areas has fallen, the number and size of towns has grown, as has the population of rural areas. One result was that in the 1980s about 15,000 hectares (37,000 acres) of land each year was being covered by new development. Meanwhile, much old industrial land in cities has been left derelict.

• Nearly one-fifth of Britain's plant species and many of its animal species are threatened, mainly by loss of habitat: the draining of wetlands, the removal of hedgerows and forests, the expansion of development, and the use of chemicals in agriculture.

On the positive side of the ledger, the area of protected land has increased substantially since the Second World War. At the heart of nature protection efforts is a network of twelve national parks, including the Lake District and the Yorkshire Dales in northern England, Snowdonia in Wales, and Exmoor and Dartmoor in the south-west. There are also 42 Areas of Outstanding Natural Beauty, 40 National Scenic Areas in Scotland, 17 forest parks, more than 200 country parks, protected coastlines, designated areas of special scientific value, and greenbelts around cities where building is strictly controlled. Together, they cover more than 20 per cent of the land area of Britain. Levels of protection vary, however, and many of these areas are protected as much for recreation as for conservation. And unlike national parks in other parts of the world, where permanent habitation is not allowed, British national parks were already settled and farmed, and continue that way, albeit with restrictions. Ironically, the BSE and foot-and-mouth crises may actually have long-term benefits for the countryside, because they emphasized the links between agriculture and other parts of the rural economy, such as tourism. There is also more sympathy for those working and living in rural areas, and lobbying organizations with an interest in rural issues have become more active.

Meanwhile, there is both good news and bad news on the relationship between transport and the environment. The good news is that Britain's air is cleaner than it has been since pre-industrial times. After many years of being known as 'the dirty man of Europe', and being heavily criticized by Scandinavian governments for its major role in the production of acid pollution, Britain took action during the 1980s and 1990s to clean its air, much of that action required by European Union law. The result is that nitrogen oxide emissions, most of which come from road traffic, are down by one-third on 1989 levels, and are projected to fall another 70 per cent by 2015. Meanwhile, sulphur dioxide emissions, coming mainly from power stations, have been reduced by 80 per cent since 1970, and carbon monoxide emissions have been halved in the same period. Finally, emissions of carbon dioxide – the primary constituent in climate change – fell by nearly 15 per cent between 1990 and 1999.

The bad news is that road traffic is worsening, threatening the quality of the air and making inroads into land as new roads and all their subsidiary services are built. There are 29 million vehicles on British roads, the highest volume of road traffic per kilometre of road of any EU country except Italy and Portugal. Despite the fact that only 48 per cent of homes have the regular use of one car, travel by road vehicle has doubled in the last 30 years. More traffic causes more congestion, which is worsened by the constant need to maintain roads to meet the needs of traffic. New roads have been built – such as the M25 motorway surrounding London – but they have added to the problem by encouraging more people to travel by road. Meanwhile, the quality of public transport has declined. In 2003, London introduced a system under which drivers in central London had to pay a daily charge, but there was little certainty about what effect this would have, and the problems of road transport in Britain only promise to become worse.

As with all other EU member states, environmental policy standards in Britain are now driven more by the requirements of European law than by those of British law. The EU has been an active and productive source of new regulations and standards on environmental quality, and Britain's goals are the same as those of the EU. European policy has focused most of its attention on improving the quality of water and air, reducing the production of waste, improving the management of chemicals and pesticides, conserving energy, and managing forests and fisheries (for more details see McCormick, 2001).

## The People of Britain

Like most of its European neighbours, Britain is a crowded country. In mid-2002, the population was estimated to be about 59.8 million, which was roughly the same as France, but living on a land area half the size of France. Population density runs at nearly 250 people per sq km (650 people per sq mile), although there is considerable regional variation: more than 280 people per sq km (730 per sq mile) in England and just 65 per sq km (170 per sq mile) in Scotland. The most densely populated parts of the country are in and around

**Illustration 2.3  Terraced Houses**

Britain is both highly urbanized – with nearly 90 per cent of its people living in towns and cities – and densely populated. These terraced and detached homes in Devon in southwest England are typical of dwellings in many small British towns.

London, the environs of Birmingham and Coventry in the Midlands, a crescent in the old industrial areas from Liverpool to Manchester and Sheffield, and small clusters around Newcastle, Glasgow, Cardiff and Belfast. The most sparsely populated regions are southwest and northern England, Wales, and most of Scotland.

England is the dominant partner in the United Kingdom, not just by land area (54 per cent of the total), but also by population and by demographic change. Nearly 84 per cent of the British population lives in England, which has also had the greatest population increase over the past century (64 per cent, compared to just 14 per cent in Scotland), and is expected to continue to grow for many years while the population of Scotland has already started to decline. Most of the major cities of the UK are in England, including London, Birmingham, Manchester and Liverpool, and – like cities everywhere – it is to these that people migrate in search of jobs, wealth and opportunity.

Typically for a post-industrial society, the rate of population increase in Britain has been declining, and currently stands at just 0.1 per cent annually. At this rate, the population is expected to peak in about 2040 at nearly 66 million before beginning to decline. An increasingly important determinant in population numbers has been the change in rates of migration. Natural change – the difference between births and deaths – accounted in the first half of the twentieth century for nearly all the increases in Britain's population, with average annual increases running in the range of 250–500,000 people. By the end of the century, the rate of natural change had fallen to just 60–100,000 people per year, while migration rates over the same period changed from a net outflow of 60–100,000 (in other words, more people were leaving Britain than arriving) to a net inflow of 130–160,000 people per year.

The patterns of international migration have had a significant impact on the diversity of Britain. Until the Second World War, it was a predominantly white country – most immigrants to Britain over the centuries had come from continental Europe, or from the white dominions of the so-called Old Commonwealth: Australia, Canada, New Zealand and South Africa. New arrivals, however, were greatly outnumbered by those leaving for the dominions and for the United States. This has all changed since 1945. In addition to the fact that more people are now arriving in Britain than are leaving, the postwar years have seen three significant changes in the patterns of migration:

- The increase in immigration from the New Commonwealth, notably the Indian sub-continent (India, Pakistan, Bangladesh) and the Caribbean. Since the Second World War, the number of non-whites living in Britain (Northern Ireland excluded) has grown from about 75–100,000 (0.2 per cent of the population) to 4.1 million (7.2 per cent of the population).
- The increase in migration to and from other EU member states. The average annual inflow of people from the EU during the 1990s grew from 71,000 to 89,000, and the number of Britons moving to other EU countries grew in tandem. Unlike old-style migration, where people moved because of economic necessity, or the general need to improve the quality of their lives, more recent migration flows have included work-related factors (companies moving workers to foreign offices) or 'lifestyle choices'; many Britons, for example, have retired to the south of France and Spain, and to Portugal.

- The increase in the number of people seeking asylum in Britain. Thanks to some of the loosest laws on asylum in the European Union, Britain has attracted asylum-seekers from a growing variety of countries. Annual applications rose from 33,000 in 1992 to 101,000 in 2000, placing Britain second only to Germany in the EU in terms of the number received (*The Economist*, 8 September 2001: 61). Annual average arrivals have grown from about 4000 in the early 1980s to about 80,000 today. Most recent asylum-seekers have come from the Balkans, the Middle East, and South Asia (particularly the former Yugoslavia, Iraq, Iran, Afghanistan and Sri Lanka), adding to the social diversity of Britain.

The British have also become increasingly mobile within Britain. Until the early part of the twentieth century it was typical for people to be born, to live, to work and to die in the same city, town or village, which would likely have been where their parents and grandparents before them had lived. The pace of mobility changed with the industrial revolution, when thousands were drawn over time to mining towns and to the factories being built in the rapidly growing urban centres of Scotland, south Wales, and the English midlands (for details, see Rubinstein, 1998, chapter 16).

During the twentieth century, social mobility greatly increased, and combined with improvements in transport and a revulsion against life in the city to produce more change. The most notable general trends have been (a) the move away from the old centres of heavy industry in northern England, Scotland and Wales towards jobs in light industry and services in southern England and the Midlands, and (b) the move away from the old city centres to the suburbs and to neighbouring towns, with a resulting increase in the number of people commuting to work.

In recent years, the most important net movement has been out of London: driven off by congestion, worsening traffic problems, the growing costs of property, and rising rents, there has been a significant outflow of people, many of them moving to cheaper, quieter and cleaner towns in the areas surrounding London. The population of the capital has continued to grow however, the place of internal migrants being taken in large part by the inflow of people moving to London from outside Britain, most notably from other EU member states.

As with all post-industrial societies, the population of Britain is becoming older as birth rates decline and people live longer. In 1901, just over a third of Britons were aged under 16, while 10 per cent were aged older than 55; today, the respective figures are 21 per cent and 23 per cent. Nearly one-quarter of adults are of pensionable age (60 for women, 65 for men), which represents an increase of 18 per cent since 1971. Present trends suggest that the number of people aged 65 or older will surpass those aged 16 or younger in the next 12–14 years. In this respect, Britain fits with trends across the European Union and in other industrialized countries outside Europe. There will be important political and economic ramifications:

- Increased pressure will continue to be placed on the health-care system as people live longer, as more must be spent on the provision of health care, and as the demand for doctors and nurses continues to grow.
- The workplace is being affected as the number of retirees who opt to continue to work for financial reasons continues to grow.
- Younger people will bear an increased burden of the social security system as proportionately fewer working-age Britons make contributions into the system and proportionately more retired Britons make withdrawals.
- Most important is the potential political power of the elderly. Given that there are more older people, and that voter turnout in this age group is high (80–87 per cent for those aged 55 and above as compared to 50–60 per cent for those aged 35 and below), retirees are becoming an increasingly important political group. Concerns about the welfare of the elderly (or 'pensioners' as they are typically called in Britain) have long been a hot-button issue, but despite the existence of many organizations representing the interests of the elderly, such as the National Pensioners Convention, Help the Aged, and Age Concern, they have not yet become an effective lobbying movement. This is likely to change as the population of Britain becomes older.

## Nationalism and Regionalism

The relationship among the four partners in the United Kingdom has not always been an easy one, with ongoing memories about the way in which England subjugated the three others, concerns about the cultural, economic and political dominance of England, and efforts to protect and rebuild minority cultural identity. Despite the existence of a 'United' Kingdom, regionalism is a factor in national politics, and there are even those in Scotland and Wales who support the idea of complete independence.

Wales lost its independence in 1285 and was united with England in 1536–42, as a result of which its early political institutions and processes developed along English lines, and the two countries today have the same legal and administrative systems. Scotland was different: the Scottish and English crowns were united in 1603, but political union did not come until 1707, and even then the two countries retained many separate features, including different religions, different legal codes, and separate educational structures. As for Ireland, the partition that came in 1922 with the creation of the Irish Free State left behind Northern Ireland, which has since been governed mainly as a semi-autonomous state, with its own civil service, its own political parties, and (except when direct rule from London was imposed in 1972-99) its own Parliament at Stormont.

What are the differences among the four countries?

• Each has its own flag*, its own culture, and its own writers and artists. Each country even has its own sports teams, so that while English, Scottish, Welsh and Northern Irish athletes at the Olympics wear the colours of Great Britain, there are separate national football and rugby teams (although the national rugby teams occasionally combine with Ireland under the colours of the British Lions). For its part, though, cricket is predominantly an English sport.

• Scotland, Wales and Northern Ireland have their own regional political parties: the Scottish National Party (SNP), Plaid Cymru in Wales, and a cluster of Northern Irish parties. All have representation both in the national British Parliament and in the new regional assemblies.

• Class and regional differences overlap, a result of the development of industry in the eighteenth and nineteenth centuries in Scotland, Wales and the north of England. These regions saw the rise of the new industrial class of manual labourers, and have since suffered the worst effects of industrial decline and economic adjustment. So while England has a per capita GDP slightly above the average for

---

* The old flag of Northern Ireland – a red hand inside a white star on a red cross – has strong connections with the Protestant community, and is no longer official but is still occasionally flown. The official flag of Northern Ireland is the Union Flag of the United Kingdom.

the UK, the figures for Scotland, Wales and Northern Ireland are all lower than average (see Table 2.1).

● Scotland and Northern Ireland have legal and educational systems that are separate from that used in England and Wales, and the Church of Scotland – created in 1560 – is also separate from the Church of England (see Chapter 7).

● Wales is officially bilingual. About 20 per cent of the population of Wales (that is, about 500,000 people) speaks Welsh, which has had equal status with English since 1993, and Wales also has its own Welsh-language radio and TV stations. (By contrast, only about 8 per cent of the people of Northern Ireland speak or write Irish Gaelic, and a bare 50,000 people in Scotland – about 1 per cent of the population – speak Scottish Gaelic, and forecasts have been made of its imminent extinction.)

England dominates the relationship between these four countries, of which it is the largest (see Table 2.1); is wealthier per capita than the three other countries, and is itself dominated by London, which plays a key role in national affairs (see Box 2.2). At the same time, Scotland and Wales have several advantages over England. First, they are slightly overrepresented in the national British Parliament, Scotland having just under 9 per cent of the population but 11 per cent of seats (although this is due to change soon), and Wales having 5 per cent of the population but 6 per cent of seats. Second, Scottish parliamentary districts on average have 10,000 fewer people than those in England. Third, Scotland in particular benefits from 20–25 per cent more public spending per head of population than England.

*Table 2.1*  The four nations compared

|  | Population millions | % | Population density per sq km | Land area '000 sq km | % | Per capita GDP (UK=100) |
|---|---|---|---|---|---|---|
| England | 50.0 | **83.7** | 283 | 130.4 | **54.0** | 102 |
| Scotland | 5.2 | **8.6** | 65 | 78.8 | **32.6** | 96 |
| Wales | 2.9 | **4.9** | 142 | 20.8 | **8.6** | 81 |
| N. Ireland | 1.7 | **2.8** | 125 | 14.1 | **5.8** | 77 |
| Total | 59.8 |  |  | 244.1 |  |  |

*Source*:  Office for National Statistics (2002). Per capita GDP figures are for 2001.

**Box 2.2   The dominating role of London**

Not all capital cities play a major role in national affairs, because power is often dissipated and shared among multiple major urban areas. For example, Washington DC may be the capital of the United States, but it is a relatively provincial city: New York has a population 15 times greater, Los Angeles a population seven times greater, and they are thus more nationally significant.

The situation is very different in Britain, where London plays a dominant role in almost every aspect of British life, so much so that Britain is not only dominated by England, but in many respects is also dominated by London. More than one-third of the British population lives in and around London, and as well as being the seat of national government, it is also the national hub for the following:

- *Communications*: it is the home of all the major national newspapers and radio and TV stations.
- *Finance*: it is the home of the Bank of England, the London Stock Exchange, and most of the major banks and financial corporations.
- *Transport*: the rail and motorway systems centre on London, which is also home to Britain's two major airports, Heathrow and Gatwick.
- *Culture*: London has world-class theatre, opera, ballet, symphony orchestras, and is home to recording studios and major rock concert venues.
- *Sports*: the national football stadium was for many years at Wembley in north London, and the capital is also home to Wimbledon for tennis, Twickenham for rugby, and Lords and The Oval for cricket.

Inner London – including the shopping and cultural districts of the West End, and the financial district of the City of London – is the wealthiest region in the European Union. For statistical purposes, the EU is divided into 211 regions; taking 100 as the average per capita gross domestic product for those regions, the poorer parts of the EU have a per capita GDP in the range of 45–70, while the figure for inner London is 233 (figures from Eurostat, the EU statistical service). Unfortunately, inner London is also one of the most expensive places to live in the world, topping comparative tables for the cost of renting and buying property, for eating out at restaurants, and for going out to the theatre or the cinema.

The strength of the relationship between the four countries has ebbed and flowed, but talk of the potential break-up of the United Kingdom is exaggerated, although there has been pressure since the 1960s for devolution (the transfer of selected powers from the national government in London to regional governments). The Conservative Party was traditionally opposed to the idea, seeing it as

**Illustration 2.4   Trafalgar Square, London**

Trafalgar Square in the heart of London, with the National Gallery in the background. London is the political, financial, communications and cultural capital of Britain, and about one-third of Britain's population lives within 80km (50 miles) of its centre.

the thin end of a wedge that would eventually lead to full independence, at least for Scotland. Meanwhile, the Labour Party for many years promised constitutional reforms leading to devolution, and – upon coming to power in 1997 – the Blair administration moved quickly to hold referendums in Scotland and Wales on a proposal to create regional assemblies. Nearly 75 per cent of Scots voted in favour, while a bare majority of the Welsh (50.3 per cent) were in favour. The result was the creation in 1998 of assemblies for Scotland and Wales, followed in 1999 by the re-establishment of an assembly for Northern Ireland (see Chapter 4 for more details).

Supporters of devolution long argued that it would reduce demands for independence, particularly in Scotland. While the Scottish independence movement has grown in recent decades, opinion polls are inconclusive on the issue of how far it has gone, with recent surveys finding between one-third and one-half in favour, depending on how the question is worded. Whatever the balance of opinion, there is without question a measure of resentment against the national government in London, strongest in the poorer parts of Scotland and Wales. An indication of the priorities of voters is provided by the support given to the regional political parties at regional and national elections: at the regional assembly elections in 1999, the Scottish National Party won 27 per cent of the vote while Plaid Cymru won 31 per cent of the vote. At the 2001 general election, by contrast, the SNP won just 20 per cent of the Scottish vote while Plaid Cymru in Wales won 14 per cent of the Welsh vote. These figures suggest that the majority of the Scots and the Welsh still support national political parties, and therefore continued union, but that larger proportions want to see local issues taken care of by local parties.

It is also important to appreciate that regionalism is not simply about national frontiers, but that Scotland, Wales and Northern Ireland are divided within themselves. The Scots have different religions, and there are cultural rivalries between highlanders and lowlanders, and between Glasgow and Edinburgh. The Welsh are divided economically between the old industrial centres and coal-mining communities of the south and the agricultural regions of the north, and between those who speak Welsh and those who do not. For its part, Northern Ireland suffers a variety of religious, economic and cultural divisions, and is split between those who support continued union with Britain and those who do not.

Meanwhile, England is characterized by its own regionalism, and by a recent rise in sympathy for the idea of English nationalism. Surprisingly for so small a country, there are distinctive regional identities that set the English apart from each other. The values, attitudes and priorities of people who live in the economic powerhouse of London and its suburbs are different from those who live in the rural and small-town environment of the 'home counties' around London, in the farmlands and the tourist meccas of the south-west, in the old industrial areas of the midlands and the north, and in the dales of Yorkshire and the mountains and lakes of Cumbria. Most unusual of all is the enclave of Cornwall on the southwestern tip of England: the Cornish are related to the Celts of Ireland, Wales and Scotland, have a distinctive culture, and – although very few now speak it – have their own language.

Nationalism has had its most damaging effects in Northern Ireland. The province was created in in 1922, when Ireland won its independence and was partitioned: while the 26 southern and largely Catholic counties were reconfigured as the Irish Free State, the six northern counties had Protestant majorities (tracing their roots back to the arrival in the seventeenth century of Scottish Presbyterians) and opted to remain part of the United Kingdom. Protestants discriminated against Catholics in the province, notably marginalizing them in schools, jobs, the police and local government. In 1968, Northern Irish Catholics held demonstrations in support of improved civil rights, to which the Protestant-dominated local police responded with force. British troops, dispatched to the province to maintain peace, were quickly accused by Catholics of taking the side of the Protestants.

Over the following 30 years, about 3500 people died and many thousands more were injured in the conflict, which saw the rise of political parties representing the different communities, and of paramilitary groups prepared to use terrorism as a means to achieving their political ends. While the Ulster Unionists and the Ulster Defence Force (UDF), among others, promoted the Protestant cause, Sinn Fein and the Irish Republican Army (IRA) promoted the Catholic cause. Assassinations, bigotry and tribalism became the tragic norm, and every attempt to bring peace to Northern Ireland failed. Most Catholics identified with the nationalist cause, demanding a reunification of Ireland, while most Protestants remained loyalists or unionists, insisting that the province remain part of the UK. Successive British governments meanwhile found themselves caught in between, pleasing neither side, and occasionally making the situation worse.

A troubled peace now prevails in the province. The Blair government underwrote negotiations between the warring factions, which after the agreement of concessions by all sides, led to the agreement of an accord in April 1998, which in turn owed much to the personal and diplomatic skills of Tony Blair (Aughey, 2001). It brought about a cease-fire between the warring sides, set up a regional assembly for Northern Ireland in which Protestants and Catholics shared power, and created cross-border councils that would bring members of the new assembly together with members of the British and Irish parliaments. The new Northern Ireland regional government finally met for the first time in November 1999, and – despite subsequent suspensions of its functioning, squabbles between the two sides, the emergence of splinter IRA groups, and continued (but much reduced) sectarian violence – the prospects for a lasting peace in the province have improved.

## Immigration and Race

Racial diversity is a relatively recent issue in Britain, despite many centuries of movement of people across its borders. Throughout the nineteenth century, Britain was a net exporter of people, most of them emigrants to the United States and to the white dominions of the Old Commonwealth. There were few foreigners living in Britain, so the issue of immigration barely registered on political, cultural or economic radars. The situation has been quite different since the 1950s, however, because of the rise in the numbers of non-white immigrants from the New Commonwealth, notably India, Pakistan, Bangladesh, West Africa and the Caribbean (see Figure 2.1). In particular, immigration and race have become synonymous issues.

As recently as the beginning of the nineteenth century, there was virtually uncontrolled movement of people throughout Europe, and passports and immigration controls were all but unknown. However, only the wealthy could afford to travel, and since they were not seen as an actual or potential drain on national economies, they were not seen as posing any kind of threat. This began to change with the era of mass emigration that began in the late 1800s, prompting governments to begin restricting movement. The first significant immigration control imposed by Britain came with the Aliens Act of 1905, directed mainly at limiting the immigration of Jews from Eastern Europe.

Under a 1948 law, citizens of the Empire and Commonwealth were considered British subjects with the right of entry to Britain. This elicited little controversy because the vast majority of immigrants were white. Then, labour shortages in the 1950s encouraged British industry to recruit workers from the New Commonwealth, particularly to work in public transport, in the National Health Service, and in northern factories. This raised the first widespread concerns about race. The law was changed in 1962 to require that Commonwealth immigrants have work permits, and was further tightened in 1968 when East African Asians holding British passports lost their automatic right to live in Britain, a move that was widely (and rightly) condemned as racial discrimination (Clarke, 1996: 326). The growth of the non-white community led to an increase in racial tensions, and to the infamous warning by Conservative politician Enoch Powell in 1968 of the threats posed by immigration to the 'British way of life', and the prospect of the streets running with 'rivers of blood'.

Non-white immigration became a hot-button issue in the late 1960s with the influx of Indians and Pakistanis from Kenya, who were joined in 1971 by more Indians and Pakistanis expelled from Uganda by the notorious military dictator, Idi Amin. The law was changed in Britain in 1971 to limit immigration to those who were born in Britain or whose parents or grandparents were of British origin. The cumulative result of these changes in the law was that by the late 1970s, only 75,000 immigrants were entering the country each year, a number that was smaller than the number of emigrants leaving each year. By the early 1980s, the number had fallen to 54,000 annually, of whom just over half were from New Commonwealth countries.

Also in the 1960s and 1970s, a number of new pieces of legislation made it illegal to discriminate against anyone on the basis of race, and set up a Race Relations Board (replaced in 1976 by the Commission for Racial Equality) to which anyone could appeal who felt that they had been the target of discrimination. Many non-white immigrants initially had difficulty being integrated into British society, and lived in economically depressed inner-city areas. Tensions peaked during the spring and summer of 1981, when violent clashes broke out between police and minorities in the Brixton and Southall districts of London, the Toxteth district of Liverpool, and in Manchester, but it is debatable whether or not these were race riots. The violence was directed against property and the police, and the rioters were both

*Figure* 2.1   Racial minorities in Britain

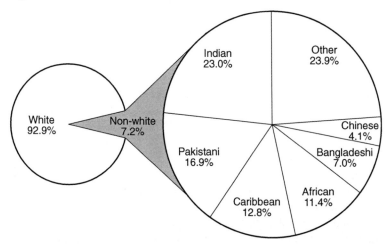

black and white. Racial prejudice was a factor in the violence, it is true, but so was economic recession, job losses, the decline of inner cities, and concerns about crime. A government enquiry into the violence (the Scarman enquiry of 1981) was critical of policing methods, and led to a substantial reformation of police–community relations.

Today, just over four million people – or about 7 per cent of the population of Britain – belongs to an ethnic minority, and an increasing proportion of the non-white population consists of people born and raised in Britain, and who have been more fully assimilated into British society than their immigrant parents. Racism has not gone away, however, as reflected in cases of racial harassment and a number of controversies in recent years involving the police and non-whites in London, where 20 per cent of the population is from an ethnic minority. The issue of race was at the heart of a particularly notorious incident in April 1993, when a black teenager named Stephen Lawrence was beaten to death by a group of white teenagers in south-east London. Failures in the policy enquiry that followed led to charges of systematic corruption and institutionalized racism in the police force, and to the passage of 1998 legislation introducing new assault, harassment and public-order offences, applying higher penalties in the case of those that are racially aggravated.

Immigration has become a touchstone political issue again in recent years with the growing pressure for Britain to admit new waves of arrivals from Eastern Europe and the Middle East, drawn by the lure of Britain's strong economy. The issue was exemplified by the large number of refugees crowded into the Sangatte camp near Calais, trying to stow away onboard trains as they entered the Channel tunnel (the camp was closed in December 2002). Opinion polls in 2002 found that immigration had become the second-ranking issue of public concern after the state of health care, with more than 40 per cent of respondents expressing concern, up from just 10 per cent in 1999 (*The Economist*, 29 June 2002: 53).

Political leaders approach the issue cautiously, worried about creating a backlash that would strengthen support for far-Right anti-immigration political parties, as it has done in Austria, France, Germany and the Netherlands. They are also concerned about a backlash from minorities themselves, who suffer economic inequalities, have an unemployment rate that is three times that of whites, and still often live in run-down suburbs. Non-whites have not yet been prompted to develop their own movement for political change,

Racial diversity has only come to Britain since the 1950s, but already it has made Britain one of the most multicultural societies in Europe. This girl is taking part in the annual Notting Hill Carnival in London, the biggest event of its kind in the European Union.

**Illustration 2.5   Notting Hill Carnival, London**

instead mainly preferring to work within the established Labour Party. Minority cultures (with the partial exception of the Muslim culture) have in many respects become a part of mainstream British culture, and there is more social mobility for non-whites. Non-whites have also become more prominent in British popular culture and professional sports: the England World Cup football squad in 1966 had not a single non-white player, whereas the 2002 squad had seven.

Two interesting anomalies complicate the issue of immigration into Britain. First, there is the unique status of the Irish. As a left-over from the time when Ireland was part of the United Kingdom, Irish citizens still have all the same rights as British citizens, including free entry, no limits on employment, and even the right to vote in British elections and run for office. There are still considerable numbers of Irish in the UK, but there has also been the beginning of reverse immigration as Irish and British citizens have been attracted to Ireland by its recent economic renaissance.

Second, citizens of other European Union states also have the right of free entry into Britain, and can vote in local or European elections. Britain has proved a magnet in recent years to nationals of other EU states, several hundred thousand of whom now live there. London in particular has become more diverse as locals finding it too expensive have moved out, and their place has been taken by continental Europeans moving to London with their jobs, or seeking to profit from the new opportunities the city offers. Where the issue of immigration and emigration once underpinned Britain's cultural and political links with Australia, Canada, New Zealand and the United States, it is slowly becoming representative of the growing economic, social and cultural links between Britain and its EU partners.

# 3

# The Social System

Britain is predominantly urban, middle-class, English-speaking and white. However, like all major industrialized countries it is a divided society. Its long early history of invasions from the continent have combined with England's incorporation of its neighbours and more recent waves of immigration from the Commonwealth and other parts of the European Union to create important cultural and religious divisions. The economic divisions that began with feudalism and that were only partly addressed by the industrial revolution live on in a society divided by class and opportunity, where the creation of a welfare state and the expansion of educational opportunities has so far failed to create a level playing field. These divisions in turn have had an impact on the distribution and expression of political and economic power.

British society is both fascinating and complex. One study (Obelkevich and Catterall, 1994, p. 1) puts it this way:

> British society is a complicated affair, full of loose ends and bits that don't fit. This may be a good thing for the people who live in it, but it is a source of frustration for those who study it and try to understand it. Every attempt to sum it up in a simple formula – as a 'class society' or whatever – has proved to have so many exceptions and qualifications that it was more trouble than it was worth. The first thing to understand about British society is that there are no short-cuts, no master keys.

Perhaps the key concept in any discussion of British society is 'change'. The structure of society, the way in which people relate to one another, the kinds of opportunities available to Britons, and the quality of their lives when measured by personal safety and by access to health care and education have all undergone considerable change since the Second World War, and even since the era of Margaret Thatcher and her programme of rolling back the frontiers of the state.

In spite of such complexities, this chapter sets out to paint a social portrait of Britain. It begins with an assessment of the class system, which – while weaker than ever before – nonetheless plays an important role in the way the British relate to each other. It then looks at the changing structure of the family, and the impact of the trend towards smaller families, changing rates of marriage and divorce, and the growing number of children born outside marriage. It examines the welfare system, the impact of social security, and the trials and tribulations of the National Health Service, which is both widely cherished and widely criticized. It looks also at the education system, elements of which are renowned around the world, but yet which still fails to provide some Britons with even the most basic skills. The chapter ends with a discussion of the performance of the criminal justice system in maintaining law and order.

**Social Class**

Not surprisingly for a society that evolved out of feudalism and still has an aristocracy, the class system in Britain is alive and well. There are those – such as Margaret Thatcher and John Major – who deny that class divisions exist, but there are others – such as Tony Blair – who, while they might not use the term 'class', make much of the social divisions that characterize Britain. Several key elements of Blairite policy (notably education and welfare) are based on the argument that there are significant inequalities of opportunity in Britain, and that the removal of the barriers to social advancement must be a central element of the actions of government.

The distinctions that set one class apart from another have declined, to be sure, most notably with the rise of the postwar middle class. However, enough remain for many Britons – consciously or subconsciously – to relate to each other on the basis of class differences. During the feudal era the system revolved around relationships with land and the monarchy: the lords managed the land, while the peasants worked the land, and were obligated to the lords in almost every way. Political and economic power was focused in the hands of a landed elite.

Even during the industrial revolution, which saw the rise of urban entrepreneurs who often accumulated huge fortunes, 'new money' made by hard work and application was still seen as worth less than inherited 'old money', and class distinctions continued to be driven more by heritage, occupation and social values than by relative monetary worth. You could be a moneyless minor aristocrat, but you were still socially superior to a wealthy factory owner. Meanwhile, the class system became more complicated. Instead of a landed aristocracy and a peasantry, a distinction now had to be made between the urban working class and the rural peasantry.

Where the class system was once divided simply into upper, middle and working class, it is today more complex than ever before, and the narrowing of wealth and income differentials have made it increasingly difficult to make generalizations about class (Jones and Kavanagh, 1998: 12–14). There is still a pyramid of social layers recognised by the government, ranging from managerial and professional occupations, to lower supervisory, semi-routine and routine workers, to the long-term unemployed (see Table 3.1). However, the balance of power and opportunity among classes has changed, the most notable development of the last 50 years being the rise of the middle class: about 60–65 per cent of Britons today describe themselves as middle-class (non-manual and managerial), up from about 20 per cent in 1914. Meanwhile, about 30 per cent describe themselves as working-class (skilled and unskilled manual workers), a significant reduction from 1914 when the figure was closer to 80 per cent.

Class differences remain, it has been argued, because Britain has not experienced the kinds of revolutions, wars or periods of mass immigration that allowed greater social mobility in other European states (Budge *et al.*, 2000: 37). Although most Britons will deny it, many still see each other through the lenses of economic status, family background and lifestyle. Many of the determinants of class are not easily observable or quantifiable, and are based as much as anything on what one person instinctively feels about another. But other determinants are more obvious, and include education, the jobs that people do, their social habits, the communities in which people live, and even the newspapers they read – broadsheets such as *The Times* and *The Guardian* are identified with the upper and middle class, while tabloids such as the *Sun* and the *Daily Mirror* are identified with the working class.

For many Britons, accent is the most obvious (if simplistic)

*Table* 3.1   Social class in Britain

---

1  Higher managerial and professional

   1.1   Employers and managers in larger organizations (company directors, senior bureaucrats, senior military officers, etc.)

   1.2.  Higher professionals (doctors, lawyers, clergy, teachers, etc.)

2  Lower managerial and professional (nurses, journalists, actors, musicians, lower military and police ranks, etc.)

3  Intermediate occupations (clerks, secretaries, etc.)

4  Small employers and own account workers (farmers, taxi drivers, painters and decorators, etc.)

5  Lower supervisory, craft and related occupations (printers, plumbers, butchers, etc.)

6  Semi-routine occupations (shop assistants, bus drivers, cooks, etc.)

7  Routine occupations (labourers, waiters, refuse collectors, etc.)

8  People who have never had paid work, and long-term unemployed

---

determinant of class, and there is still some truth to the sentiment expressed more than 80 years ago by the playwright George Bernard Shaw in *Pygmalion*: 'It is impossible for an Englishman to open his mouth without making some other Englishman hate or despise him'. At the same time, accents are misleading. The standard upper-class accent for much of the early and middle twentieth century was Received Pronunciation (RP), otherwise known as Oxford or BBC English; this is the kind of accent with which members of the royal family speak. Despite the fact that no more than 5 per cent of the population ever had such an accent (a proportion that has been halved in recent years), RP was the benchmark against which all other accents were measured. It was widely – if undeservedly – interpreted as a badge of education, authority and trustworthiness. Meanwhile, almost anyone speaking with a regional accent was assumed to be working or lower middle class. Thus the accents of Devon and Yorkshire were associated with the rural working class, and the scouse accent of Liverpool or the cockney accent of London were associated with the urban working class.

The BBC perpetuated the distinction, for many years employing only those announcers with an RP accent. But the BBC has also done much to undermine the dominance of RP since the 1980s, making efforts to employ announcers with regional accents, particularly on local radio and TV stations. Accents are still something of a social straitjacket, however, and anyone who speaks with an accent that does not correspond with his or her social credentials is immediately regarded as suspect. In a telling incident in 1999, Prime Minister Tony Blair – who is soundly middle-class – appeared on a television chat show hosted by a singer and comedian named Des O'Connor. Blair began the interview speaking in the clipped middle England tones for which he is known (despite the fact that he was born in Scotland), but as he relaxed he began to adopt so-called Estuary English, named for areas of southeastern England, including suburbs and towns lying along the Thames estuary, where words are often shortened and key vowels are dropped. There was much comment in the national media the next day about the significance of this, with Blair being accused of hiding his middle-class heritage.

Social mobility – usually defined as the ability to move from one class to another with a change of generation – has increased significantly since the 1960s, reflecting new access to education, a growth in the proportion of Britons in managerial and professional jobs, a decrease in the number of people employed in manual labour, the effects of the welfare system, and a weakening of the class system. The rich tend to remain rich, it is true, and the gap between the rich and the poor is substantial (see Box 3.1). Studies also suggest that there is less social mobility in Britain, France, Germany and the United States than is generally supposed, or than there is in Australia, Japan or Sweden (*The Economist*, 6 April 2002: 47). However, the British middle class is bigger and more stable than in the past. Where children would typically follow the occupational path (and the social status) of their parents, it has become more usual for offspring to move up the occupational ladder, and for those who have been able to create new wealth or status for themselves to change their class identity. This has been possible in part because welfare and improved education have helped reduce the chances of downward mobility. There has also been a decline in the value once accorded to inherited wealth – in today's more egalitarian and meritocratic Britain, 'new money' attracts more respect.

The emergence of the consumer society has also made a significant difference. The idea of 'going without' and of avoiding conspicuous consumption – a hangover from prewar years when most Britons were too poor to own their own homes or to furnish them with more than the basic necessities – was extended by postwar austerity and rationing. Even the boom of the 1950s reached relatively few people,

**Box 3.1   Poverty and affluence**

Poverty is a troubling issue in every industrialized country, in part because of the debates over how it should be defined, and in part because of the large numbers of people who are apparently still 'poor' in the midst of growing wealth. In Britain, as in most other comparable countries, the overall quality of people's lives has improved dramatically since the Second World War. People have higher incomes, better job security, more access to education and health care, and more of them own homes and cars. However, not all is well:

- If the government definition is accepted (people living in households with less than 60 per cent of median national income, after housing costs), then Britain has the second highest rate of poverty in the EU: 22 per cent (or 13 million people), compared to the EU average of 15 per cent (only Greece has a higher rate) (New Policy Institute, 2002).
- The number of people living below the poverty line is twice what it was 20 years ago, and has not changed since 1995/96.
- The rich have become richer, and the poor are falling behind. Despite the doubling of real household disposable income since 1971, the income gap in Britain grew rapidly in the late 1980s, fell slightly in the early 1990s, then rose again in the late 1990s. The average income of the top 20 per cent of households in 1999–2000 was nearly £55,000 (€/$82,500), or 19 times the average income of the lowest 20 per cent.
- Single-parent families and retired people are overrepresented in lower income groups, as are households with children. At the bottom of the scale, about 150,000 people are homeless according to official government figures, although unofficial estimates suggest that the figure may actually be twice as high.

Meanwhile, affluence has become more visible in the last generation as the net worth of the upper middle class has expanded. The amount of money that people had left to save or spend after taxes and other deductions, adjusted for inflation, doubled between 1971 and 2000. This was made possible by lower income and estate taxes, substantial increases in the value of homes, and profits from shares and other investments. The wealthiest 10 per cent of the adult population now owns 56 per cent of household marketable wealth. Symbolic of the change has been the growth of business for home improvement stores, the increase in the number of people taking overseas holidays, and the growth in the number of individual shareholders, up from 8 per cent of households in 1980 to 20 per cent in 1987 to 26 per cent in 2003.

and certainly the British were a pale shadow of middle-class Americans when it came to being more adventurous with their leisure time, or acquiring material possessions. It was only in the early 1970s that low-cost travel allowed more people to spend their holidays in Spain or Greece or Morocco rather than seaside English resorts. It was only in the 1980s that consumption began to move into high gear, and people spent more money installing central heating and double-glazing in their homes, buying new cars, TVs, stereos and video recorders, and going on holiday to the United States, Africa, or the Far East and Australia.

The British class system has also been impacted by several other developments:

• Changes in occupational structure. The number of jobs in labour-intensive heavy industry has fallen, to be replaced by jobs in more automated and lighter industry, and particularly by jobs in the service sector. This has altered the balance of population numbers between the working and middle classes.

• A substantial increase in private home ownership. In 1900, just 10 per cent of the population owned their own homes, but in 2003 the figure is more than 70 per cent. A breakthrough came in the 1980s with the decision by the Thatcher government to sell off council houses (state-owned housing stock) to their tenants, creating over a million new owner-occupier families almost overnight. The value of homes has grown dramatically, going through booms in the mid-1980s, the early 1990s, and again in 2000–03, increasing the net worth of homeowners and blurring the distinctions between different social classes.

• The rise of the upper middle class. Increases in incomes and benefits and improvements in working conditions for managerial and professional staff have increased the buying power, financial options and political influence of the upper middle class, even going so far as to create a 'super class' of senior professionals and managers with new power, who are increasingly separated from the rest of society by money, education, values, residence and lifestyle (Adonis and Pollard, 1997).

The changing nature of the class system can be seen in the changing relationship between class and political activity. While the Labour Party was for many decades the champion of the working class, and the Conservative Party attracted more support from the middle class, the link between class and voting has declined. The share of the middle-class vote for the Conservatives has fallen from 80 per cent to 60 per cent since the early 1970s, while the share of the working-class vote for Labour has fallen from 60 per cent to 50 per cent. Labour under Tony Blair realized that economic changes meant that it could no longer rely on the working-class vote, so the policies of 'New' Labour were more geared to middle-class needs, as a result of which its share of the middle-class vote in 1997 equalled that of the Conservatives (Kavanagh, 2000: 127–8). Sociological factors are now less of an explanation of voting behaviour than are political factors (see Chapter 5).

## The Changing Structure of the Family

The definition and the place of the family has changed in Britain in recent years, as it has in most other industrialized countries. The British have the same worried conversations about the breakup of the nuclear family, about the failure to provide for elderly and disabled family members, and about the supposed decay of moral values in the wake of reduced parental guidance. Yet they fail to realize that family size has been falling steadily for more than a century. In the 1860s, the live birth rate for married women was 5.7. By the 1920s, the figure had fallen to 2.2, where it has more or less remained ever since. The nuclear family – a mother, a father and dependent children – was already relatively unusual 30 years ago (accounting for just one-third of British households) and has become even more so today (just under one-quarter of households). So the idea of 'traditional family values' has been a misnomer for decades, and it is really only social pressure – and perhaps the portrayal of families in television dramas, sitcoms and commercials – that keeps the spirit of the nuclear family alive.

There are several reasons for changes in the structure of families:

- There has been a trend towards smaller families. There was a time when people had more babies because of higher mortality rates, and because children were needed to work the land for the family. But mortality rates have fallen, children are no longer needed for their labour, there is less social pressure to have children, and – indeed – having a child has become an expensive proposition. To feed, clothe, house, educate and take care of the health of a child is

**Illustration 3.1  Maple Infant School**

The size and nature of British families has changed dramatically in recent years, as fewer people marry, more are divorced, women delay having children, and family size decreases. These children are taking part in a class at an infant school in Surrey.

now a significant financial commitment. As a result, the average completed family size in Britain has fallen from 3.2 children in 1951 to less than 2.0.

- Women are putting off having children. Many more of them are taking their education further, and many more are looking to establish a career before starting a family. As a result, the mean age at which British women have their first child has risen from 26.2 years in 1972 to 29.1. At the same time, the number of women opting not to have any children at all has increased; about one-fifth of women born after 1965 are projected to remain childless.
- There have been changes in attitudes towards marriage. The majority of British men and women still get married, but the proportion has been declining, with more people living together before getting married, and more people simply living together without getting married: about one-sixth of the non-married adult population of England and Wales is estimated to be living together. It is now as

common to hear British adults coyly referring to their 'partner' as to their husband or wife.

• There was a sixfold increase in the divorce rate between 1961 and 1999. This has happened in part because of a decline in the social stigma attached to divorce, in part because couples in an unhappy marriage are more likely to break up rather than struggle on as their parents might have done, and in part because women are earning higher wages and better qualifications, and so developing more independence.

• The number of children born outside marriage has increased, the rate in Britain now being among the highest in the industrialized world: nearly 40 per cent of children were born outside marriage in 2000, a 50 per cent increase over the rate in 1990, and a 500 per cent increase over the rate in 1971. Only Iceland, Sweden, Denmark and France have higher rates, while the rate for the United States is about 33 per cent, and the rate for the European Union as a whole is 27 per cent (*The Economist*, 6 July 2002: 49).

• The number of people living alone has grown, up from 18 per cent of households in 1971 to 29 per cent. One factor in this has been increased life expectancy, contributing to growing numbers of empty-nesters (parents whose children have grown up and left home) and of widows and widowers. However, the biggest growth has been in the number of men under age 65 living alone, which has tripled since 1971 to account now for one in ten households.

The cumulative result of all these changes has been a reduction in the average size of the household over the last 50 years, from 4.6 people to 2.4 people, and projections that it will fall to 2.2 by 2021. The 'unconventional' household has become much more common than the nuclear family, with important effects on the way people relate to one another, on the structure of communities, on the provision of social services, and on the upbringing of children. The most alarming implications have been for the number of children living in poverty – approximately four million British children, or one in three, are members of families that live below the poverty line. By no means do all of them live in single-parent households, but there is a close link between being a single parent and being poor. The Blair government made a pledge in 1999 to end child poverty within a generation, and although the number of children living in poverty has fallen, the extent of the problem is still unconscionable for a wealthy industrialized society like Britain.

## Social Services and Health Care

Like all modern industrialized societies, Britain is a welfare state, or one in which government makes provision under the law for those in need, particularly the elderly, the sick, the poor, the disabled and the indigent. There have been elements of a welfare system in place since the sixteenth century, when a Poor Law provided limited support for those in need, although churches continued to provide most of the services needed to help the poor and the unemployed. With industrialization, the population of Britain grew rapidly, as did the number of people working in cities, which became overcrowded, filthy and polluted. The expanding working class lacked basic amenities such as adequate housing, sanitation, health facilities and utilities such as a clean water supply. Working conditions were often appalling, child labour was common, the poor were exploited and typically denied the vote, and when the government finally did take action in 1834 to provide assistance for the indigent, the solution was to create a network of workhouses where inmates lived in prison-like conditions, worked long hours for little reward, and were separated from their families.

Responding to decades of pressure for social reform, the Liberal government that was swept into power in 1906 laid the foundations of the modern welfare state by creating state schools, providing a state pension, providing free school meals for children, and creating unemployment benefits. However, it was not until after the Second World War – on the recommendation of the 1942 Beveridge Report (see Chapter 1) – that a comprehensive welfare system was finally developed. Entering office in 1945 on the crest of a wave of reforming zeal, the new Labour government of Clement Attlee oversaw the passage of legislation that created a social security system designed to provide help for the unemployed, widows, and the retired, and a National Health Service that would provide mainly free medical services to anyone not already covered by other programmes.

The calculations made about welfare needs in the 1940s were quite different from the realities that have emerged since then. For example, it was assumed that unemployment would mainly be a short-term problem and affect few people, that families would typically be supported by a male breadwinner while wives would stay at home, and that the number of contributors to social insurance would greatly exceed the number of dependents (Mohan, 1999: 135). In fact,

**Illustration 3.2    St Thomas' Hospital**

St Thomas' Hospital in London. The British live longer and healthier lives than ever before, but problems in the health-care system have been high on the political agenda, with concerns about staff shortages and long waits for patients needing operations.

Britain has witnessed long-term unemployment, changing patterns of participation in the labour market, smaller families, and increased life expectancy.

Thanks in part to changes such as these, the social security system has become the single biggest item on the national government budget, accounting between 1995 and 2001 for about 28 per cent of annual government spending. In 2001, the government spent £105 billion (€/$158 billion) on social security, or nearly £1800 (€/$2700) for every man, woman and child. About half of spending goes on retirement pensions, which are paid to anyone who has made a certain number of contributions into the social security system while they were working. The pensionable age for women is 60, and for men is 65, although starting in 2010 the age for women born after 1950 will be gradually increased to 65. Payments are not substantial (£3770 annually for a single person and nearly £6030 for a married couple (respectively €/$5655 and €/$9045)), but then the system is intended only to act as a safety net to avoid the kind of poverty that particularly afflicted elderly people before the advent of the welfare state. Other items in the social security budget include payments to long-term sick and disabled people (about one-quarter of spending), support to families (including maternity pay and child benefits), unemployment pay, and support for widows and widowers. In all, just over a quarter of the population receives benefits of some kind.

The second key element in the social security system – and a matter of considerable political controversy in recent years – is the National Health Service (NHS). Created in 1948 by the National Health Service Act, the NHS provides residents of Britain with a health-care system in which services are either free or heavily subsidized; pregnant women, new mothers, children, the elderly, full-time students, and those on low incomes are exempt from most charges. The service is paid for out of public funds, with all taxpayers, employees and employers paying into the system, and services being provided on the basis of need rather than the ability to pay. The single biggest employer in Western Europe (with a total workforce of about one million people), the NHS cost about £50 billion in 2001 (€/$75 billion), and is projected to cost close to £60 billion annually by 2004 (€/$90 billion). Health-care professionals – such as doctors, dentists, optometrists and pharmacists – are mainly self-employed, provide services on behalf of the NHS, and are compensated by health authorities for providing those services.

Public opinion on the NHS is divided. While few question the principle of universal free medical care, and there is much pride in the concept of the NHS, the quality of service it provides has been the subject of growing criticism. Most complaints focus on poor standards, bureaucracy, low pay and long hours for doctors and nurses, the amount of time it sometimes takes for a patient to see a doctor, and the waiting time in accident and emergency departments in hospitals. Most controversial of all have been the infamous waiting lists for patients seeking operations; it can take up to 18 months for someone to receive non-urgent surgery, 9–12 months to receive hip- or knee-replacement surgery, and even several months for cancer patients to start receiving treatment. Waiting lists at times have numbered in the tens of thousands, and there have been well-publicized (albeit rare) instances of patients dying before being able to receive care.

Every British government in recent decades has had to face the issue of reforms to the NHS. Unlike, for example, the United States, where 'socialized medicine' is politically and publicly unpopular, and where public health-care services are provided only to the elderly and the poor, Britain runs in tandem with all its European neighbours, where the principle of national health care is unquestioned. However, it is clearly in need of reform. Most critics of the British system have argued that the best response is to spend more money, and the Blair administration has responded accordingly. Spending on the NHS is increasing at an annual rate of 6.4 per cent in the period 1999–2004 (although Britain still only spends roughly half as much on health care – as a percentage of GDP – as the United States). In its 2000 NHS Plan, Labour focused on the need to modernize the NHS, to pay more attention to the needs of patients, to provide a system of rewards for the best-performing hospitals and NHS services, to encourage more students to enroll in medical schools, to recruit more doctors and nurses, and to make significant cuts in waiting times and waiting lists.

Other critics argue that the shortfall of staff is the real problem, citing OECD figures which show that Britain in 2000 had fewer doctors per head of population than any other OECD member state except Turkey and South Korea (see Figure 3.1). Some of the methods used to address this issue – such as launching overseas recruitment drives for doctors and nurses, or sending patients to other European countries for treatment – have created their own controversies.

Alongside the NHS, Britons can take out private health insurance and attend private clinics; roughly 10 per cent of the population is covered by private medical insurance taken out with organizations such as the British United Provident Association (BUPA). The Conservative governments of the 1980s and 1990s encouraged the development of the private health-care sector, in part to take pressure off the NHS but also to provide patients with choice, and to promote the most effective use of expensive facilities and treatments. But the private sector still tends to cover only relatively minor treatments, and most long-term expensive health care is provided by the NHS.

Despite all the debates about the NHS, the indicators typically used to measure quality of life show that the effects of health care have improved significantly in Britain. For example, life expectancy is now 75 years for men and nearly 80 years for women, putting Britain above countries that spend more on health care (such as Germany and the United States) and even above Mediterranean countries with their healthier diets (see Figure 3.2). Meanwhile, healthy life expectancy (defined as life expectancy in good general health) has increased by two years for men and women since 1981. Death rates from cancer and coronary heart disease – while still high – have fallen in recent years, the number of people smoking has been nearly halved since the mid-1970s, and there have been marked improvements in the British diet, with a decline in the consumption of red meat and foods containing fat, increased consumption of fruit, and greatly increased public awareness about the chemical content of food (leading to a rising demand for organic food combined with widespread rejection of genetically-modified products).

While health trends are positive in some areas, in at least two others they are generating increased concern:

• Britain has the worst drugs problem in Western Europe. Where drug-related deaths in most European countries are either falling or holding steady, they are climbing in Britain, to a rate of nearly five deaths per 100,000 people in 1999, compared to about two in Italy and Germany, and less than one in France and the Netherlands. Addicts are becoming younger, consumption of hard drugs such as heroin and cocaine is the highest in Europe, and drugs are a central

*Figure* 3.1 **Numbers of doctors in selected OECD states, 2000**

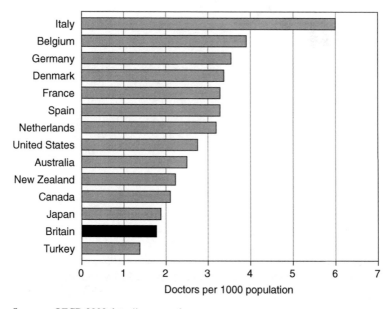

*Source*:    OECD 2002, http://www.oecd.org

*Figure* 3.2   **Life expectancy in selected OECD states, 1999**

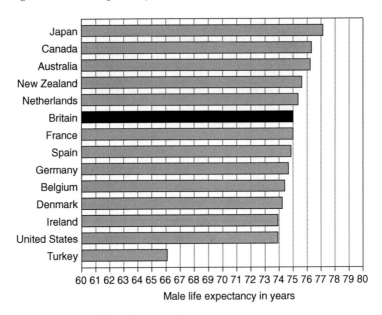

Male life expectancy in years

*Source*:   OECD 2002, http://www.oecd.org

factor in crime: about two-thirds of all those arrested for mugging, burglary, robbery, shoplifting or car theft test positive for drug use. The rise in the number of drug offences is also one reason why Britain has a higher per capita prison population than any other European country except Portugal (*The Economist*, 12 January 2002).

- Britain is witnessing the emergence of a public health problem that until recently has mainly been associated with the United States: the rising number of people who are overweight or obese. In 1980, just 6 per cent of British men and 8 per cent of women were classified as obese, but by 1999 the numbers had increased (respectively) to 21 per cent and 19 per cent. Part of the problem lies in the Northern European diet, which is lower in fruit, vegetables and fish than the Mediterranean diet. Other causes include lack of adequate exercise, obesity running within families, and increasingly sedentary lifestyles.

One of the legacies of Thatcherism has been a new consensus in Britain since the 1990s, that there should be a change away from the attitude that the state must be responsible for providing a safety net, and a move instead towards a 'stakeholder' ethic. This has been defined as the notion that while everyone should benefit from membership of society, they should do so only to the extent to which they have played by the rules of society (Finer, 1997). This is a remarkably Thatcherite concept, but was adopted enthusiastically by the Blair government, which moved towards a reduction in the reach of the welfare state. Among other things, it encouraged more people to join private health-care schemes and to take responsibility for their own retirement needs rather than relying on social security, and encouraged private funding for education. It also launched a 'welfare to work' scheme in 1998 that was aimed at encouraging the non-employed (such as mothers who choose to stay at home) to move back into the workplace as a means of reducing the welfare bill and tackling the social problems that sometimes come with workless households.

Despite assurances by the Blair administration that its priority was to focus more time and energy on improving the quality of public services, the British public remained largely unconvinced. Polls in early 1999 suggested that conditions in the National Health Service were regarded as the dominant issue of concern by 49 per cent of the electorate, and the quality of education by 32 per cent of the electorate, and that nearly half of all Britons believed that the Blair administration had not kept its pre-election promises to address problems in these areas. In its first two years in office, the strategy of the Blair administration was to blame such problems on its Conservative predecessors, but this became increasingly unviable, and expectations among voters – and criticism of the Blair administration – began to rise. However, trying to encourage a fundamental change in public attitudes toward the provision of basic services has proven a tall order.

## Education

When asked to outline his priorities in the lead-up to the 1997 election, Tony Blair frequently replied that they were 'education, education and education'. The Labour government argued that education was a critical investment in social capital, that improved education offered people the ability to escape social exclusion and to take part in economic activity, and that it was not only good for individuals but for society at large (Alcock, 2000). Conscious that fewer people were being educated in Britain than in many other industrialized countries, Labour promised to cut class sizes, invest in building repairs, give incentives to good teachers, and make education more accessible. Unfortunately, the changes have been slow in coming, and studies continue to reveal a worrying state of affairs:

- A government-sponsored report published in 1999 found that nearly a quarter of adults were classified in the lowest literacy level (being unable, for example, to use the index in a *Yellow Pages* phone directory), and in the lowest numeracy level (being unable, for example, to calculate the change they would receive from a simple shopping list). Among European countries, only Poland and Ireland had worse records (*The Times*, 26 March 1999: 14). Sweden had the best record, at 7 per cent in each category.
- Comparative data from the OECD published in 2001 revealed that Britain spent significantly less on schools than comparable countries: 4.9 per cent of GDP in 1999, compared to an industrialized-country average of 5.3 per cent, and as much as 7–8 per cent in Denmark, New Zealand, Norway and Sweden. At the same time, its ratio of pupils to teachers does not compare well: nearly 23:1, compared to an industrialized-country average of 18, and figures as low as 11–17 in Denmark, the Netherlands, and Sweden (OECD, http://www.oecd.org).

Of course, for every study that reaches one set of conclusions, there is another that reaches another set of conclusions. For example, the significance of the OECD report has been undermined by studies which conclude that more spending does not necessarily mean better education. Thus, the jury is still out on just how well the British education system performs. Labour nonetheless felt that there was need for change in order to help people find work and stable income sources in a competitive global market, and to break the cycle of welfare dependency (Kendall and Holloway, 2001). A common criticism made against British education is that its quality varies so much, and that national statistics disguise the fact that most of the problems have come in the more troubled state schools, while the better state schools and those in the independent sector have been doing well, with exam results improving in recent years. The number of young people entering higher education during the 1990s grew from one in five to one in three, but instead of promoting social mobility and reducing differences in opportunity for the advantaged and the disadvantaged, nearly 75 per cent of university students still come from the top half of the economic and social spectrum.

Since 1972, the law has required that British children receive full-time education between the ages of 5 and 16 (in Northern Ireland they are required to start at age 4). About 70 per cent stay on in full-time education beyond 16, obtaining further schooling or going on to higher education (where women outnumber men by 11 to 9). About 20 per cent go into government training programmes, and the balance enter the workplace. Schools are divided into two groups: state schools that are operated by public funds, and independent schools that are privately-financed. Education at state schools is free, and about 93 per cent of children in England and Wales take this option. By contrast, education at independent schools is often expensive, and is usually an option only for wealthy families or for children with scholarships or financial aid.

The 1944 Education Act created a system for England and Wales in which children in the state system attended primary school until age 12, at which point – on the basis of a standardized exam – the more academically gifted were channelled into grammar schools, while those who failed the exam went to less academic secondary-modern schools. Grammar schools prepared children for national exams that qualified them to go on to higher education or for entry into the professions, while secondary moderns did not. Critics charged that this system was socially divisive, perpetuating the class system, and determining life choices for children at too young an age. Beginning in the 1960s, the local education authorities that administered schools were allowed to decide whether they wanted to keep the dual system or to replace it with non-selective comprehensive schools which would provide an education for children of all ability levels and different social backgrounds. Although barely one-third of parents support the idea of comprehensive schools, complaining that bright children suffer from being in classes with less-able children, comprehensives are now attended by nearly 90 per cent of children in the state system, and there are few grammar schools and secondary moderns left.

Meanwhile, Scotland and Northern Ireland have their own education systems. Schools in Scotland have long been comprehensive, and have a different system of exams from those in England and Wales;

only about 5 per cent of Scottish pupils attend private schools. In Northern Ireland, state schools are selective, with about 40 per cent of children attending grammar schools and the rest attending non-grammar schools. State schools are supposed to be open to all religions but tend to be divided into Protestant and Catholic schools, and single-sex education is more common than in England and Wales. State schools in England and Wales use a National Curriculum which includes English, maths, science, history, geography, art, music and a modern foreign language. Northern Ireland has its own curriculum, but Scotland does not.

Independent schools are both more expensive and more exclusive, and tend to give their students a better-quality education overall (although there are many fine state schools in the system). Confusingly, they are known as 'public' schools, because they were long designed to train pupils for public service, in either the military or the government. As a result they are often run on semi-military lines, with compulsory chapel every day, younger pupils acting as valets for older pupils, and compulsory involvement in sports and military-style cadet corps. They are mainly boarding schools, although the number of day pupils has increased, and they were once almost exclusively for boys, although the number of coeducational public schools has increased. Entry is determined by examination and is not restricted by social class or connections, although the ability to pay the often high fees is critical. British public schools include such famous establishments as Harrow, Eton, Winchester and Marlborough, and over time have produced many of the leading figures in British political, commercial and military life. Their influence is declining, though, as Britain becomes more egalitarian and meritocratic (see below).

Higher education is provided by an extensive network of universities and of more specialized colleges offering, for example, teacher training and other vocational skills. Britain has 87 universities, which can be categorized into four types:

- The ancient universities that have existed for centuries, and for a long time were the *only* universities, all of them restricted to men. The oldest English universities include Oxford and Cambridge (founded in the twelfth century), and the oldest Scottish universities include St Andrew's and Glasgow (founded in the fifteenth century), and Edinburgh (sixteenth century).
- The so-called redbrick universities founded mainly in the late nine-

teenth and early twentieth centuries, including Birmingham, Leicester, Liverpool and Sheffield.

- The universities founded in the 1960s, often in rural areas, and including Essex, Surrey, Sussex and East Anglia.
- The 'new universities' that were once vocational polytechnics but were given university status in 1992, including Greenwich, Thames Valley, and West of England.

Where British universities – and a British university education – were once considered among the best in the world, their status has been undermined in recent decades by a combination of an enormous increase in student numbers and misplaced government policy. The good news is that there has been a dramatic increase in the number of students in higher education. In 1960, barely 5 per cent of school-leavers went on to university or college, and there were just 200,000 students in higher education. In 2003, the figure is closer to 30–40 per cent of school-leavers, most of the growth in numbers having come since the late 1980s, and there are more than 1.2 million students in British universities. Thus, higher education has ceased to be some-thing available only to an elite few. The Blair administration wants to take this further by ensuring that as many as half of all those in the 18–30 year age range experience some form of higher education, a figure that would put Britain in the same rank as the United States.

Unfortunately, this growth – and the talk of plans for additional growth – has taken place against a background of falling government spending on higher education. Just as the number of 18–21-year-olds doubled in the period 1989–2000, so spending per student was cut by two-thirds (*The Economist*, 16 November 2002: 52). As a percentage of GDP, spending on higher education in Britain today is less than half what it is in Canada or the United States, ranking alongside France and Germany at about 1.2 per cent. The universities receive support from the government, but they are independent institutions and – particularly since the Thatcher administration – have been expected to depend less on public funding and instead to raise a large percentage of their own financial support. The positive results have included more attention being paid to marketing, fund-raising, and academic performance. However, administrators and staff complain that many problems remain:

- A reduction in staff numbers, with the student–lecturer ratio down from 9:1 in 1990 to about 16:1;

**Illustration 3.3   Student demonstration**

A student from Goldsmiths College in London taking part in a protest
against government plans to change university fees. There has been
dramatic growth in the number of students going on to higher education,
but government spending has lagged.

- A reduction in research money, Britain having the dubious distinction of being the only industrialized country spending less on
  research in 1995 than in 1981;
- A declining share of top-level research output, leading to much
  hand-wringing about the declining numbers of British scientists
  winning Nobel prizes (down from 13 in the 1970s to two in the
  1990s);
- A deterioration in the quality of buildings and other facilities;
- A brain drain as academics have left to work overseas.

A thorough review of higher education is currently under way,
much of the discussion centring on the extent to which the government should subsidize student fees. Perhaps, however, the state of
higher education would improve if there was less concern about
creating an egalitarian system and more about the need to allow a
tiered arrangement in which different institutions catered to different
student needs and aptitudes, and in which some institutions were

publicly funded while others were funded more by student fees, income from applied research, and other non-governmental sources of support, including alumni donations, and corporate/private donations.

Overall, education in Britain has become more widely available, and there are signs that the tiered structure of the education system is having less of an effect on society and politics than it has had in the past. Where once it was almost required that anyone wanting to advance to the highest levels of the professions or government should attend the 'best' schools and universities, a private education is no longer as much of an advantage over a state education as it once was. This is reflected in an informal study undertaken by the weekly news magazine *The Economist*. In 1972, it looked at the educational background of what it defined as the 100 'top jobs' in Britain, which included positions in politics (including the prime minister, senior government ministers, and party leaders), business (the heads of major companies), academia, the media, the professions, sports and the arts. It found that 67 per cent of the jobholders had attended a private school and that 52 per cent had attended either Oxford or Cambridge. It carried out the same study in 1992 and found the figures little changed. However, when it replicated the study in 2002, the results were noticeably different: only 46 per cent of jobholders had attended a private school, and only 35 per cent had attended Oxford or Cambridge (*The Economist*, 7 December 2002: 53–4). If the survey reveals greater educational equality, it reflects little progress on gender equality – only five of the jobs in 2002 were held by women.

## Law and Order

Debates about law and public safety in Britain have tended to veer back and forth between, on the one hand, conservative concerns about the breakdown of order and allegations of an intergenerational reduction in the quality of life and, on the other hand, liberal arguments that the problem is one of too much order rather than too little. Reiner (1999: 163) argues that 'the British have long been regarded as peculiar in relation to order', the peculiarities shifting with time: in the eighteenth century they were regarded as ungovernable, then in the Victorian era the national image 'was one of unflappable self-discipline and orderliness . . . symbolized by institutions like the queue, or the imperturbably stiff-upper-lipped gentleman', and in the last generation there have been 'a succession of law-and-order panics' ranging from football hooligans to urban and rural riots, stimulating agonized discussions about 'vanished virtues'. The structure of the British legal system is described in Box 3.2.

By comparison to the relatively tranquil quarter-century following the Second World War, the last 30 years or so has seemed to many older Britons to have been marked by relatively high degrees of disorder and indiscipline, at least if headline-grabbing events are any indication: the often violent confrontations between management and striking workers in the 1980s, the unfortunate reputation for hooliganism that British football has won because of the behaviour of a minority of 'fans', race riots in a number of major cities, the troubles caused by 'lager louts' in bars on the continent, the growing number of cases of road rage caused in part by frustration with traffic congestion, and everyday violence and destructive or anti-social behaviour. The impression has been created that such problems are widespread and worsening, but the popular perception may in fact be quite different from the reality, because trends in the crime rate in Britain are (at worst) not dramatically different from those in other industrialized countries, and Britain is in many ways still a paragon of orderliness and good manners.

Britain is the birthplace of the organized police – the oldest police force in the world is London's Metropolitan Police, created in 1829 by Prime Minister Sir Robert Peel, after whom the police were long known as 'Peelers'. There is no national police force in Britain, but instead there are 52 independent forces based either around major urban centres or around counties and regions. They answer to local police authorities made up of a combination of elected officials, magistrates, and independent members – the authorities in turn appoint chief constables to run the force, taking responsibility for policy, promotion and discipline.

Statistics and trends in crime are controversial because of the difficulties of developing an accurate measure. According to the figures of crimes reported to the police there were 5.2 million offences in England and Wales in 2000–2001. However, the figure was nearly three times higher according to the British Crime Survey, which has been conducted annually since 1982 and which asks representative groups of people about their experiences with crime. Of the cases reported to the police, theft and burglary account for nearly 60 per cent, physical violence for nearly 12 per cent, drug offences for 2 per

**Box 3.2   The legal system**

The British legal system is based on a combination of criminal and civil law, the former dealing with wrongs affecting the community and the latter with disputes involving two or more parties. No clear distinction is made between the two in England, Wales and Northern Ireland, where courts have jurisdiction in both areas. There is no common national system of law, England and Wales having its own system which is distinct from those in Scotland and Northern Ireland.

There are four main sources of national law: statutes passed by Parliament, common law in the form of precedents set through decisions made by courts, laws adopted by the European Union and the decisions of the European Court of Justice, and international treaties of which Britain is a signatory. For example, the European Convention on Human Rights – which provides for the right to life, liberty, personal security, privacy, and freedom of thought, speech, religion, assembly and association – was incorporated into British law by the 1998 Human Rights Act. (In Scotland, statutes passed by the Scottish Parliament – the old one that existed before 1707 and its modern counterpart – are an additional source of law.)

The law is enforced by professional judges and part-time unpaid magistrates (or justices of the peace), the former being qualified lawyers and the latter being given enough training to oversee a trial and apply the law. Magistrate's courts deal with about 95 per cent of all criminal cases, all of them less serious; the magistrates typically sit in benches of three members, are advised by trained law clerks, and have limited powers of punishment. Indictable cases such as rape and murder are passed on to higher Crown courts for trial by jury. Parties in a case are usually represented either by barristers (advocates in Scotland) or solicitors; the former practise as individuals and tend to be trial lawyers, while the latter work in partnerships and deal with general legal matters, such as wills, estates, taxes and the transfer of property.

cent, and sexual offences for less than 1 per cent (although it is sexual offences which are typically underreported). According to the Survey, there have been decreases in almost every form of crime in recent years, the number of burglaries, for example, being down 21 per cent in 1999 from 1997 levels, and reaching its lowest level since 1991.

While the extent of the problem of crime is debatable, as is the appropriate response, there are elements of life in Britain which still support Reiner's notion of 'unflappable self-discipline and orderliness'. In their dealings with one another on a daily basis, most Britons still display courtesy, good manners and consideration. They may appear stand-offish to Americans (notorious for their willingness to strike up personal conversations with complete strangers), they may appear stolid to Spaniards and Greeks (with their Mediterranean expansiveness), and they may appear controlled to Italians (who appear unable to form and maintain a queue), but they have created a society in which cooperation and order are still more common than confrontation and disorder.

# 4

# Politics and Government

Britain is the birthplace of the parliamentary system, which – if the extent to which it has been exported is any measure – is the most successful of the world's different systems of government. Otherwise known as the Westminster model, after the area of central London where the British Houses of Parliament are situated, the key elements of parliamentary government include the following:

- a fusion of the executive and the legislature;
- a symbolic head of state and a political head of government;
- an executive made up of a head of government and a cabinet of ministers;
- representative democracy, in which elected officials are accountable to voters;
- responsible government, where government ministers are held collectively accountable for their decisions and for running their departments;
- a multi-party system based around strong party discipline within the legislature.

Because Britain has a long history of parliamentary government, has avoided revolutionary change, and has one of the world's oldest monarchies, it is often assumed that its political system is both stable and predictable. Nothing could be further from the truth. Even the most cursory glance at history shows a system in a constant process of mutation. For centuries, the most important changes were driven by the struggle for power between the monarchy and Parliament. More recently, changes have been driven by debates over the appropriate role of government in the lives of citizens, and by the fluctuating balance of power between prime minister and Parliament.

The pace and the extent of change have been particularly notable during the administrations of Prime Ministers Margaret Thatcher and Tony Blair. If Thatcher altered the style of government, taking a more hands-on approach to leadership and more fully exploiting the powers of her office, Blair not only continued to redefine the place and the character of the office of prime minister, but also made many significant changes to the institutions of government (such as his reforms of the upper chamber of Parliament, the House of Lords) and to the balance of national and local government (notably his creation of regional assemblies for Wales, Scotland and Northern Ireland).

This chapter examines the structure of the British system of government. It begins with a discussion of the constitution, and then looks in turn at the monarchy, the prime minister and cabinet, Parliament, the judiciary, the bureaucracy and local government, explaining their relative roles in the process by which Britain is governed. It identifies the institutions with the most and least influence over the political process, discusses changes in the balance of power among those institutions, examines the centralization of power in national government and in the office of prime minister, and critically assesses the nature of the British model of parliamentary democracy.

## The British Political System

Just as there has been a debate since the Second World War about British economic decline (see Chapter 6), so there has been much talk about the decline of the British state (for example, see English and Kenny, 1999). Critics have charged the government with a failure to deliver economic growth and the kind of political stability and social cohesion demanded by citizens of a modern democratic, capitalist system. They have also raised concerns about the lack of controls on an ambitious prime minister, the relevance of the monarchy and the House of Lords, an electoral system that misrepresents the balance of support for competing political parties (see Chapter 5), and the lack of a codified bill of rights for citizens. The term 'decline' became so fashionable in academic discussions about the British political system that it raised questions about the very legitimacy of that system.

However, while Britain certainly witnessed its share of political and social upheavals during the 1960s and 1970s, so too did many other countries. It is also important to bear in mind that, in a world where democracy and successful free-market economic policies have taken root only in perhaps two or three dozen countries, the Westminster model stands out more for its strengths than its weaknesses. Those strengths have inspired political development around the world, and the institutions of British government have been directly copied in most of the world's richest and most successful countries, including almost all European states, Japan, Australia, Canada and New Zealand. Even the United States, whose system of government at first appears very different from that of Britain, reflects many of the core principles of parliamentary government.

The British system has not declined since 1945, but has simply continued to change. The change can be seen most clearly in the gaps between the theory and the practice of government in the Westminster model, which is based on six key principles:

- *Balanced government.* In theory, the powers of the executive, consisting of a prime minister and cabinet, are balanced by those of the legislature, to which the executive is constantly accountable. In practice, while the prime minister cannot take for granted the support of Parliament, the balance of power has shifted away from Parliament.
- *Parliamentary sovereignty.* In theory, only Parliament has the right to make laws, and its powers are not limited or constrained by any other authority. In practice, Parliament has seen its powers reduced because British law in many policy areas is now superceded by European Union law, and party discipline in Parliament has meant that most decisions are now taken within the executive. Thus, Parliamentary sovereignty has become executive sovereignty (Smith, 1999: 11).
- *Representative democracy.* In theory, the people rule, while the work of government is carried out by their elected representatives, who stay in office only as long as they have the support of voters in their local districts. Government is directly accountable to the people in what it does. In practice, it has long been debatable just how far elected representatives feel obliged to respect the view of their constituents, even assuming that they can always be sure what their constituents want. Also, turnout at general elections has been

falling, suggesting an increasing disconnection between voters and their representatives.

● *Responsible government.* In theory, government ministers are responsible to Parliament for running their departments, and they make decisions that are then implemented by a neutral bureaucracy. In practice, the actions of ministers are driven more by personality, ideology, obligations to the prime minister, and concerns about the next election, and the bureaucracy has much more influence over government policy than most people realize.

● *Collective responsibility.* In theory, the cabinet is responsible as a group to the public and to the prime minister for its conduct and for its policies. Ministers routinely disagree over policy within the cabinet, but if a minister cannot support government policy, he or she will either be dismissed or be expected to resign. If the government loses an important vote in Parliament, or if there is a vote of no confidence in the government, the cabinet as a whole is expected to resign (Kavanagh, 2000: 50). In practice, cabinet government has become less important with time, and recent prime ministers – notably Margaret Thatcher and Tony Blair – have often made decisions without first checking with the cabinet, and have relied more on outside advisers.

● *Constitutional monarchy.* This is perhaps the only one of the principles where theory and practice still coincide. Britain has a monarch, and government is carried out in the name of the monarch (whose permission is technically needed for most key political decisions), but the monarch actually has very little real power. Any attempt by the Queen to actually use her powers – for example, by vetoing a new piece of legislation – would probably result in uproar and a constitutional crisis.

If the old Westminster model no longer exists, what has replaced it? Several analysts have recently suggested that it makes more sense to see British government not as a simple model based around a few key institutions, but as a complex network of interdependent institutions, where power is distributed horizontally rather than vertically, and is no longer concentrated in a limited number of institutions. In this 'core executive' model, the rules are often informal, institutions are less important than culture and values, and the decision-making system is less hierarchical (for more discussion, see Smith, 1999).

**The Constitution**

A constitution is an instrument that outlines the rules by which a government functions. It usually explains the general principles underlying the process of government, describes the structure of the major government institutions and their responsibilities, explains the process by which laws are made, and spells out the rights of citizens and the limits on the powers of government. The vast majority of countries have constitutions that are codified: there is a single written document in which the powers of government and the rights of the governed are outlined.

However, there is another way of looking at constitutions. Instead of simply being a set of principles and rules, they can be a summary of how a society is politically constituted or how its legal and political order fits together. Rather than starting with a formal statement of norms and then looking at how they are applied, Johnson argues,

> the constitution is treated as the outcome of shared experiences and practices, the result of a common history rather than a founding declaration . . . It is not so much a set of instructions on how to do things as a set of precedents and notes of guidance extracted from past experience . . . [It] is unlikely to have special rules for its amendment, chiefly because it is the outcome of adaptation and evolution in response to changing circumstances and needs. (Johnson, 1999: 46)

This model of a 'customary constitution' applies to Britain, where – instead of a single, written document – government operates on the basis of many different documents and traditions (Kavanagh, 2000: 47–9):

- *Common laws.* These are the product of custom and of judgements handed down over time by British courts. Among the most important are those dealing with freedom of speech, the power to make treaties and declare war, and the sovereignty of Parliament.
- *Statute laws.* These are Acts of Parliament which override common law and have the effect of constitutional law. Many of the details of Britain's system of government – including the relative powers of the two houses of Parliament, the expansion of the vote, and British membership of the European Union (EU) – have been established (and can be changed) by the passage of new statutes.

- *European laws.* As a member state of the EU, Britain is subject to all laws adopted by the EU, which override British laws in those policy areas where the EU has primary responsibility. These include trade, agriculture, social issues, consumer protection and the environment, but they exclude tax policy, foreign policy, education and criminal justice, because these are policy areas over which the EU does not have jurisdiction, or has only limited or shared jurisdiction.

- *Traditions and conventions.* Many of the actions of government in Britain (and in other democracies) are based on custom and tradition; there are no laws that spell them out, but instead they have simply developed as habits over time. For example, nothing in the British constitution says that the prime minister and cabinet should come out of the majority party in the House of Commons; this is simply a tradition that has become an accepted part of the political process.

- *Scholarly commentaries.* Many of the principles and practices of British government have come out of commentaries written by constitutional authorities, such as Walter Bagehot (author in 1867 of *The English Constitution*, and one-time editor of the news weekly *The Economist*) and Albert Venn Dicey (author in 1885 of *An Introduction to the Study of the Law of the Constitution*). Dicey was influential in confirming three of the basic features of the British system: the sovereignty of Parliament, the rule of law, and the importance of conventions and customs (Thomas, 1999: 144–5).

It would be wrong to assume that government is based solely on the rules found in constitutions, even in those countries – such as the United States – where the constitution is regarded as being at the very heart of the nature of government. Much of what happens in government is driven by many other forces, including judicial interpretation, political feasibility, opportunism, muddling through, loopholes in the law, and public opinion. But constitutions provide the blueprint against which the theoretical expectations and the practical actions of government can be compared, better understood, and given some structure and order.

In contrast to the constitutions of France or Germany, which spell out in detail how government should work, and whose gaps are filled in by the rulings of the national constitutional courts, Britain takes a more pragmatic approach to government. As Philip Norton puts it, the rules of British government are determined 'on the basis of what has proved to work rather than on abstract first principles' (Norton, 2001: 57). This approach allows for greater flexibility, and avoids the need for the government to make formal amendments to the constitution. An example of a change introduced by the Blair government, which has now become an accepted part of constitutional practice, is the referendum. These have been used before in Britain, particularly when the government has been divided on an issue (for example, over membership of the European Community in 1974, and over devolution in 1979), but they have been used so often since 1997 that all major constitutional changes are now likely to be put to a referendum (Jones and Kavanagh, 1998: 59). Blair used them on the question of assemblies for Scotland and Wales (1997), on an elected mayor for London and the Northern Ireland peace agreement (1998), and promised to use one on the question of whether or not Britain should adopt the euro.

Flexibility has its advantages, but critics of the current system in Britain argue that there is too much potential for the abuse of powers by a strong prime minister, and there have been concerns about the ways in which leaders such as Thatcher and Blair have challenged the conventional way of doing business. The result has been growing support for a written constitution, which is now favoured by about 80 per cent of Britons. This is all very well in theory, but it would be difficult to codify laws, legal judgements and traditions dating back several hundred years, and to reach political agreement on both the principles and the details of a written constitution for Britain. Many constitutions in other countries were written at a time when those countries were moving from one system of government to another, a process which focused the minds of the authors. Such a focus would be lacking in the British case.

## The Monarchy

Britain is a constitutional monarchy. This means that, in contrast to an absolute monarchy (where almost all power lies in the hands of a single ruler) or an aristocratic monarchy (where the ruler governs with the support of aristocrats, both parties relying on each other for power and support), the powers of the British monarch are limited and controlled by law. The actions of government are carried out in the name of the monarch, who acts as something like the living

The splendour of the State Opening of Parliament, an annual event at which the Queen – before members of both Houses of Parliament – outlines the government's programme for the upcoming year in a speech written for her by the prime minister and his advisers.

**Illustration 4.1    State Opening of Parliament**

embodiment of the state. But the monarch herself does very little that could be defined as exercising independent judgement over government.

Except for a brief spell between 1649 and 1660 when the Cromwellian republic was proclaimed, Britain has been a monarchy since the ninth century and the rule of Alfred the Great (871–99). Like their continental European counterparts, British kings and queens once had a virtual monopoly on political power, but – as noted in Chapter 1 – their control began eroding with Magna Carta in 1215, and the 1689 Bill of Rights finally confirmed that Parliament was supreme. Queen Elizabeth II (Box 4.1) is now little more than a ceremonial head of state. It is often said that the British monarch reigns but does not rule; in other words, she is expected to be a neutral and non-political symbol of the state, the government and the people, and a living embodiment of history, stability, tradition and national identity. At the same time, though, the Queen has several so-called reserve powers that have political significance:

- She can dissolve Parliament and call new elections, although in practice she does this only when asked to by the prime minister. At the same time, the prime minister must ask her permission, which – theoretically – could be denied. But it never is.
- Before a bill can become a law, it must be signed by the Queen (that is, given the Royal Assent). Theoretically she could veto a piece of legislation, but the last time this happened was in 1707 (Norton, 2001: 308).
- If no one party has an absolute majority of seats in the House of Commons after an election, the Queen can step in as an arbitrator, and – on the advice of the prime minister – name the person she thinks is most likely in practical terms to be able to form a government. Queen Elizabeth has had to do this three times. A famous example came at the February 1974 election when Prime Minister Edward Heath lost his majority, and failed to agree a coalition with the Liberal Party. Harold Wilson was invited by the Queen to form the first minority government since 1931.
- Every year she presides over the State Opening of Parliament, giving a speech in which she outlines the government's programme for the next year. The speech is written by the government, and the Queen simply reads it aloud, but it still symbolizes the fact that government is carried out in her name.
- She meets weekly with the prime minister at confidential meetings, during which she has the right 'to be consulted, the right to encourage, and the right to warn' (Bagehot, 1963). She is briefed on the government agenda, and can share her thoughts on the decisions of government, although there is no obligation on the prime minister to do as the monarch says.
- The Queen is the Head of the Armed Forces, and it is she alone who can declare war and peace, although this can only be done on the advice of her ministers. There was a time when monarchs raised and equipped armies, and led them into battle. King George

II in 1743 was the last to do that, but the symbolic link remains, and
all members of the Army, Royal Air Force and Royal Marines (but
not the Royal Navy) must swear an oath of allegiance to the Queen.
- Above all, the Queen is the embodiment of 'the Crown', a term
  which in some respects is akin to 'the state'. The government does

---

**Box 4.1   The Monarch: Queen Elizabeth II**

Queen Elizabeth came to the British throne unexpectedly. Her uncle
David had been heir to his father George V (1910–36), and would have
been crowned King Edward VIII in 1936 had he not decided to abdi-
cate so that he could marry a commoner, the American divorcee Wallis
Simpson. His younger brother Albert instead succeeded to the throne as
George VI, and when he died in 1952, he was succeeded by his eldest
daughter Elizabeth.

The Queen was optimistically expected to rule over a new Elizabethan
age in which Britain's military, technological and cultural achieve-
ments would mirror those of Queen Elizabeth I (1558–1603). But while
the British economy prospered during the 1950s, and Britain led the
way on the development of the jet engine, nuclear power and other new
technologies, significant changes were already underway that would
radically alter Britain's place in the world. It had already begun to
dismantle its empire, and decolonization accelerated during the 1950s.
The economies of the United States, West Germany, France and later
Japan all offered new competition to Britain, which slipped down the
league of the world's major economic powers. Racial tensions also
grew as workers were invited to come from the Caribbean and the
Indian subcontinent to meet Britain's labour shortages. Then came the
social and cultural revolutions of the 1960s that altered the balance of
power, by class, gender and age.

With Britain undergoing social, political and economic change, the
reign of Queen Elizabeth took on an entirely different meaning. The
role of the monarchy changed as anti-monarchists began to question the
place of heredity in a modern state. The decision was taken to modernize the royal family and to allow unprecedented media and public
access to its inner workings. Unfortunately the revelations did not
always reflect well on the monarchy – the Queen's three eldest children
and her own sister underwent messy and public divorces, and the
Queen herself seemed unable always to keep up with popular demands
for the monarchy to become more in tune with a changing society. As
an individual, Queen Elizabeth is popular, as reflected in the outpouring of support for her during her golden jubilee celebrations in June
2002. However, opinion polls suggest that public support for the
monarchy has slipped since the mid-1980s from 85–90 per cent to
about 75–80 per cent today.

its work on behalf of the Crown, bureaucrats are servants of the Crown, judges dispense justice in Crown courts, and government ministers are conferred with the powers of the Crown (Johnson, 1999: 50–1).

The monarchy was long surrounded by an air of mystery, and very little was publicly known about the private lives and personalities of members of the royal family (although the rumour-mill was kept busy with stories). This was seen as an important part of the stability, success and exceptionalism of the monarchy; in the words of the constitutional authority Walter Bagehot, it was important not to 'let in daylight upon magic'. All has changed in the last 15–20 years as the private lives of the royal family have become the focus of intense media coverage and public interest all over the world. The very public troubles of the heir to the throne – Prince Charles – and his late wife Princess Diana in particular helped dull a great deal of the gloss that surrounds British royalty.

The role of the monarchy and its relevance to modern Britain has been the topic of much debate, and the monarchy has changed in response. The once unthinkable – that a divorced heir to the throne could become king – has now been accepted, and attempts have been made to end the ban on the heir marrying a Catholic, to abandon primogeniture (under which a first-born daughter is overtaken in the line of succession by a younger brother), and to expect the monarch to be head of the Church of England. One of the great strengths of the British monarchy – and the major reason why it has lasted so long – is that it has been more adaptable than many of its now-extinct continental European counterparts (although change is coming much faster now to remaining continental monarchies, such as those in the Netherlands and Sweden). The adjustments being made by the British monarchy are just the latest in a long series of adjustments it has had to make to meet new styles, expectations, and political realities.

## Prime Minister and Cabinet

While the monarch provides symbolic leadership for Britain, government is run by the prime minister, who provides policy leadership and oversees the implementation of law through a cabinet of senior ministers. By definition, the prime minister is the leader of the political party or coalition with the most seats in the lower chamber of Parliament, the House of Commons. As long as he can keep the support of his party in Parliament, the prime minister has considerable power over deciding which laws will be passed, and which policies adopted.

At first glance, those powers can seem almost dictatorial. Critics of Margaret Thatcher complained that she abused the powers of the office (or at least used them to a far greater extent than her predecessors), and that she manipulated government by appointing ministers to her cabinet who were easily controlled. Similarly, critics of Tony Blair have complained that he is too much of a micro-manager, that he has become more like a president than a prime minister, and that he has moved the centre of power away from Parliament and the cabinet and into his own office, where he relies on political and media advisers. However, the prime minister ultimately relies for his power and his credibility upon support within the cabinet and within his political party, and on his standing in the court of public opinion.

The fall of the Thatcher government stands as a important lesson to all prime ministers. Thatcher had first won election in 1979, and won two more elections in 1983 and 1987. Not long into her third term she had disagreements over Europe with her foreign secretary Geoffrey Howe, and over economic policy with her Chancellor of the Exchequer Nigel Lawson. Howe was moved to a less important position, then Lawson resigned from the cabinet, then Howe resigned as well, weakening Thatcher's authority. She won the largest number of votes in the normally routine annual party leadership contest in November 1990, but did not have a big enough margin to be declared outright winner. Her credibility undermined, she resigned and was replaced by John Major. She fell because of a complex combination of unpopular policies, disagreements with key cabinet allies, an unwillingness to heed the advice of ministers, and a failure to maintain alliances in the cabinet to ensure that she had support for her policies (see Smith, 1999: 97–100).

As with all government leaders in democracies, prime ministers have a combination of formal and informal powers. Formally, they act as the head of government, appoint senior members of government, chair the cabinet, oversee the security services, lead their parties, choose the date for the general election, report to Parliament in a weekly Question Time, and represent Britain in political dealings with other countries. Informally, they are the driving force in setting the national political agenda, are responsible for managing crises, set

*Table* 4.1   Postwar British prime ministers

| Date | Prime Minister | Governing Party |
|---|---|---|
| July 1945 | Clement Attlee | Labour |
| February 1950 | Clement Attlee | Labour |
| October 1951 | Winston Churchill | Conservative |
| May 1955 | Anthony Eden | Conservative |
| January 1957* | Harold Macmillan | Conservative |
| October 1959 | Harold Macmillan | Conservative |
| October 1963* | Alec Douglas-Home | Conservative |
| October 1964 | Harold Wilson | Labour |
| March 1966 | Harold Wilson | Labour |
| June 1970 | Edward Heath | Conservative |
| February 1974 | Harold Wilson | Labour |
| October 1974 | Harold Wilson | Labour |
| April 1976* | James Callaghan | Labour |
| May 1979 | Margaret Thatcher | Conservative |
| June 1983 | Margaret Thatcher | Conservative |
| June 1987 | Margaret Thatcher | Conservative |
| November 1990* | John Major | Conservative |
| April 1992 | John Major | Conservative |
| May 1997 | Tony Blair | Labour |
| June 2001 | Tony Blair | Labour |

\* In these years, leadership of the governing party changed – through health, resignation, or loss of political support – without a general election being held.

the style and tone of government according to the policies they adopt, the management methods they use, and the people they appoint to the cabinet, and – as the examples of Thatcher and Blair show – can become leading actors on the global political stage, if they choose.

There are two key foundations to the authority of a prime minister:

• The power to call elections to the House of Commons. These must be held at least once every five years, but they can be called any time within that period, at 3–4 weeks' notice. Unlike leaders in countries where elections are held on a fixed timetable – such as France, Germany, or the United States – prime ministers can use elections strategically, perhaps using the threat of calling an election to bring uncooperative cabinet members into line.

If they have the luxury of time, prime ministers will always call an election when the polls suggest that their party has the best chance of winning (John Major was up against the five-year limit in 1997, and had to call an election despite unfavourable poll figures). More rarely, a prime minister may have to call an election because he has lost a critical parliamentary vote, has lost a vote of confidence, has lost his majority in Parliament, or has lost the support of his party. The last time an election was called because of the loss of a vote of confidence was in March 1979, when the Labour government of James Callaghan – which had lost its majority two years earlier and governed in a pact with the small Liberal Party – lost the support of the Liberals, then lost a Parliamentary vote.

● The power of appointment. As well as leading their party, prime ministers decide the size of the cabinet, call and chair cabinet meetings, appoint and remove members of the cabinet and other senior government officials (about 100 people in all), regularly reshuffle cabinets (bringing in new members and either removing existing members or moving them to new posts) and can even reorganize government departments. The power of appointment allows the prime minister to manipulate the cabinet, alter the personality and character of the government (for example, revitalizing it by bringing in new blood), reward supporters, penalize or undermine the position of opponents, marginalize those who pose a threat to his tenure, and cultivate potential successors.

British prime ministers are normally experienced national politicians who have worked their way up through the ranks of party and Parliament. They must be members of the House of Commons, and usually serve a lengthy apprenticeship before winning the leadership of their parties. Margaret Thatcher served 16 years as a Member of Parliament before being elected leader of her party in 1975, and another four years as leader before being elected prime minister in 1979. By contrast, John Major and Tony Blair rose to the top relatively quickly, serving as members for 11 years and 14 years respectively before becoming prime ministers.

Prime ministers run the country with the help of the cabinet, a group of about 20–22 men and women who head the major government departments, including the Foreign and Commonwealth Office, the Home Office, the Treasury, the Ministry of Defence, and the Department of Trade and Industry. Together, the prime minister and the cabinet constitute Her Majesty's Government: they run their departments, plan the business of Parliament, discuss and attempt to resolve policy differences among departments, oversee and coordinate government policies, and take collective responsibility for the decisions and actions of government (Kavanagh, 2000: 238–9). While a prime minister is technically no more than a 'first among equals' in the cabinet, his powers of appointment and agenda-setting mean that loyalty to the leader is an essential prerequisite for cabinet members. Once the cabinet makes a decision, all members are expected to support it in public, whatever their personal feelings may be. If they cannot, they must either resign or – more rarely – may be removed. Cabinet members are all members of Parliament (mainly of the House of Commons), and the cabinet is an important testing ground for anyone with ambitions to become prime minister.

The relationship between prime minister and cabinet – and the role of the cabinet in the process of government – is very much driven by the personality of the prime minister (for more details, see Hennessy, 2001):

- Margaret Thatcher led from the front, was noted for her forceful-ness, particularly after her landslide victory at the 1983 general election, and was famous for stretching the powers of her office almost to their limit. She took key decisions outside the cabinet, reduced the number of cabinet meetings, and removed 12 ministers in 11 years.
- John Major was in a weaker position, serving out two years of Thatcher's last term before winning his own mandate in 1992, but even then presiding over a tired and divided party, and often having to react to problems rather than leading the way. He made more use of his cabinet, allowed a greater variety of opinion, emphasized collegiality and consensus, and intervened less in the affairs of departments.
- Tony Blair (Box 4.2) has imposed strong discipline on his party and his cabinet, helped by his huge Parliamentary majority since coming to power. He has delegated discretion to strong ministers prepared to follow the government line, has relied less on the cabinet than on a small inner circle (a kitchen cabinet) of advisors and aides, and has given an important role to his press and commu-nications staff.

There has been much debate in recent years about the extent to which the office of prime minister has become more like the office of a president. Analogies are made with the presidency of the United States, reflecting the extent to which prime ministers have become

**Box 4.2   Prime Minister: Tony Blair**

Tony Blair has been an unusual prime minister and an unusual leader of the Labour party. Born in Scotland in May 1953 of Scottish and Irish parents, he was raised in middle-class comfort in England, attending private schools and studying law at Oxford. He was elected MP for Sedgefield in northern England in 1983, and was appointed to the shadow cabinet in 1988, holding first the energy portfolio and then the job of shadow home secretary (dealing with issues such as policing). In 1994 – at the age of just 40 – he was elected Leader of the Labour Party, and moved quickly to abandon some of its more left-wing policies and to bring it closer to the centre of the political spectrum. In May 1997, he ended 18 years of Conservative government to become the third youngest prime minister in British history, the first prime minister born after the Second World War, and the first truly post-imperial prime minister.

Blair quickly made the prime ministership his own, confounding those who predicted that – like several of his predecessors – he would lose control of left-wingers in his party and enjoy only a short honeymoon with voters. In fact, he became the most popular prime minister since opinion polling began in the 1930s, keeping a 50–55 per cent approval rating well into his first term. As well as working hard to achieve peace in Northern Ireland, and improving Britain's relationship with the European Union, Blair used his 177-seat majority in the House of Commons to bring changes to the structure and character of British government. He was elected to a second term in office in June 2001, his majority barely changed – this was the first time that the Labour Party had won two consecutive full terms in office.

On foreign policy Blair proved to be among the most visible European leaders of his time, supporting US policy on Iraq, committing Britain to a leading role in the NATO bombing of Serbia in 1999, providing important moral and diplomatic support to the Bush administration following the September 2001 terrorist attacks on New York and Washington DC, and playing a leading role in efforts to develop a European defence capability (see Chapter 8). However, while he appeared to relish the role of international statesman that came in the wake of the September 2001 attacks, he was criticized at home for his willingness to support the plans by President George W. Bush to go to war with Iraq, and for being too slow to deal with the decay of Britain's public services, notably health care and the transport system.

**Illustration 4.2   Tony Blair and Iain Duncan Smith**

Prime Minister Tony Blair talks with the Leader of the Opposition, Iain Duncan Smith. The powers of the prime minister have grown in recent years, with critics charging that the office – and Blair's use of it in particular – has become too presidential.

independent from their cabinets and from Parliament. The prime minister's office has developed more of a life of its own, with an increasing number of advisors, aides, speechwriters, spin doctors and liaison staff, and the emergence of a staff that looks much like the staff clustered around the US president in the White House. Meanwhile, the cabinet has played a less important role in policy-making. Smith (1999, pp. 76–7) notes several reasons for this:

- It is confined largely to rubber-stamping decisions rather than developing government strategy.
- Ministers are too concerned with the work of their departments – where their reputation will rise or fall – to be involved in other areas of policy.
- The cabinet is less a place where strategy is developed than a place where departmental interests are protected.

The result has been to put the prime minister in an advantageous position over his ministers. At the same time, though, the support of the cabinet and Parliament is still the critical element in the ability of prime ministers to govern, and – as the case of Margaret Thatcher shows – they forget this at their peril.

## Parliament

Parliament is the pivot of the Westminster model. It is the British legislature, where proposals for new laws are introduced, discussed and either rejected or accepted, where existing laws are amended or abolished, and where votes are taken on taxing and spending. It may seem powerful, but because a prime minister with a good majority can normally count on the loyalty of party members, Parliament usually spends most of its time debating or confirming the government's programme, rarely voting against the government.

As the main link between citizens and the executive, Parliament plays a key role in legitimizing government. Strictly speaking it consists of the monarch and the two houses of Parliament, but the monarch has only a symbolic role and the upper House of Lords has only limited powers over law and policy, so the real focus of political power lies with the lower House of Commons. As noted earlier, the principle of Parliamentary sovereignty means that only Parliament has the authority to make laws, but this power has been reduced since 1973 by the growing importance of European Union law: where British and European law conflict (in policy areas for which the EU has responsibility), British law is superceded by European law. The result has been that Parliament has lost powers to the lawmaking bodies of the EU: the European Commission, the Council of Ministers, and the European Parliament.

The British Parliament has two chambers:

### House of Lords

The so-called upper house, the Lords was once a powerful part of government, and is a throwback to the days when Britain was ruled by aristocrats: its members were almost all hereditary peers, including dukes, barons and earls. The idea of hereditary privilege was increasingly at odds with a modern democracy, however, so the House steadily lost its powers in tandem with the diminishing role of the monarchy. In 1958, membership was expanded to life peers: mainly people who have been in public service, and are rewarded with a title by the Queen on the recommendation of the prime minister, the title dying with them.

Pressures grew in the 1960s and 1970s for more change, and the Labour Party even promised during the 1980s to abolish the House when it came to power. It later abandoned that pledge, but the Blair government moved quickly to make staged reforms to the chamber. The automatic right of hereditary peers to sit in the House ended in 1999, and a government commission was appointed to develop suggestions for where to go next. It reported in 2000, recommending a largely nominated chamber, limiting its members to 12–15 years of service, and retaining its existing powers. As this book went to press, no final decision had yet been taken on how to proceed.

The Lords has never been elected, but it has little real power. About two to four of its members are usually appointed to the cabinet, it has its own select and *ad hoc* committees (but no standing committees), and every parliamentary bill must go through the Lords, which spends most of its time revising bills sent from the House of Commons. The chamber can introduce and revise proposed legislation, but most of its decisions can be overruled by the Commons: money bills do not need the approval of the Lords, and while it can delay approval of other bills for up to a year, they can be reintroduced in the Commons which can pass them without the approval of the Lords. It does have its uses: it has more time to debate issues than the Commons, it often debates controversial issues that the Commons would prefer to avoid, it can force concessions from the Commons, and it is a useful point of access for lobbyists.

With the ending of the right of hereditary peers to sit in the chamber, the transitional House of Lords now has four remaining kinds of members:

- A rump of 92 hereditary peers who have been allowed to stay on pending the next stage in the process of reform.
- Religious leaders: the two archbishops and 24 bishops of the Church of England.
- The law lords: 28 nominated judges who function as the supreme court of appeal for civil and criminal cases (except criminal cases in Scotland). Headed by the Lord Chancellor they hold their positions until the age of 70. The House of Lords Constitution Select Committee also plays a role in legal issues, reviewing all public

The Houses of Parliament on the banks of the Thames in central London. Parliament is at the core of the British system of government, but it has lost powers as those of the prime minister have grown, and as European law has superseded British law in many key areas.

**Illustration 4.3   The Houses of Parliament**

bills going through Parliament that have constitutional implications.

The law lords made headline news around the world in 1998 when they upheld the decision of lower courts to detain the former Chilean dictator Augusto Pinochet during a visit to Britain. He was held at the request of the Spanish government, which wanted to try him for crimes against Spanish citizens living in Chile. (He was eventually allowed to return to Chile on the basis that he was too ill to stand trial.)

- Life peers: about 600 people who have been given peerages as a reward for public service. Typically in the past they have included former prime ministers and Speakers of the House of Commons, and people prominent in public life, such as actors, musicians, and entrepreneurs. Political appointments continue to be made, but are now subject to vetting by an Appointments Commission. Also, 15 'people's peers' have been created, chosen from more than 3000 applicants who had to show that they could bring integrity and experience to the job.

Members of the House are not paid, but can claim expenses for attending its sessions. The transitional House of Lords has about 700 members, who are organized along party lines. In late 2002, there were about 220 Conservatives, 200 members of the Labour Party, 60 Liberal Democrats, and 180 'cross-bench' (independent) peers.

*House of Commons*

Although it is the 'lower' house, the Commons is the more powerful chamber of Parliament, and the real focus of law-making. It consists of 659 Members of Parliament (MPs) elected by direct universal vote from single-member districts. Debates are presided over by a Speaker, who is elected by the House from among its members, and usually comes from the majority party. The Speaker is not allowed to vote, and is expected to remain strictly non-partisan.

The chamber of the House is small, with benches rather than seats (see Figure 4.1). The governing party sits on the left, with the prime minister and members of the cabinet on the front bench. MPs without government office, or with only junior office, sit behind the front bench, and are known collectively as backbenchers. The next biggest party in Parliament sits across from the governing party. Its leader sits directly opposite the prime minister, beside a shadow cabinet of opposition MPs responsible for keeping up with – and challenging – their counterparts in the cabinet. The leader of the opposition and the shadow cabinet are formally recognized and salaried positions. If the opposition wins a majority in an election and becomes the government, its leader typically becomes prime minister, and many members of the shadow cabinet become the real cabinet. In other words, the shadow cabinet is a government in waiting.

The process by which a bill becomes a law begins in government departments, which identify issues that merit changes in the law, and develop proposals that are circulated to all other interested departments. The cabinet then looks over the proposals, and those that are accepted go to the Parliamentary Counsel, which drafts bills. The

*Figure* 4.1  **The House of Commons: who sits where?**

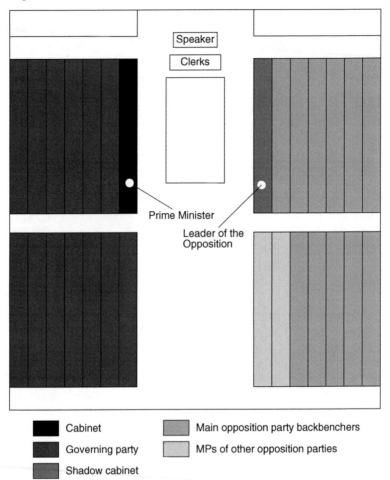

plan to introduce a bill is then normally announced in the Queen's Speech at the State Opening of Parliament in October. The bill is then introduced to Parliament (either chamber), and after initial debate is sent almost immediately to the relevant standing committee, where most of the real work of Parliament is done: specialists go over the details, outside experts are invited to give testimony, and changes are made to the bill.

Once a bill has passed through committee, it goes back to Parliament for more debate and amendments, and a final vote. Bills must be passed by both chambers (except money bills, which only need the support of the Commons), but the House of Lords has no standing committees, and all it can really do is delay legislation. If it demands amendments to a bill and the Commons disagrees, then the bill fails, but it can be reintroduced by the Commons and does not need the support of the Lords. Once a bill is accepted, it is sent to the Queen for her signature.

Party discipline is tight, but discontent is not unusual and party revolts have led to seven of the 11 Conservative leaders since 1900 being removed by a vote within their own party. This last happened when Margaret Thatcher lost the leadership of her party. A breakdown of party cohesion – usually dubbed a 'backbench rebellion' if the breakdown is big enough – is normally interpreted as a sign of weakness, and can lead to the fall of a government, the resignation of a prime minister, or even a general election.

**The Judiciary**

Constitutional courts – such as those in the United States and Germany – typically exist to defend and interpret the constitution, and act as the final court of appeal on cases calling for judicial review: the process by which a judgement is made on the constitutionality of a law or the action of an elected official. Since Britain does not have a codified constitution, it does not have a distinct constitutional court. Instead, judicial review is carried out in a complex system of courts topped by a Court of Appeal and the House of Lords, where law lords will hear final appeals in five-person benches. Appointments to the higher courts are made either by the Lord Chancellor (who presides over the Lords, is a member of the cabinet, and comes closest to being Britain's 'Minister of Justice') or by the prime minister after consultation with the Lord Chancellor, and hence they are highly political.

The role of judicial review in the British system is changing with the growing powers of the European Court of Justice. One of the key institutions of the European Union, the Luxembourg-based Court does not yet have a codified European constitution to interpret, although work was under way on one as this book went to press. But it does have a series of treaties and a growing body of European law, whose primacy over national law in many areas of policy is established. It also has the power to bring cases against the governments of EU member states who have not properly applied particular EU laws. The influence of Europe is also felt in the field of human rights, guarded by the Strasbourg-based European Court on Human Rights. Britain was one of the original signatories of the 1951 European Convention on Human Rights, and while this was not eventually incorporated into British law until 1998, many cases were successfully brought against the British government.

## The Bureaucracy

Britain has about half a million bureaucrats (or civil servants), who carry out the typical responsibilities of bureaucrats everywhere: most are responsible for collecting government revenues (mainly in the form of taxes) and for making payments in the form of benefits and pensions, and for running key government services. Like most of its counterparts elsewhere, the British bureaucracy – sometimes known as Whitehall after the part of London where many government departments are headquartered – is hierarchical in structure and nature, and is expected to execute the laws of government and the wishes of government ministers.

The British civil service – like all other elements of government – has undergone substantial change in recent years as attempts have been made to reform it by borrowing ideas from the private sector designed to make the service more efficient and responsive to consumers. The most important of these ideas have included the contracting-out of jobs previously done by bureaucrats, pay tied to performance, improvements in management methods, and techniques designed to provide a better service for less cost. In the view of Kavanagh (2000: 296–300), the effect has been a fundamental change to the characteristics of Whitehall:

- Beginning in the early nineteenth century, bureaucrats were able to assume that their jobs were permanent. Careers in government and the civil service were treated as separate, and bureaucrats were regarded as servants of the monarch rather than of the political leadership of the day. In recent years, though, performance has been linked to pay, and the movement of staff between the public and private sectors has been encouraged, undermining the idea of jobs for life.
- As servants of the Crown, bureaucrats must be impartial and recognize that their responsibilities are above party politics. For this

reason, they are not allowed to stand for political office or to express political opinions in public, and – if they decide to enter politics – they must resign from the civil service, not just take a leave of absence as their counterparts in France and Germany are allowed to do. This impartiality was easier during the period of consensus government in the 1950s, 1960s and 1970s, but became less so with the growing ideological distance between the two major parties in the 1980s and 1990s. There are also allegations that recent governments have been more aggressive in involving themselves in decisions on the appointments of senior civil servants.

- The principle of responsible government means that ministers receive confidential advice from civil servants, but must take public responsibility for the work of their departments, and so bureaucrats remain largely anonymous. This principle has been eroded by a combination of public enquiries that have been more willing to name names, by greater media inquiry into the workings of the bureaucracy, and by greater openness in the memoirs of former ministers and their aides.

The greatest changes to the bureaucracy were brought by Margaret Thatcher, who cut the number of civil servants by 28 per cent, began a programme of departmental efficiency audits, questioned senior civil servants more aggressively about policies, took a close interest in high-level promotions, and imposed her views more aggressively on the civil service (Jones and Kavanagh, 1998: 174). The most notable change in recent years has been a trend away from large government departments under the control of ministers to more than 150 small, independent agencies responsible for delivering services directly to the public. These include the Benefits Agency, the Environment Agency, the Health Development Agency, and the National Youth Agency. Instead of being subject to ministerial control, the agencies are led by chief executives who control budgets and staffing, and are held accountable by performance targets. Policy advice and the development of legislation are still the responsibilities of government departments, but executive and administrative duties have been handed over to these agencies, where four out of five bureaucrats now work. The old notion of 'Whitehall' is increasingly at odds with reality.

## Local Government

Britain has long been a unitary state, where political power has been focused at the national level, and local government has had few significant political powers. Local government until recently has been responsible mainly for providing a variety of basic services that most people take for granted, including refuse collection and road maintenance. Most Britons show little interest in local politics, turnout at local government elections is usually low, and local government officials are not as well known as national politicians. So weak is local government that it can be reformed, restructured or even abolished by the national government.

Changes made over the last 30 years (the most recent in 1998) have created a complex and confusing system of local government authorities. In England and Wales, most areas come under a two-tier system of counties and districts, each with locally elected councils responsible for such issues as education, transport, housing, highways, local services, refuse disposal, and the police. In selected areas, mainly larger cities, county and district functions have been combined into new unitary authorities. London has its own elected government (see below), and six other metropolitan counties – such as Greater Manchester and Merseyside – have no county councils but are instead divided into district councils. Meanwhile, Scotland has unitary councils, Wales has unitary authorities, and Northern Ireland has unitary districts.

The picture has been further complicated by the recent creation of elected regional assemblies for Scotland, Wales and Northern Ireland, but not for England. Thus, Britain – while still claiming to be a unitary state in which power is focused at the national level – has actually become a semi-federal system of government. The word 'federal' has negative connotations in Britain, mainly because of fears expressed by Eurosceptics about the possibility of a federal Europe in which many of the powers of British government are taken over by EU institutions. Interestingly, it is rarely mentioned in academic studies of the changes that have come to local government in Britain. It has been more fashionable to talk instead about 'multi-level governance', defined as 'negotiated exchanges between systems of governance at different institutional levels' (Pierre and Stoker, 2000: 30).

The Scottish and Welsh regional assemblies were created in 1998, following public referendums, and the first elections were held in May 1999. Both are elected for fixed four-year terms, and have powers over local issues such as education, health services, housing, transport and policing. The 129-member Scottish Parliament has control over most domestic policy matters, including health, education, justice, local transport and the environment, can make primary legislation in these areas, and has limited tax-raising powers. The 60-member National Assembly for Wales has control over a similar range of issues (except justice and policing), but has no taxing powers. Meanwhile, Northern Ireland – which had its own Parliament from 1921 to 1972 – has, since 1998, also had its own 108-member Assembly with powers over local issues, and also has two Ministerial Councils that address joint policy-making with Ireland and with the British Parliament. (The UK government retains control over economic, monetary, employment, foreign, defence and security policy.)

London – which, with its surrounding suburbs, is home to about one-third of the British population – was at one time governed by the Greater London Council, led by a left-wing Labour politician named Ken Livingstone. Illustrating the powers of national government over local bodies, Margaret Thatcher abolished the Council in 1986. The Blair administration felt that a city the size of London should have its own local government, so the ceremonial office of Lord Mayor of London was joined by a new elected office. The first elections were held in 2000, and – much to the chagrin of the Blair administration, which promoted its own 'official' Labour candidate – Ken Livingstone was restored to power. He governs with a 25-member elected Greater London Assembly.

# 5

# Civil Society

The term *civil society* is usually used to describe a community of individuals or citizens capable of acting separately from the state on the basis of pluralism, tolerance, civility and mutually accepted rules, and the patterns of association they endorse and accept. If the state consists of the rules and institutions by which a community is governed and controlled, then civil society is made up of all the voluntary and spontaneous forms of political association that evolve within that state, which are not formally part of the state system, but show that citizens can operate independently of the state. In this regard, 'civil society' should be distinguished from 'society' more generally.

Vibrant democracies such as Britain have many channels through which citizens can associate, and use their numbers and common sets of goals either to achieve their objectives without government, or to put pressure on government. These channels include elections, political parties, interest groups, the media, and a host of other conventional and non-conventional forms of participation, ranging from direct contact with elected officials to protests, boycotts, strikes and demonstrations. Like other democracies, Britain has a varied and active civil society in which many of its residents engage with the political process and create organizations that either complement the work of government, or provide services where government has failed to do so.

This chapter begins with a survey of political culture in Britain, outlining the norms and attitudes of the British towards politics and civic responsibility: the views they hold regarding their role in the political system, their expectations of that system, and their responsibilities to the political community in which they live. It then looks at elections and political parties, explaining the electoral process, comparing the structure and implications of the winner-take-all system with those of the proportional representation system used for elections to regional assemblies and the European Parliament, and examining the policies and the recent fortunes of the major political parties. It finishes with a discussion of the role of interest groups and the media in politics.

It argues that the changes that have come to political institutions – described in Chapter 4 – are reflected in the sphere of civil society. Concerns about the fairness of the winner-take-all electoral system have led to the recent introduction of proportional representation in local and European elections. The two-party system that has long been a feature of British politics remains, but the balance between the two major parties has shifted as Labour has moved to the centre, and the Conservatives have struggled to find a new identity in response, so far without much success. Meanwhile, the British have turned their backs in growing numbers on two of the most traditional forms of political participation – party membership and voting in elections – and have instead become more involved in the work of interest groups, and more willing to use unconventional channels to express their political views.

**Political Culture**

The term *political culture* describes the norms, values and expectations of a society as they relate to politics and government. Political culture helps explain what leaders and citizens regard as acceptable and unacceptable regarding the character of government, and the relationship between government and people. Tying down the political values of a society is always a challenge, especially for a country like Britain, with its multinational identity and its long and convoluted history. Generally, though, most political scientists agree that the British tend to be pragmatic and deferential, to have faith in their political system (if not necessarily politicians), to be patriotic, and to be politically moderate. At the same time, government has a reputation for not being sufficiently transparent, in the sense that the people do not have as much access as they might to the workings of government. This, however, has begun to change in recent years.

*Pragmatism*

The British tend to be pragmatic when it comes to their expectations of government and their aspirations for their own lives. They take an empirical approach to problem-solving, shying away from theory and looking instead at tried and tested approaches, and at the practical reality of policies. In the United States, argues Vivien Hart (1978: 202–3), 'the emphasis has been on what democracy is and should be, while Britain has been characterized by a more pragmatic and less urgent emphasis on what democracy is and can be'. This is not to suggest that the British do not dream, or aspire to achieve change, or that they are opposed to innovation. Quite the opposite is true, and the details of the political system have changed constantly over time.

Particularly among older Britons, and particularly in the 1970s and 1980s, realism spilled over into pessimism. There was more than a hint of truth to the joke that the national motto should be 'mustn't grumble', or 'things could be worse' (given how often some Britons use this as the answer to the greeting 'How are you?'). The media have tended to perpetuate the problem by their fascination with everything from lowered educational performance to rising crime and the mixed record of the English national cricket and football teams. Until recently at least, academics made the situation worse with their misplaced emphasis on the 'decline' of Britain. In fact, the view that life was better and safer in 'the old days' is not supported by the facts; in terms of health care, education, economic wealth, individual freedoms, gender equality, consumer protection and the state of the environment, life for most Britons has improved significantly in the last 30 years. Fortunately, there are now signs that more people are beginning to realize this, and the gloom of the 1970s and 1980s is lifting.

*Faith in the Political System*

Despite the pessimism that some feel, the British tend to have relatively high levels of faith in their political system, reflected in the fact that most feel that they can influence government (Almond and Verba, 1989). These feelings are tied closely to the long history of relative political stability and evolutionary change in Britain, which contrasts with the often revolutionary and violent change that has come to political systems in other European states. Faith in the political system was long bound up in the class system and the strong feelings of political and social deference that this promoted. Cynics occasionally described Britain as a Nanny State, or one in which the government acted like the archetypal Victorian nanny, insisting that it knew what was in the best interests of the people, and preferring not to be questioned too much. However, deference is on the decline (Hall, 1999: 453), for several reasons:

- Changes in the class system have weakened the authority of the establishment.
- There is a growing respect for succeeding through effort and hard work, and a declining respect for privilege and old money.
- The British are becoming more self-reliant and less dependent on the state.
- The political system is seen as being less responsive than it should be.
- There has been a declining respect for elected officials.

These changes may represent a decline in faith in government, or they may represent a change in the *expectations* of government, tied in with a growing belief in self-determination and support for alternative methods of engaging with government and expressing political opinions. On the one hand, membership of political parties has been falling, as has turnout by voters at elections. At the same time, there has been a growth in the membership of interest groups, and recent studies have suggested that the British are more willing to use unconventional forms of political participation than the citizens of any other democracy: a recent survey found that 56 per cent were prepared to sign petitions, 35 per cent to attend lawful demonstrations, 25 per cent to join a boycott, 15 per cent to join a wildcat strike, 13 per cent to refuse to pay taxes, and 9 per cent to block traffic (Wallace and Jenkins, 1995).

It is important to make a distinction between levels of faith in political institutions and levels of faith in political leaders. With regard to institutions, the two for which there is the least public respect – the monarchy and the House of Lords – have undergone substantial change in recent years. At the same time, criticisms of the political system have also been addressed: government has responded to concerns about the electoral process, about excessive power in Westminster, and about too much secrecy in government by introducing proportional representation in regional and European elections, and by passing legislation aimed at making government more open. So there is reason to believe that levels of faith in institutions will improve over time.

Faith in political leaders seems to be on the decline, however, as it is in several other democracies. Corruption and the abuse of powers have always been a factor in British politics; one of the most infamous such cases came in 1963 when it was revealed that John Profumo, the Minister for War, had been having an affair with a woman named Christine Keeler, who had also been having an affair with a Russian diplomat. More recently, the reputation of Britain's politicians has continued to be sullied by a series of scandals affecting both the Conservative and the Labour Parties. These included the discovery in 1994 that two Conservative MPs received payments in return for asking questions in the House of Commons, the revelation that a high-ranking Labour minister had failed to declare a loan received from another minister for a house purchase, and charges that the Blair administration had given British citizenship to a wealthy Indian businessman who had made major donations to Labour Party funds. The result has been a tendency to see political leaders less as public servants and more as political adversaries out for personal gain.

*A Confused National Identity*

Although they are not as patriotic as the Americans and the French, the British take high levels of pride in their history and institutions, which is part of the reason why so many have little enthusiasm for the European Union. Polls regularly find that the majority of Britons describe themselves as either 'proud' or 'very proud' of being British. However, the notion of patriotism has been muddied by the rise of Scottish and Welsh nationalism (see Chapter 2), which has raised questions about the definition of 'Britain' and 'British'. Recent polls have found that about 65–75 per cent of Scots think of themselves primarily as Scottish and only 25 per cent as equally Scottish and British, and that 50 per cent of the Welsh think of themselves primarily as Welsh and only 30 per cent as equally Welsh and British. Identities are even more confused in Northern Ireland, where 65–75 per cent of Protestants regard themselves primarily as British, while 60 per cent of Catholics think of themselves mainly as Irish (figures quoted by Meehan, 1999).

While the Scots, the Welsh and the Irish have long defined their identities in relation to their dominant neighbour, the English have defined themselves more in the context of the meanings of 'Britain' and 'British'. This has begun to change in recent years, though, with more residents of England defining themselves as 'English' rather than 'British', and with calls for the recognition of St George's Day (23 April) as a national holiday, for greater recognition of what makes England different from Scotland and Wales, and even for England to preempt the Scots by breaking away from the UK first. But these kinds of views are held by only a very small minority, and are controversial because they are criticized for playing into the hands of supporters of Scottish independence. Also, because of the long and interspersed histories of the four countries, it is difficult to distinguish the national features of England from those of the United Kingdom.

*A Closed Society*

The British tend to be a private people, hence the often-quoted phrase that an Englishman's home is his castle. Perhaps because Britain is such a crowded country where a premium is placed on personal space, the British can often seem a little stand-offish to visitors. This sense of privacy was long reflected in the secrecy that often surrounded the functioning of government in Britain. Issues of national security are subject to secrecy in every democracy, but critics of government in Britain charged that state secrets were too narrowly defined in Britain, and that this helped increase the power and reduce the accountability of the police, weakened the power of Parliament at the expense of the executive, promoted the use of surveillance and reduced the right to personal privacy, and allowed the government to interfere with media freedom.

The result has been a movement in recent years for greater freedom of information. Successive governments have provided more open government, and information has become more freely available, particularly with the development of the internet. In 1997, the Labour government promised new legislation, leading to the passage in 2000 of the Freedom of Information Act. This provides a statutory right of access to recorded information relating to the work of Parliament, government departments, local authorities, the health service, and other publicly-funded organizations. Critics charge that there are too many important exceptions – including information related to policy-making, and to matters where legal action may be likely or pending – and that the Information Commissioner responsible for enforcing the Act has powers only to recommend rather than compel the release of information. Nevertheless, it has helped make government more accessible, and has helped encourage citizens to be more interested in the activities of government and in gaining access to official information.

## Social Liberalism

In line with many of their European neighbours, but in notable contrast to Americans, the British as a whole tend to take liberal positions on social issues. For example, the basic principles of the welfare state are unchallenged, capital punishment has been outlawed since 1964, homosexuality and abortion have both been legal since 1967, there is very little censorship on television, and unmarried couples living together and having children are not only tolerated but are steadily becoming the norm. Where political debates in the United States are often based around the question of the extent to which government should become involved in determining the personal choices of citizens – either through regulation on such relatively trivial matters as mandating the use of seatbelts by drivers, or through bigger issues such as access to legal abortion or prayer in schools – these are rarely discussed in Britain, if only because liberal social values are so ingrained in national life. Attempts have been made to spark debates about the decline of 'family values' or to make access to abortion illegal, but such arguments attract little broad-ranging public support or sympathy.


## Elections

Like all liberal democracies, Britain has many channels through which its citizens can take part in politics, express their opinions, and try to have their views reflected in government policy. These include regular elections, a variety of political parties representing different ideological and regional positions, a broad and active community of interest groups, and one of the most diverse media establishments in the world. The options have increased in recent years as the number of elective offices and the number of parties has grown, the electoral system has diversified, and the number of sources of political news has increased. Only about one in ten Britons has a sustained interest in politics, but most take some periodic, intensive interest (usually in the lead-up to elections), and most are well-informed about national and international issues.

Elections serve the dual purpose of maintaining the legitimacy of the system of government, and of offering citizens a means of effecting peaceful political and constitutional change (Kavanagh, 2000: 116). Because Britain is a small country with a unitary system of administration, and because it is almost alone in Western Europe in using the winner-take-all electoral system (Box 5.1), British elections are simple, cheap and quick. Parties choose who will run in their name, no party has more than one leader, and because those leaders are well-established public figures, they do not need to spend time and money making themselves known to the public.

British voters are faced with three sets of elections as described below.

### The General Election

This is the election by which members of the lower chamber of Parliament – the House of Commons – are chosen, and so by which the national government of Britain is determined. It is by far the most important event on the electoral calendar, and attracts the most political activity, and the greatest media and public interest. It is not held on a fixed schedule, but must be held at least once every five years, on a date chosen by the prime minister and confirmed by the monarch. The election campaign itself is very short, lasting just 18 days (excluding weekends and public holidays).

The UK is divided into 659 constituencies (electoral districts) of roughly equal population size, each represented in the House of Commons by a single Member of Parliament. All 659 seats must be contested in the general election, and voters make a straight choice among the candidates from the different parties standing in their district. The choices are made easier by the fact that parties have strong ideological consistency (although the distinctions have become more blurred in recent years) and that there is strong party identification among voters, who will tend to vote more for parties than for individuals. Once the results are in, the monarch asks the leader of the party with the largest number of seats to form a government. If there is no one clear winner, then the party leaders negotiate among themselves to form a coalition. This rarely happens in the British system, because the structure of the electoral system usually produces clear winners (see Box 5.1).

Constituency boundaries are revised periodically to make sure that the number of voters in each is roughly the same. Until 2000, there

---

**Box 5.1  British elections: are they fair?**

There are two major kinds of electoral system: (a) the winner-take-all system (sometimes known as first-past-the-post) under which a winning candidate does not need a majority, but prevails simply by winning more votes than any other candidate, and (b) proportional representation (PR), under which the number of seats that parties win is in proportion to the number of votes they win. Winner-take-all has the advantage of being quick and simple, and tends to produce stable and accountable one-party governments, while PR tends to produce sometimes unstable multi-party coalitions. However, winner-take-all is not always fair. It tends to work in favour of parties that have large blocks of concentrated support, and against the interests of parties whose support is more thinly spread; the former tend to win seats, while the latter more often come second or third.

Britain uses winner-take-all for its general elections, and the kind of skewed results it can produce were most glaringly obvious in the 1983 general election, when the ruling Conservatives won 42 per cent of the vote but 62 per cent of seats in the House of Commons. Meanwhile, Labour won 28 per cent of votes and 32 per cent of seats (a more equitable result), while the third-placed Liberal-SDP Alliance won almost as many votes as Labour (25 per cent) but just 4 per cent of seats in the House. This meant, mathematically speaking, that the votes of Alliance supporters were worth only one-tenth as much as the votes of Conservative supporters.

Almost every other European country uses PR, whose introduction in Britain was first proposed as early as 1917, but until recently found few supporters within the Conservative and Labour Parties, because they benefited the most from winner-take-all. However, pressure from within the European Union for a common EU-wide electoral system has combined with a change of heart within the Labour Party to push reform further up the political agenda. Following on a campaign pledge, the Blair administration appointed a commission in 1997 to look into the options, and it came back with a recommendation for a mixture of winner-take-all and PR.

British voters had their first taste of PR in 1998–99 with elections to the Scottish, Welsh and London assemblies and to the European Parliament (although Northern Ireland had already used PR for European and local elections). However, there is little sign of PR being used for the general election, because of a lack of public enthusiasm, opposition from the Conservatives, and antagonism even from members of the Labour Party (Fielding, 2000: 27).

were separate boundary commissions for England, Scotland, Wales and Northern Ireland, but they were then absorbed into an independent national Electoral Commission, which is also responsible for supervising the financial restrictions on parties and for overseeing referendums. One change due to come at the next boundary review will be a reduction in the number of seats in the UK Parliament for Scotland. There is a statutory minimum of 71 at the moment, but this will be abolished, potentially reducing the number of Scottish seats to about 57–60.

A worrying feature of recent general elections has been falling voter turnout: from a high of 83–84 per cent in 1950–51, it fell to 76–79 per cent in the 1970s, and to 71 per cent in 1997. These figures were respectable, placing Britain around the average for most European countries, with the notable exception of those where voting is compulsory such as Belgium and Italy. Then came the 2001 election, when turnout in Britain fell to a new low of just 59 per cent. Was this a sign of a new long-term trend in British politics, or was it an anomaly, to be explained by the particular circumstances of the 2001 election, in which the opposition Conservatives were unable to put up a real contest to Labour? It is not yet an issue that much concerns British political analysts, but this may yet change.

*European Elections*

On a fixed five-year cycle, Britain elects 87 representatives to the 626-member European Parliament (EP) in Strasbourg, France. Candidates for EP elections are fielded by the same parties that contest general elections at home, and they run on a mixture of domestic and European issues. The first direct elections to the EP were held in 1979, since when British voters have shown a remarkable lack of interest in turning out: after running at about 36 per cent (far below even the modest EU average of about 57 per cent), British turnout fell in 1999 to an all-time low of 23 per cent (less than half the EU average of 49 per cent). The lack of interest is explained by a combination of the Eurosceptic views of many British voters, and of the limited powers of the EP itself – it can neither introduce nor take the final decision on adopting new laws.

European elections are notable for the extent to which opposition parties usually do much better than the governing party. The main explanation for this lies in attitudes towards different levels of elections. Elections that decide who runs the national government – or 'first-order' elections – always draw the most media and public inter-est, and the highest turnout. By contrast, 'second-order' elections – such as European or local elections, where the stakes are lower – are usually seen as an opportunity to comment on the performance of the governing party. Thus, its supporters are less inclined to vote (adding to the low turnout figures), and many other voters will cast their ballots for parties they would not normally support (Hix, 2000: 64).

At the 1994 elections, the governing Conservatives – plagued by divisions over Europe – won just 18 of the British seats, while the opposition Labour Party won 62. By contrast, the 1999 elections were a major blow for Labour, by then in government, whose share of seats fell to 29, while the Conservatives won 36 seats, and the balance was won by smaller parties including the Liberal Democrats (up from 2 to 10), the UK Independence Party (3), and the Greens (2). The turn-around was part of the typical inclination of voters to cast their ballots for the opposition, but it was also a reflection of a Europe-wide shift to right-wing parties calling for a slow-down in European integration, and was also affected by Britain's decision to adopt for the first time the same system of proportional representation used for EP elections in the other 14 EU member states. Instead of having 87 single-member districts and declaring the candidate in each district with the most votes the winner, Britain was divided into several much larger multi-member districts, competing parties put forward lists of candi-dates, and the seats were divided up among the parties according to the proportion of the vote each received.

## Local Government Elections

Because Britain is a unitary state (in theory, at least), and local authorities have limited power, local elections are seen as 'second-order' contests, and have traditionally been ignored by most voters. Members are elected to district, county, city and town councils on a fixed four-year cycle, but the few voters who turn out usually make their choices on the basis of national issues and the performance of the national government, and turnout is rarely more than 40 per cent. However, the situation may change as the new regional assemblies become more settled. Because they have their own powers over a variety of local policy issues, the stakes in the elections have been raised. Turnout at the first elections in 1998–99 was not inspiring – 70 per cent in Northern Ireland, 58 per cent in Scotland, and 46 per cent in Wales – but this may improve with time. Scottish and Welsh

Some of an estimated one million people on Britain's largest ever demonstration – in London on 15 February 2003, against war on Iraq. While less prone to vote, Britons now seem more willing to take direct action to express their political views.

**Illustration 5.1   Stop the War March**

assembly elections are based on a combination of winner-take-all and PR, while regional and European elections in Northern Ireland use PR.

## Political Parties

Britain has a broad range of political parties, covering a variety of ideological positions. However, while 73 parties contested the 2001 general election, and nine won seats in Parliament, Britain has for a long time been a two-party system. During the nineteenth century, it was the Conservatives and the Liberals that took turns at governing, their dominance occasionally threatened by Irish nationalist parties. Since the end of the First World War, Labour has replaced the Liberals, and they and the Conservatives have dominated, typically winning about 70–75 per cent of the vote between them and about 90 per cent of the seats in Parliament (see Table 5.1). The remaining share of votes and seats has been taken up by the old Liberal Party and its successors, and by regional parties; as well as Scottish and Welsh nationalists, Northern Ireland has its own parties which do not campaign on the mainland.

The winner-take-all electoral system has allowed the British party system to be one of the most stable in Western Europe. Where most other EU countries wholly or partly use PR, and so are commonly ruled by coalition governments, Britain spends most of its time under the administration of a single political party. There were coalition governments between the wars, and there have been the occasional minority governments since 1945, but otherwise one party has always been firmly in control.

## Labour

The Labour Party was founded in 1900, and first came to prominence in the 1920s when its leader Ramsay MacDonald led two coalition governments. Labour won outright power for the first time in 1945 under the leadership of Clement Atlee, and immediately set about building a welfare state and a managed economy, nationalizing key industries, and creating a national health service, a social security system and a subsidized education system. It lost power in 1951, but returned in 1964–70 and again in 1974–76 under the leadership of Harold Wilson, and then of James Callaghan (1976–79). It went into opposition in 1979, losing four straight general elections and under-going a crisis of confidence before finally regaining power in 1997 under the leadership of Tony Blair.

Its failures in the 1980s were blamed on a combination of the political shrewdness of Conservative Prime Minister Margaret Thatcher, 'unelectable' party leaders such as the old-style socialist Michael Foot, and the growing unpopularity of many of its more traditional socialist policies, including state-ownership of key industries, support of labour unions, and the redistribution of wealth through taxation. The extent of its internal problems was emphasized in 1981 when a group of moderate members of the party broke away to form the Social Democratic Party (SDP). This merged with the Liberal Party

*Table 5.1* General election trends in Britain

|  | 1987 | | 1992 | | 1997 | | 2001 | |
|---|---|---|---|---|---|---|---|---|
|  | % vote | seats | % vote | seats | % vote | seats | % vote | seats |
| Labour | 31 | 229 | 35 | 271 | 42 | 418 | 41 | 412 |
| Conservative | 42 | 376 | 42 | 336 | 30 | 165 | 32 | 166 |
| Liberal Democrats | 23 | 22 | 17 | 20 | 16 | 46 | 18 | 52 |
| Regional parties | 4 | 23 | 4 | 24 | 5 | 29 | 5 | 27 |
| Other | >1 | 0 | 2 | 0 | 7 | 1 | 4 | 2 |
| Total |  | 650 |  | 651 |  | 659 |  | 659 |
| Turnout (%) |  | 75.3 |  | 76.3 |  | 71.4 |  | 59.4 |

*Source*: % share and turnout figures from National Statistics web site, 2002.

in 1988 after having helped force Labour to rethink and moderate its policies.

Tony Blair was elected party leader in May 1994, and made it clear that he was opposed to many of the party's old positions. He moved quickly to 'modernize' Labour and to distance it from its more traditionally socialist ideas by adopting what he called a new 'left-of-centre agenda'. One of his first successes was to encourage the party in 1995 to abandon the controversial Clause Four of its constitution, which pledged 'common ownership of the means of production, distribution and exchange'; Labour thereby gave up its promise to undo privatization, one of the most successful of Margaret Thatcher's policies, and has since stood for more overtly free-market economic policies of the kind associated with the 'third way' in politics (see Box 5.2).

The victory of 'New Labour' in May 1997 was remarkable in almost every sense. Labour won a 177-seat majority, while the Conservatives lost half their seats in the Commons and all their seats in Scotland and Wales. Even senior members of the cabinet – including several future contenders for the leadership of the party, such as former Defence Secretary Michael Portillo – lost their seats. Debates subsequently raged about the reasons behind the Labour victory and the Conservative defeat. Britain at the time had rates of

---

**Box 5.2  The Third Way**

One of the hallmarks of the Blair administration has been its shift towards the centre of the political spectrum, and its adoption of a set of goals and values known as the Third Way. While the term has never been clearly defined, it is understood to mean an approach to government, politics, economics and social issues that lies somewhere between the kind of right-wing conservatism/capitalism associated with the Thatcher government, and the left-wing liberalism/economic management associated with more mainstream socialist parties in Western Europe. It has also been described as 'capitalism with a conscience' or 'market socialism', and has been associated with social democratic German chancellor Gerhard Schroeder, former US president Bill Clinton, and former socialist French Prime Minister Lionel Jospin.

It became more widely known in Britain when Tony Blair's New Labour adopted many of the policies usually associated with the middle ground of politics, encroaching into traditionally Conservative territory. For example, Blair embraced the market economy, opposed traditional socialist ideas of taxing and spending, developed a closer relationship with business, reduced the influence of trade unions in the Labour Party, committed his government to developing a balanced budget, instituted a more pro-European policy (Labour was for many years hostile to the idea of European integration), and moved Labour toward foreign policy positions that were pro-globalization, pro-NATO and pro-US. Blair also claimed that improved education, reform of the national health-care system, a tough position on crime, and constitutional reform were among his priorities.

The novelty value in the Third Way is debatable. It is rare to find a socialist party in a democracy that does not use elements of the free market to achieve its objectives, and even the conservative administration of Margaret Thatcher was prepared to use the state when it suited. But whether this was truly a new set of prescriptions, or simply a repackaging of an old set, it not only won Blair two elections with convincing majorities, but also apparently confounded the Conservatives, who found it more difficult to show how they were different from Labour.

---

unemployment and inflation that were among the lowest in Europe (6 per cent and 3 per cent respectively). The Conservatives were also the party of Margaret Thatcher, whose policies of privatization and undermining the powers of labour unions had been popular and effective.

The change of fortunes symbolized a widely-felt need among Britons for new ideas in government, and a concern that

**Illustration 5.2  Labour Party Conference**

The annual Labour party conference in 2001. After 18 years in opposition, Labour under Tony Blair moved away from its traditional leftist policies and won a convincing election victory in 1997. In 2001, it won its first ever second full consecutive term in government.

Conservatives had paid too little attention to social problems. Labour had also moved itself towards the centre of the political spectrum (for example, promising not to raise income taxes), and the Conservatives had suffered from internal squabbles and the monetary crisis of 1992, when the pound was ejected from the European exchange-rate mechanism (Dunleavy, 2000: 131). Furthermore, there was clearly much tactical voting in the election, with Labour and Liberal Democratic supporters voting for the other party in districts where one of them was in a strong position to challenge the incumbent Conservative (Sanders, 1997). Finally, a new generation of young people who had known nothing but Conservative government was voting for the first time; 52 per cent of under-25s voted Labour, up from 35 per cent in 1992. Many analysts also argued that the vote was ultimately less for Labour than against the divided Conservatives.

Remarkably, Blair was able to prevent damaging in-fighting from breaking out within the party between supporters of two currents of thought: left-wingers with a preference for public ownership and intervention in the economy, opposed to nuclear weapons, and cool on the transatlantic alliance, and right-wingers prepared to take a more pragmatic approach, in favour of nuclear weapons, and in support of the transatlantic alliance. The right tends to have the ascendancy when Labour is in office, and the left tends to dominate when Labour is in opposition (Kavanagh, 2000: 147). Labour maintained its commanding position at the 2001 election, when its majority was reduced by just 12 seats, and its percentage share of the vote fell from 43 to 41. However, voter turnout fell to 59 per cent, suggesting that enthusiasm for Labour was waning, and that it was being returned to office partly because the Conservatives had failed to offer a strong alternative.

*The Conservatives*

The origins of the Conservatives (also known as the Tories) date back to the late seventeenth century. Since the end of the Second World War they have held power for a total of 36 years, under the leadership of Winston Churchill, Anthony Eden, Harold Macmillan and Alec Douglas-Home (1951–64), of Edward Heath (1970–74), and of Margaret Thatcher and John Major (1979–97). However, despite the number of their postwar election victories, and despite their status as one of the longest-serving political parties in any democracy, they have never won more than 45–50 per cent of the national vote, their share fell to a new low of 31–32 per cent in the 1997 and 2001 elections, and today they find themselves in a state of crisis.

The Conservatives are a pro-business, anti-regulation party with so many shades of opinion that it is often charged that British conservatism lacks consistency or coherence. Much like Labour, there have been two distinctive strands in Conservative thinking in recent years. Right-wingers in the party emphasize limited government, low taxes, self-reliance, social discipline, authority, continuity and morals, and are critical of the EU, while moderates emphasize the creation of wealth, efficient economic organization, a more active role for government in the economy, and a more progressive role for Britain in Europe. Between 1945 and 1975, Conservative policies changed little, irrespective of the leader. Then Margaret Thatcher became leader and broke with tradition, and for more than a decade the party developed policies that reflected her values. She supported monetarist economic ideas (such as controls on government spending, reducing the role of government in the marketplace, low taxation and a free market), promoted private enterprise and private ownership, believed in a strong global role for Britain and close Anglo-American relations, and was hostile to many aspects of European integration. Although the Conservatives under the leadership of Prime Minister John Major fought the 1997 election against the background of a strong economy, they faced an electorate that was tired of internal party squabbles. The party had become particularly divided over the issue of Europe, with some of its members arguing in favour of greater support for European integration, and some arguing that the process of integration had gone too far. The Conservatives had also been hurt by a number of financial scandals involving prominent backbenchers (in what became known as the 'sleaze' factor). Major was unable to pull the party together, it went into the election 20 percentage points behind Labour in opinion polls, and it sustained its worst election defeat since 1832.

Following his defeat, John Major resigned the party leadership (although he stayed on as an MP), and was replaced by the 37-year-old William Hague, who faced the difficult task of uniting the Conservatives and making them a true party of opposition. The task proved a hard one, however, given the substantial majority enjoyed by Labour, and the popularity of Tony Blair and the Labour government. As they approached the 2001 election, the Conservatives were in a state of confusion, many of their more popular policy positions having been coopted by Labour. There was also a squabble within the party over Europe, and questions about how long Hague would remain leader.

The 2001 elections barely made a dent in Labour's dominance, and the net number of Conservative seats rose by just one. William Hague quickly resigned the leadership, and a new election was held which drew more attention to the polarization within the party. The vote was open to all party members, more than two-thirds of whom are aged 55 or older, and barely 5 per cent of whom are 35 or younger. They made a questionable tactical error in rejecting strong candidates such as Michael Portillo (who undermined himself when he publicly admitted to having had gay experiences when younger) and the pro-European former finance minister Kenneth Clarke, instead electing the right-wing and inexperienced Iain Duncan Smith. Just as Labour had been led in the 1980s by 'unelectable' leaders who were too ideologically extreme, so it seemed that the same was now happening to the Conservatives; their new leader had views that were close to those of the party grassroots, but too far from the middle ground of British politics. Though he has tried to temper his image and focus on party modernisation and delivery of public services, Duncan Smith made very little impact, prompting much speculation of possible leadership challenges if the party continued to 'flat line' in opinion polls, well behind Labour.

## Liberal Democrats

A small moderate centre party, the Liberal Democrats were created in 1988 when members of a Labour Party splinter group (the Social Democratic Party, or SDP) joined forces with the Liberal Party, one of the oldest parties in Britain and for many years until the 1920s the major opposition to the Conservatives. The last Liberal prime minister (David Lloyd George) left office in 1922, and Liberal support declined as the working class shifted its allegiance to Labour. Surprise by-election victories in the 1960s and 1970s had media pundits talking about the Liberals being on the verge of a breakthrough, and for a while in the mid-1980s, the SDP-Liberal Alliance seemed poised to take over from Labour as the major opposition party.

The Liberals and the SDP merged in 1988 to form the Liberal Democratic Party, which contested its first general election in April 1992. It won an impressive 17 per cent of the vote, but the peculiarities of winner-take-all meant that this converted into just 20 seats (3 per cent of the total). In the 1997 election the party again won about 18 per cent of the vote, but more than doubled its representation in Parliament, winning 46 seats, the best result for a third party since the 1920s. New attention was paid to the Liberal Democrats by political analysts, especially given that their support and cooperation has been actively encouraged by the Blair government. They have been led since 1999 by Charles Kennedy (b. 1959), who was able to continue to build modestly on party growth at the 2001 election, where the party won an additional six seats. Kennedy has claimed that the Liberal Democrats are on the verge of taking over from the Conservatives as the effective opposition to Labour, but critics ask how this can be when Liberal Democratic policies are so close to those of Labour in many areas.

## Other Parties

There are many other smaller political parties in Britain, but among them they rarely win more than 3–5 per cent of the vote in general elections. The most important of the minor parties represent regional interests. The Scottish National Party (founded in 1934) campaigns for devolution for Scotland and has undergone a revival since the 1950s, increasing its representation in the UK Parliament to five seats. It won 35 seats (27 per cent of the total) in the Scottish Parliamentary elections in 1999, which gave it the balance of power and allowed it to become the opposition to the Labour–Liberal Democratic coalition government. Its then-leader, Alex Salmond, went so far in September 1999 as to predict that Scotland would be completely independent before 2007, the 300th anniversary of the political union of England and Scotland. Meanwhile, its Welsh counterpart Plaid Cymru (founded in 1925), which has in recent years had two to four seats in the UK Parliament, also won just over a quarter of the seats in the Welsh assembly in 1999.

There are also nearly a dozen parties which are active only in Northern Ireland, and whose key differences revolve around their positions on the relationship with Britain. The biggest is the Ulster Unionist Party, which represents the Protestant cause of continued union for Northern Ireland with Britain, while the smaller Sinn Fein represents the Catholic/nationalist cause and has campaigned in the past for the reunification of Ireland (a goal officially rescinded by the 1998 Northern Irish peace agreement). The Social Democratic and Labour Party meanwhile takes a more balanced line between the two positions.

While candidates for the larger parties must go through a rigorous selection procedure, British law allows almost anyone to stand for Parliament under almost any guise, and even from prison. The only formal requirements for candidates are that they are residents of Britain, are aged over 21, are citizens of Britain, Ireland or a Commonwealth country, have collected the signatures of 10 electors, and have paid a deposit of £500 (about €/$800), which is returned if the candidate wins more than 5 per cent of the vote. (A candidate who fails to cross the 5 per cent barrier is described as having 'lost their deposit'). Everyone over the age of 18 can vote except convicted felons, the criminally insane, and aristocrats (but including citizens of Ireland or Commonwealth countries resident in the UK).

## Interest Groups

As with most modern liberal democracies, interest groups play a key political role in Britain. There are thousands of such groups, ranging from multimillion-member pressure groups to charities with more limited objectives. Several of Britain's mass movements and interest groups have spread to other countries. For example, the movement against cruelty to animals began in Britain, long famous as a nation of animal lovers, and produced the Royal Society for the Prevention of Cruelty to Animals (RSPCA). (Ironically, it was founded in 1824, 65 years before the National Society for the Prevention of Cruelty to Children.) Similarly, Save the Children, Oxfam (famine relief), the World Wildlife Fund, and Amnesty International were founded in Britain and have since become international.

As voters have become disillusioned with elections and political parties, the membership of interest groups has grown – more than half the adult population is now a member of at least one group, and many people belong to multiple groups (Kavanagh, 2000: 178). Interest groups have also become more professional and the methods they use have diversified. Where they once focused their efforts on ministers and bureaucrats, they have worked increasingly to mobilize media and public opinion, and have intensified their lobbying of Parliament, providing information to MPs, making presentations to parliamentary committees, and trying to influence the development of legislation. The European Union has provided new channels for lobbying: groups try to have input into the development of new EU laws and policies, and report failures by the government to implement EU law to the European Court of Justice.

A number of groups have developed such a close relationship with government that they are routinely consulted on policy decisions. Described as 'insider' groups by Grant (1989 and 2000), they have earned this status by providing information and expertise, by speaking with authority for a particular sector, by having goals compatible with those of the government, and by having a reputation for discretion, responsibility and confidentiality. Examples include the National Farmer's Union and the British Medical Association.

Interest-group activity in Britain has occasionally added up to broader movements aimed at bringing political, economic or social reform, and there have been three particularly important movements in Britain in recent years.

*The Labour Movement*

Britain has about 300 trade unions, the biggest of which are affiliated to the Trades Union Congress (TUC), founded in 1868. Unions were for a long time closely affiliated with the Labour Party, having a 40 per cent share in the electoral college which elected the party leader, and sponsoring about 40 per cent of Labour candidates in general elections. The TUC has also in the past made agreements with Labour governments whereby – in return for concessions – it agreed not to make big wage claims or to go on strike. By 1974, unions had so much power that a general strike was called which ultimately obliged Edward Heath's Conservative government to call a general election, which it lost.

The failure of the Labour governments of Harold Wilson (1974–76) and James Callaghan (1976–79) to reach agreements with the unions on prices and wages led to another near-general strike in 1979. This made Labour so unpopular that it lost the 1979 election, ushering in a Thatcher government bent on reducing union power. Laws were passed requiring union leaders to ballot their members before taking strike action, and unemployment reduced union membership during the 1980s. In addition to a lengthy and divisive strike by coal-miners in the mid-1980s, print and journalists' unions also went on strike – all three groups failed to meet their goals. In recent years, unions have lost much of their support and many of their members, and their political influence has declined further as their influence on the Labour Party has weakened.

### Business Groups

If the TUC represents workers, then employers are represented by the Confederation of British Industry (CBI), founded in 1965. Financial institutions are politically important, mainly because of the influence of the financial district of the City of London (see Chapter 6). While City interests are kept separate from those of industry, and while there are no formal links between business and the Conservative Party (such as those that once existed between unions and the Labour Party), many senior managers in the City and Britain's larger companies had significant influence within the Conservative Party during the Thatcher and Major years. They have not been ignored by the Blair government, which has made a point of cultivating contacts with business as part of its philosophy of increasing productivity and promoting British economic influence in the EU.

### The Environmental Movement

Green political parties have not been as successful in Britain as they have in several other European countries, the pressure for environmental change instead expressing itself through support for a large community of environmental interest groups. Britain has what may well be the oldest, best-organized and biggest (per capita) community of such groups in the world, which – by one estimate - had a combined membership in 2002 of 3.2 million (Royal Society for the Protection of Birds, 2002). Much of the growth in its size and levels of activity has come since the late 1980s, and the groups with the fastest growth include those that have been most activist, such as Greenpeace and Friends of the Earth.

It took some time for activity to be translated into political influence. Several studies in the 1980s suggested that environmental groups had only limited political influence (see, for example, Lowe and Goyder, 1983: 58), but in recent years the new emphasis on the role of the individual in the creation of environmental problems has led to a new level of activism both among groups and individuals. Three issues in particular are credited with prompting much of the political activity in the late 1990s: the anti-roads movement, direct-action protests in 1998–99 against the use of genetically-modified foods, and concerns about rural issues and the state of the countryside (Margetts, 2000: 189–91). The latter issue prompted an estimated 100,000 people to turn out in a London protest in 1997, and 250,000 to turn out in 1998. A MORI poll found that 80 per cent of the participants in the 1998 protest were Conservative voters, a group not usually given to protest activity.

## The Media

The British generally have a high level of political literacy and interest in national and international affairs, a situation which is sustained by one of the most diverse and well-respected mass media establishments in the world, catering to almost every taste and political persuasion. Like all European countries, Britain has mainly national or regional media, so people are interested less in local politics than in national or international politics. Important changes have come to the British media over the past decade: they are becoming more powerful political actors, they are becoming more polarized as competition increases, their independence from political parties is growing, and a greater variety of sources of information has become available.

Take the case of television. Until the late 1980s, British TV viewers had a choice of just four channels: two government-owned and commercial-free channels run by the British Broadcasting Corporation (BBC), and two independent commercial channels (ITV and Channel 4). (A new commercial channel – Channel 5 – was created in 1996.) All are editorially independent, are required to give equal air-time to the major political parties, and frequently become involved in political controversy. Users pay an annual licence fee, which goes to supporting BBC TV and five national BBC radio channels. Despite being government-owned, the BBC has a reputation for being an impartial and dependable source of news both inside and outside Britain.

During the 1990s, the television landscape changed out of all recognition:

- Cable and satellite providers became available, and the number of TV channels leapt from four to more than 60, offered most notably by companies such as BSkyB, Carlton and Granada's cooperative venture OnDigital (until its collapse in 2002) and the BBC.
- Audience share for the five terrestrial channels fell from more than 90 per cent to about 80 per cent, and is projected soon to be as low as 60 per cent.
- Scotland is increasingly opting out of carrying national programming, and is instead airing more locally produced programmes.
- While there is more 24-hour news on offer, there has been less prime-time political coverage on the mainstream commercial channels (Scammell, 2000: 171–8).

Under the circumstances, the public-service programming that was once provided by the BBC without much competition is now viewed by a smaller proportion of the audience, which is offered more entertainment options instead. The promotion of 'British' political issues has also declined as regional news plays a bigger role in the choices available to viewers. Finally, political parties have to work harder – and use a greater variety of methods – to put their message across to viewers. At one time, the major political parties were guaranteed 5-or 10-minute prime time slots on the three major terrestrial TV channels during election campaigns, the so-called Party Political Broadcasts. They still have them, but instead of enjoying the virtually undivided attention of viewers, they are now competing with the broadcasting fare of dozens of different channels.

The British broadcast market is about to undergo yet another series of changes, which promises to make it one of the world's freest, but also has critics concerned. A bill working its way through Parliament in 2002 promised to liberalize the market, deregulating commercial radio, allowing radio owners to buy television stations and vice versa, allowing a merger of independent television (currently run by two separate companies), and allowing non-European companies to buy British companies, something which they have not been allowed to do so far. It is notable that the world's media have come to be dominated in recent years by seven major companies, four of which are American (including AOL Time Warner and Disney), two continental European (Bertelsmann and Vivendi), one Japanese (Sony), and none British. The bill is designed in part to encourage the emergence of a world-leading British media company that could compete with the Big Seven. Critics charge, however, that too many other countries (notably the US) still bar foreigners from investing in their domestic industries, and that the existence of the BBC – a large state-owned corporation – could act as a barrier to the development of a large private competitor (*The Economist*, 11 May 2002: 16, 51–2).

While British broadcasting is seeing growing variety, the print market remains relatively unchanged. With the exception of major regional dailies (such as *The Scotsman* in Edinburgh), most newspapers are London-based national morning papers, which between them are read by about 80 per cent of the population. The choices have been steady for many years: there are five so-called 'quality' papers (such as *The Times* and *The Guardian*), and five mass circulation tabloids (such as the *Sun* and the *Daily Mail*), most of which have related Sunday papers (such as the *Observer* and the *People*). Where the 'qualities' provide a broader variety of news and comment, several with a particular political or social bias, the tabloids tend to be more openly partisan and to present an often simplified and exaggerated picture of politics. The popularity of the tabloids has also led to concerns that they allow their owners too much political influence. Particular criticism has been directed at Rupert Murdoch, whose News International Corporation owns Sky Television, *The Times/Sunday Times*, the *Sun*, and the *News of the World*. Murdoch is an Australian with American citizenship whose papers tended to take strongly anti-EU and pro-Conservative editorial positions, but since 1997 have in the main supported Blair, including at election time.

The media not only carry out the typical roles of helping form the national political agenda, providing people with information, helping determine political reputations, and providing the self-appointed role of watchdog. More recently, they have also been more openly manip-

**Illustration 5.3  Newspaper headlines**

Newspapers announce the death of Diana, Princess of Wales in August 1997. Britons have a wide variety of national newspapers from which to choose, from serious papers of comment to tabloids, infamous for their fascination with the private lives of celebrities.

ulated by government for political ends. In this regard, Britain has lagged some way behind the United States, where media strategies have been a critical part of political campaigns since the 1950s. It has only been since the 1970s, for example, that prime ministerial press officers have become well-known public figures. Margaret Thatcher in particular was well-known for developing a media strategy, for employing an advertising agency to develop campaign advertising, and for changing her image (even to the point of taking voice-training lessons) in order to help convey her message. Tony Blair has also had an active media programme, such that one of the most prominent members of his administration has been his press secretary, Alastair Campbell.

The availability of political information – and the opportunity for political participation – has been greatly affected in recent years by the rise of the internet, now the world's largest communications system. The British compete with Americans as the most internet-connected people in the world: the proportion of homes with internet access rose from less than 10 per cent in 1998 to nearly 40 per cent in 2001 (about the same proportion as in the United States), and many more people have access at work or in libraries, while virtually all schools in Britain are connected. Recent surveys have found that more than half of all adults have used the internet. The Blair administration has plans to ensure universal access to the internet – and to provide all government services online – by 2005. The official government website – UKOnline – has connections to virtually all government departments, and was receiving more than 20 million hits weekly in 2001.

# 6

# The Economy

Economic issues play a central role in the public life of most societies, particularly capitalist systems, but in few places has this been
more true in the last 50 years than in Britain. From being the dominant economy in the world, Britain has seen itself outperformed by its
competitors, and hurt by the policies of labour unions and management, many of the members of which were incapable of looking
beyond their sectional interests at the bigger economic interests of
their country. The contradictory inclinations of different governments
to play a greater or a lesser role in the marketplace has also caused
dramatic shifts in British economic fortunes.

The postwar Labour government favoured nationalization and
welfare, policies that promoted the reconstruction of Britain but over
the longer term contributed to a decline in productivity, efficiency
and competition. By the late 1960s, Britain's economy was in trouble,
and it became common to hear talk of a 'British disease'. The symp-
toms of this condition included an expensive welfare system, powerful trade unions, a large public sector, falling productivity, and a
declining trade surplus. Conditions worsened during the 1970s, and
for many the nadir was reached in 1978–79 with the so-called 'winter
of discontent', when it seemed that all the accumulating problems of
the previous 20 years had brought the British economy to the brink of
collapse. The media were fascinated by the booms and busts, feeding
into popular misconceptions of the economic decline of Britain.
When voters went to the polls, their decisions were driven as much as
anything by concerns about that decline and by their opinions about
which political party offered the best solutions to Britain's economic
woes.

The Thatcher government came into office in 1979 determined to reverse the trends, and arguing that government was too involved in market decisions, and that the entrepreneurial spirit of Britons had been dulled by high taxes and too much reliance on the state. It reduced taxes, sold off key industries to the private sector, and reduced the burden of regulation. Through a combination of these policies and broader changes in the global economy, by the 1990s the prospects for Britain were much improved. New wealth was being created, new businesses launched, productivity was growing, and both inflation and unemployment were down.

This chapter looks at the economic system of Britain and at the causes and effects of recent changes in that system. It begins with a survey of the structure of the economy, arguing that much of the hand-wringing about decline has been misplaced. It then examines economic trends since 1945, contrasting the boom years of the 1950s with the crises of the 1970s, assessing the content and impact of Thatcherism, and discussing the changes that have taken place over the last decade. It ends by looking at the place of Britain in the global trading system, and at the impact on the British economy of membership of the European Union.

### The Structure of the Economy

Britain has all the typical features of a modern capitalist society. It is wealthy, it makes a diverse range of products, it offers its consumers a wide range of services, the bulk of its economic wealth is generated by non-tangible services rather than industry, and it plays an important role in the international trading system. It is also a free-market system in which prices are driven mainly by supply and demand, and in which private enterprise dominates the creation of wealth. Private enterprise was at the core of the development of Britain's empire, but the postwar policies of an expanded public sector and greater government regulation broadened the frontiers of the state, which have contracted again since the 1980s as the government has withdrawn from the marketplace and placed greater emphasis on the private sector and individual enterprise.

The basic measure of national economic wealth is gross domestic product (GDP), or the total value of all goods and services produced by a country in the course of a year. Britain in 2001 had a GDP of just over $1.4 trillion, making it the fourth wealthiest economy in the world after the United States, Japan and Germany (see Figure 6.1).

*Figure* 6.1   The British economy, 2001

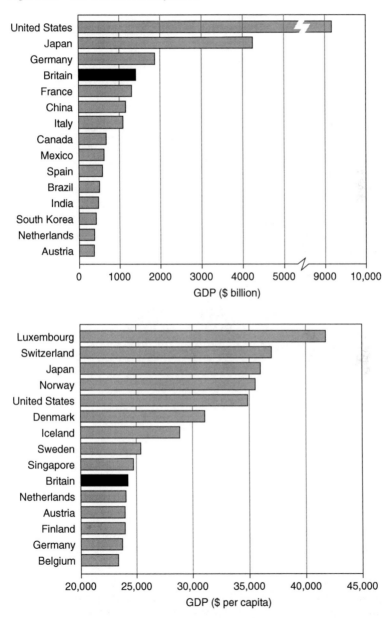

*Source*:   World Bank Web site 2002, World Development Indicators database,
http://www.worldbank.com.

Margaret Thatcher, prime minister from 1979 to 1990. She responded to concerns about British economic performance by reducing the role of the government in the marketplace: lowering taxes, privatizing government-owned business, and curbing trade union power.

**Illustration 6.1   Margaret Thatcher**

There was a time in the 1980s when its GDP fell below that of France and even Italy – when Italy overtook Britain in 1986, the Italian press dubbed the event *il sorpasso*, a recognition of the extent to which the Italian economy had progressed and to which the British economy had regressed. However, the last few years have seen a notable recovery as economic growth has helped Britain overtake both Italy and France in GDP. Even when assessed by per capita GDP, Britain has done well, and by 2001 even ranked ahead of Germany (but significantly below Japan or the United States).

In terms of how that GDP is generated, Britain's economic structure is very much the same as that found in most other liberal democracies. All economic activity falls under one of three categories:

industry, agriculture or services (the latter being activities which do not produce a tangible good or commodity). Britain was once predominantly an agricultural society, but that changed with the industrial revolution, when the contribution of agriculture to economic wealth slipped as industry grew. Since the Second World War – in line with the USA, Japan and all other European countries – the contribution of services has grown as that of industry has declined. Many of Britain's factories have closed, and manufacturing jobs have been lost to Asian and Latin American countries with cheaper labour. Britain still has an industrial sector, but where industry now accounts for just 32 per cent of GDP, and agriculture for 2 per cent of GDP, two-thirds of its economic wealth is generated by services, such as retail activities, banking, insurance, financial services, tourism and entertainment.

Public income and spending in Britain in 2001–02 each came to just short of £400 billion (€/$580 billion). Income is derived primarily from income tax (26 per cent) National Insurance (16 per cent) and value added tax (15 per cent), the balance coming from corporation, excise and local taxes (see Figure 6.2). There are three bands of income tax: a starting rate of 10 per cent for those on low incomes, a basic rate of 22 per cent, and a higher rate of 40 per cent for top-earners. Income tax rates were significantly reduced during the Thatcher years, and the basic rate is now the lowest it has been in more than 70 years. Meanwhile, tax on the income and capital gains of companies runs at 30 per cent, the lowest rate of any of the major industrialized countries. Finally, like all European Union member states, Britain imposes value added tax on each stage in the production and distribution of goods, the standard rate being 17.5 per cent.

In terms of spending, the major items in Britain – as in all advanced industrial societies – are social security, health and education, which among them account for 56 per cent of government spending. Concerns about the quality of public services have encouraged the Blair administration to increase spending on health care, education, transport, law and order, and deprived neighbourhoods. It is debatable, however, whether the problem with public services is one of too little expenditure, or of too much government involvement in their management.

One of the most distinctive features of the British economy is the special role of finance (Gamble, 1999: 34). When Britain was the centre of the global economy in the nineteenth century, and sterling

*Figure* 6.2   The national budget

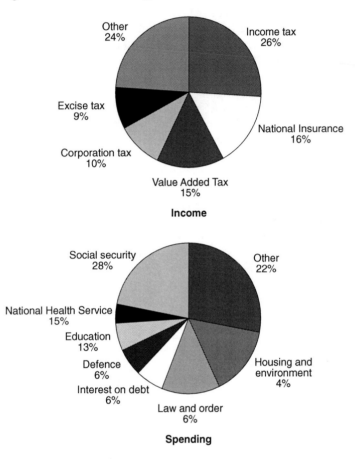

*Source*:   Office for National Statistics. Figures for 2001–2.

was the dominant currency, the position of London took on new strength, and even today the financial district of London – the City – has a role in the national and international economy which gives London a dominance unmatched by the capital city of any other country. Whenever key decisions need to be taken on economic policy, the question is often 'How will it play in the City?' The key to the power of the City is that it has developed interests in a range of international commercial and banking services which do not depend for their profitability upon the state of the national economy (Ingham,

**Illustration 6.2   Skyline of the City of London**

The skyline of the City of London, with St Paul's Cathedral on the left, the Thames in the foreground, and the International Finance Centre on the right. 'The City' is the biggest market in the world for gold, foreign exchange, and international insurance.

1984: 62–78). The statistics illustrate the economic importance of the City:

- It is the biggest market in the world for gold, international insurance and international commodities.
- It is the biggest market in the world for foreign exchange, with more than $500 billion in turnover every day.
- It has the world's third-largest stockmarket (after New York and Tokyo) when measured by value.
- Nearly $3 trillion in assets are managed by City corporations.
- It has nearly half of the global foreign equity market, and about 70 per cent of Eurobonds are traded in the City.
- More than 480 foreign banks have offices in London, as do 375 of the *Fortune 500* biggest corporations in the world.
- One-fifth of international bank lending is arranged in the City (City of London Web site, 2002, http://www.cityoflondon.gov.uk).

Perhaps the most notable change that has come to the British economy in recent decades has been in the structure of business. Nationalization and the expansion of the welfare state by the postwar Labour government greatly increased both taxation and the role of the state in the marketplace, an approach that initially brought benefits to a country exhausted by war, but that over the longer term created an atmosphere in which inefficient state-owned monopolies removed choice and stifled enterprise. The privatization undertaken by the Thatcher administration in the 1980s significantly reduced the presence of the state in the marketplace, and helped revitalize the entrepreneurial potential of British business. There are now nearly 4 million business in the UK, and – as they once were – many of them are world-ranking. The *Financial Times* survey of the world's 500 biggest companies in 2001 found that 40 were UK-based, and the survey of Europe's 500 biggest companies found that 143 were UK-based. They included Vodafone, BP, GlaxoSmithKline, AstraZeneca, Shell, Royal Bank of Scotland, Lloyds TSB, British Telecom, Cable and Wireless, Diageo, Marconi, Tesco, Reuters, and Anglo-American.

The larger British companies have been behind an increasingly active programme of joint ventures, mergers and overseas acquisitions. Acquisitions in 2000 reached a record level of more than $260 billion, surpassing the previous record – in 1999 – by 63 per cent. Among the most notable recent examples were the 1998 takeover by BP of Amoco of the United States (and the subsequent takeover by BP Amoco of Atlantic Richfield), the 1999 $200 billion takeover by Vodafone of the German company Mannesmann, and the 1999 takeover by Vodafone of the US company AirTouch Communications. There have also been record levels of mergers and acquisitions in Britain involving foreign companies: when ranked by value, Britain is second only to the United States as a target. In the first half of 2002, there were more than $80 billion-worth of mergers and acquisitions in Britain, more than the value of those in Germany and France combined (*The Economist*, 6 July 2002: 97). Prime examples in recent years have included the 1999 takeover of Asda supermarkets by Wal-Mart, and the 2000 takeover of the cell phone company Orange plc by France Telecom.

By 2002, most of the key indicators suggested that Britain's economy was in good condition (*The Economist*, various issues, late 2002); see Figure 6.3:

*Figure* 6.3    British economic performance, 2002

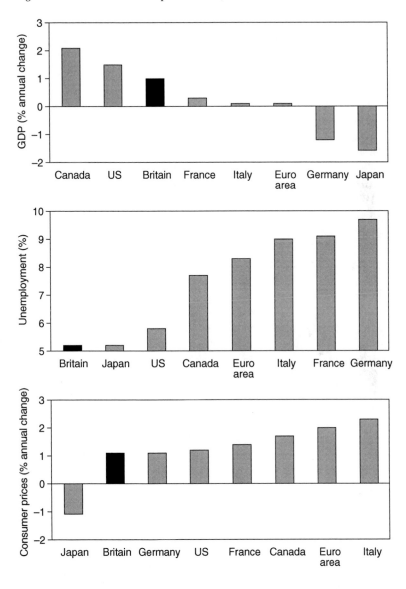

*Source*:    *The Economist*, 2002, various issues.

- After running at a lower rate than those of its EU partners in the 1970s and 1980s, annual growth in GDP in the 1990s was the same as that for the EU and the G8 group of countries. By 2002, Britain's economy was growing faster than those of France, Japan or Germany (it was falling in the latter two countries), and it had over-taken France to become the fourth-biggest in the world in absolute terms.
- The unemployment rate – after hovering in the range of 2–4 per cent between 1945 and 1975, then climbing to a peak of 11 per cent in 1985–86 – was back down to just over 5 per cent, one of the lowest rates in Western Europe.
- The inflation rate – which had peaked in 1980 at 21 per cent, fallen to 3–5 per cent in the mid-1980s, and risen again to 10 per cent in 1991 – was down to 1.1 per cent, the lowest on record. This continued the longest period of sustained low inflation in Britain since the 1960s.
- The pound had been growing steadily in value for a decade. This has caused problems for exporters by making their products more expensive, but it has greatly increased the purchasing power of British consumers and businesses.

Not all was good news, however. Questions remained about Britain's productivity, there were concerns about the low rate of personal savings in Britain, and its key public services were under-performing. Critics charged that too many barriers remained to the entrepreneurial spirit in Britain, and that while the relative decline of productivity may have ended, the British marketplace was still not as free as those of the United States and Germany. But despite the characteristic pessimism of economists, businessmen and the media, all the key indicators suggested that Britain was enjoying a level of prosperity unknown for more than two generations. As one observer noted, 'For more than a decade now, there has been something seriously right with the British economy' (Kaletsky, 2002).

### From Hands-Off to Hands-On, and Back Again

All economies are mixed, meaning that private and public enterprises coexist, often interacting and sometimes competing with one another. They differ only to the extent to which the government intervenes in the marketplace through regulation, taxes, subsidies, benefits and tariffs. The levels of intervention are determined mainly by the extent to which services and programmes are provided by government, and to which there is agreement that the government should help those in need. In terms of policy goals, the ideal is a combination of low inflation and unemployment, high productivity, a balanced budget, a low national debt, and a balance of payments on trade. There has been much debate over just how best to achieve this ideal combination of factors, and Britain – like all Western governments – has moved back and forth between intervention and *laissez-faire* over the last century.

In 1776, the Scottish philosopher and political economist Adam Smith (1723–90) published his seminal *The Wealth of Nations*, in which he argued against the mercantilist philosophy of governments intervening to promote exports and to limit imports, instead supporting the idea of trade and competition. He argued that a market economy left to itself, while not always perfect, had a natural tendency to promote economic equilibrium (a balance between supply and demand), and – by encouraging capitalists to make and sell the goods demanded by the marketplace – to promote the general welfare, 'led by an invisible hand to promote an end which was no part of his intention' (Smith, 1976). Smith's views were influential, but British governments of the late eighteenth and early nineteenth century were deeply conservative, and protected the domestic economy through tariffs on a variety of imports, notably grain. The Corn Law of 1816 – which prevented imports of foreign grain as long as the price of grain was below a particular level – was eventually repealed in 1846, contributing to an end to economic depression and the beginning of an era of massive growth and prosperity for Britain.

The prevailing view in industrialized countries for the rest of the century, and the early part of the twentieth century, was to minimize government involvement in the marketplace, and to treat economic cycles as a natural and uncontrollable part of economic life. Then came the Great Depression in the early 1930s, which forced governments to rethink their approach. Influenced by the theories of the British economist John Maynard Keynes (1883–1946), they chose to address economic downturns by stimulating demand, to which end they cut taxes or increased spending on the public sector. The wisdom of Keynesianism seemed to be borne out by the economic boom of the 1950s, which in some countries extended into the 1960s and early 1970s.

As noted in Chapter 1, the keyword in British economic policy after the Second World War was consensus: a tacit agreement between the Conservatives and Labour that – whichever was in power – they would work to maintain welfare, full employment and a mix of private and public ownership, and would agree on policies through compromise involving discussions between government and interest groups, particularly unions. This approach was credited with helping pull Britain out of the brief era of austerity that followed the war, underpinning the prosperity of the 1950s, introducing the era of mass consumption, and helping promote productivity and exports. Over the short term, the consensus on government intervention seemed both wise and productive.

By the 1960s, however, Britain was in trouble, and the words 'British disease' were often on the lips of economic and political analysts. Whether the disease was a real set of economic trends, or simply the construct of the press and popular opinion, is a debatable point, but there were clearly many critical problems afflicting the British economy:

- An overdependence on consultation as a method of governance. Most notably, the political Right felt that trade unions had become too powerful, leading to the repeated reliance of governments on consultation with – and appeasement of – the unions, the use of strikes as a first resort, and the loss of an increasing number of working days through industrial disputes.
- A welfare system that was proving expensive and was – to its critics – making too many people dependent upon the state, thereby reducing self-reliance and undermining incentives for self-improvement.
- A large public sector that had created inefficient state monopolies, and interfered with the ability or the motivation of entrepreneurs to start and build competitive private businesses.
- A declining position in world trade. Britain's share of world export trade had fallen from more than 26 per cent in 1950 to about 9 per cent between 1973 and 1977.
- A relative decline in productivity, which – during the 1950s and 1960s – had grown at 3.1 per cent annually. This compared unfavourably to annual average rates of 5.6 per cent in West Germany, France and Italy. By 1973, the situation was even worse; growth was down to just 0.2 per cent, compared to 3.8 per cent in France and 2.5 per cent in West Germany.

- A declining trade surplus. From a time in 1963 when Britain exported twice as much as it imported, its trade surplus had almost disappeared by the early 1970s.
- Little incentive for technological innovation, and a failure to apply such innovation to industry.
- For social conservatives, the 'disease' also included moral decline, reflected in the rise of a counterculture, a conspiracy to rebel, a weakening of 'family values', an increase in the incidence of crime, and the compromising of 'traditional' notions of law and order.

Booth (2001: 6, 88 ff; see also Box 6.1) takes issue with the notion of the 'British disease'. He argues that Britons were far better off at the end of the century than at the beginning, that judgements of the performance of British manufacturing trade were too harsh, and that many historians are now prepared to argue that the economic weaknesses of the later twentieth century were grossly exaggerated, and that many of the problems that caused so much concern in Britain were evident in other developed economies as well. But Margaret Thatcher was one of those who supported the popular view of decline, and – upon becoming leader of the Conservative Party in 1975 – argued that major changes were needed if Britain's problems were to be addressed. Her philosophy included several key economic features:

- The promotion of an enterprise culture through a reduction in the size of the public sector, the encouragement of a free market-orientated economy, and the reduction of government subsidies so that businesses could find their true economic level.
- The reduction or removal of government regulations on business, and the privatization of many previously state-owned industries and services, such as British Telecom, Jaguar, British Petroleum, British Airways, and British Airports Authority. Government-owned housing – known as council houses – were also sold off to their occupants. The effect of privatization was to triple the number of private shareholders between 1979 and 1989, and more people began to realize that they could increase their net worth by making well-placed investments in the market. Many of the privatized businesses also became more efficient and competitive, and more driven by consumer demand.
- A freeing of the labour market through the curbing of trade-union power, and the introduction of trade-union reforms. In the

152

**Box 6.1    The mythology of decline**

Many of the studies of British politics and economics between the 1960s and the 1990s bemoaned the 'decline' of Britain. On the political front, the concern was that the political system was not as responsive or efficient as it might have been, and that British influence in the world was waning. On the economic front, commentators worried about falling productivity and Britain's failure to rise to the new business challenges posed by Germany and Japan. Their arguments seemed to be supported by the hard data: in 1900, Britain managed the global financial and trading system, it had the highest per capita GDP in the world and by far the largest share of the world's manufactured exports (a remarkable 35 per cent), its share of world exports equaled that of the United States, and British worker productivity was second only to the US (and 150 per cent greater than the level in France) (Booth, 2001: 4). By 1973, however, Britain had dropped to fourth place on every list.

What most commentators failed to note in their analysis was that (a) Britain's global economic stature was bound to change given the end of empire, the costs of two world wars, and the accelerating growth of emerging economic powers such as the United States and Japan; (b) much of the decline could simply be attributed to other countries catching up with Britain, which had transferred resources out of agriculture much earlier than most of its competitors (Booth, 2001: 42); (c) the decline was almost entirely relative, and the absolute figures showed significant improvements in Britain's productivity and its quality of life; and (d) the decline was not general, and Britain continued to dominate and prosper in many economic sectors.

Almost all the key indicators suggest that Britain's economy, despite its many problems in the 1960s and 1970s, has kept pace with its competitors, and 'has delivered unparalleled and sustained improvements in living standards and personal economic security for the majority of its people over the past half-century' (Middleton, 2000: 25). Postwar per capita GDP has grown in tandem with that of the USA, Germany, France and Japan, the distribution of wealth has broadened with the rise of the middle class, the overall quality of life when measured by indicators such as infant mortality, life expectancy and access to education has improved dramatically, Britain has one of the freest economies in the world (when measured by such factors as personal choice, freedom to compete, and the protection of person and property), it is one of the least corrupt societies in the world, and it is both an aggressive source of – and attractive magnet for – foreign investment. Thus, the notion of decline must be questioned.

mid-1980s the Thatcher government fought and won battles with major unions, most notably the National Union of Mineworkers, whose leadership appeared bent on bringing down the government.

• The use of monetarist economic policies aimed at reducing the increase in money supply so as to reduce inflation, and cutting government expenditure so as to reduce public borrowing and income taxation.

The reduction of taxes was intended to put more money in the pockets of British consumers, and to promote savings, investment and entrepreneurial activity. At one time in the 1960s, the top rate of income tax (the so-called supertax) had stood at a remarkable 95 per cent, undermining the motivation for wealthy Britons to create new businesses and therefore new jobs, and creating a new class of tax exiles who left the country for parts of the world with more sensible tax rates. Under Thatcher, the top rate of income tax was reduced to 40 per cent, and the basic rate fixed at 35 per cent. Many new businesses were started, and while many failed, there was an average net increase of 500 new firms every week in Britain in the early 1980s, peaking at nearly 900 per week in 1987, and the number of self-employed grew from 7 per cent of the labour force to 11 per cent (Riddell, 1989: 53, 72, 75).

Thatcher's economic policies were typical of the trend among Western post-industrial countries since the early 1980s to reduce the level of government intervention in the marketplace. Support for Keynesianism declined, as support grew for the monetarist philosophy of free marketeers such as Milton Friedman and the Chicago school of economists, who argued that the role of government should be to promote the supply of labour and capital in order to promote economic growth. However, critics charged that such policies undermined key principles of the welfare state, and that they failed to take adequate note of the problems of the underclass.

Whether as a result of such policies, or for a more complex set of reasons, there is little doubt that there has been an aggregate improvement both in British economic health and in the attitudes of business towards customers. The relative decline of the 1960s and 1970s had been halted, and by the mid-1990s Britain had the fastest growing economy in the European Union. Building and road construction expanded, there were more private home-owners and shareholders, and the number of luxury cars on the roads had increased. Class distinctions declined as the middle class grew, and competition helped improve the choices available to consumers and the quality of service provided by retailers.

At least part of the problem for many years was that business was not well-regarded as a profession. This was ironic for a country where the creativity of industrialists and inventors had first driven the industrial revolution of the eighteenth and nineteenth centuries, then underpinned the commercial revolution of the twentieth century. Attitudes in Britain stand in particularly stark contrast to those in the United States, where some of the best-known names in public life are entrepreneurs, ranging from the Rockefellers and the DuPonts of a century ago to the likes of Bill Gates, Donald Trump and Warren Buffet today. And yet the history of British business is peppered with names of comparable stature, including Cecil Rhodes (founder of the De Beers diamond corporation), William Lever (whose company became the foundation of Unilever), the Cadbury family of chocolate fame, Charles Rolls and Henry Royce, Jesse Boot (whose name lives on in Boots, the national chain of chemists), W. H. Smith (founder of the chain of news and stationery stores of the same name), Michael Marks and Tom Spencer (founders of the chain of clothing and food stores), William Morris (later Lord Nuffield) (one of the founders of the British automobile industry), and Anita Roddick (founder of The Body Shop).

Americans admire those prepared to work hard to build new enterprises and create opportunities, despite recent scandals in the United States that have greatly tainted the reputation of corporate leaders, and reduced admissions to postgraduate business schools. For their part, Britons still do not particularly admire the business profession, and – despite the economic freedom they enjoy – the British are still less likely to start up a new business than their counterparts in most other industrialized countries. There are signs, however, that attitudes may be changing, and the owners and operators of large businesses are becoming increasingly prominent in public life, if not necessarily well-admired.

A prime example of the rise of modern business celebrities is offered by Richard Branson, whose Virgin business empire has grown to include many different interests. Virgin began in the late 1960s as a cut-price record store in London. Branson then moved into the recording industry, becoming known more widely for the launch of the cut-price airline Virgin Atlantic, and expanding to areas as diverse as fashions, soft drinks, publishing, property, hotels, cinemas, and even railway services. Virgin Atlantic has been in a struggle against

British Airways in its attempt to capture a greater share of the transatlantic air travel market through an alliance with American Airlines. Branson's ventures have not always been successful, but a flair for publicity has made him a well-known public figure, contributing to a reassessment of public attitudes towards business, and of business as a career option.

Despite criticism that the Thatcher administration failed to take care of the needs of the underclass, and despite continued problems with poverty, a growing income gap between rich and poor, and homelessness (see Box 3.1), the free-market philosophy had become so popular and institutionalized by the time Thatcher left office that when Tony Blair became leader of the Labour Party in 1994, he set about 'modernizing' the party and committing it to the maintenance of some of the more popular aspects of Thatcherism, most notably privatization. Indeed, many of the elements of the Labour manifesto as it went into the 1997 general election sounded more conservative than socialist. They included a balanced budget, greater independence for the Bank of England, efforts to reduce welfare dependency, promotion of the work ethic, close ties to business, and a rejection of special deals for unions. At the same time, however, the Blair government emphasized the need to deal with the problems of the underclass.

The British are generally wealthier and better-off today than they were even 20 years ago, but debates continue about the areas in which they still lag behind their European counterparts. Of particular concern in recent years has been the declining quality of public services. The British once took great pride in the quality of their public transport network (notably the railway system), the National Health Service, the education system and the police force, but recent decades have seen growing problems in almost all areas. For example, the quality of the transport system has declined as railways have become more inefficient, with public faith undermined by frequent delays and cancellations of service, and by the occasional fatal accidents. Faith in the National Health Service has fallen as patients have had to wait longer for non-essential surgery. Concerns have been raised about the education system as comparative studies have found British pupils lagging behind their counterparts in other industrialized countries. Respect for the police has been undermined by charges of racism in several police forces, notably the London force (see Chapter 3).

The Blair administration has increased spending on public services in response to the growing clamour of criticism, but critics argue that the problem is not so much a lack of spending as too much govern-ment control and inefficient management. 'Compared with the way those services are run in mainland Europe', argues *The Economist* (14 July 2002: 51), 'health and education in Britain are run by central-ized, egalitarian, socialist-style systems'. Critics argue that there is too much resistance in Britain to choice in both health care and education, and that the idea of running health care on a private or semi-private basis – or of filtering children into different educational streams according to their ability or desires – does not have enough political or public support in Britain to prompt the kinds of changes needed to make the provision of services more efficient. In this respect, Britain is on a very different path from that of most of its European neighbours.

It is not just over the question of choice in public services that Britons differ from the citizens of most other industrialized countries, but also over the question of personal wealth and financial indepen-dence. Conspicuous consumption is a concept that has come quite late to the British, to some extent because of the residual effects of 'going without' during and after the Second World War, but also because of a preference since then for allowing the state to provide many basic services rather than opting for private alternatives. Thus, most Britons prefer public health care to private health care, look to the state to provide social security rather than building their own retirement plans, and depend on state education for their children rather than private education. Among the effects of these attitudes is that Britons save very little (typically less than 5 per cent of house-hold disposable income), and they also invest relatively little.

## Britain in the Global Trading System

As an island state whose leaders and entrepreneurs have long recog-nized the need for trade, and the opportunities it offers, Britain has always been an outward-looking society. It continues to be a major actor in world trade today: it has less than 1 per cent of the world's population but accounts for 5 per cent of world trade in goods and services. It is the world's fifth-largest exporter of goods (worth nearly $300 billion in 2000), and it is the second-largest exporter of services (worth $120 billion in 2000). The value of its exports are equivalent to more than 25 per cent of GDP, and it has the highest ratio of inward and outward investment of any of major economy. It is also a leading member of all the main international trading and economic organizations, including the G8 group of countries, the European Union, the World Trade Organization, and the Organization for Economic Cooperation and Development (OECD).

British exports and imports have grown in tandem in recent years (although usually with an annual deficit), increasing from a combined value of about $450 billion in 1990 to about $810 billion in 2000. Finished manufactured goods such as machinery, equipment, road vehicles and consumer goods make up nearly half of all exports, services account for about a quarter, intermediate goods such as chemicals, pharmaceuticals and metals account for about 20 per cent, and the balance is made up of food, drink, tobacco and raw materials, notably oil – Britain is a major exporter of oil, although its reserves are rapidly running out. The European Union is its biggest trading partner, accounting for about 57 per cent of exports and 50 per cent of imports. Asia, the Middle East and Australasia account for about 20 per cent of British trade, and the United States for about 15 per cent (see Figures 6.4 and 6.5.)

One of the most notable features of the British economy is the volume of inward and outward foreign investment. In 1999, it was the world's largest outward investor, overtaking the United States for the first time since 1988. Meanwhile, in the period 1992–2001 it attracted nearly $450 billion in investment from overseas, ranking it second only to the United States as a target of inward investment. It attracted about one-quarter of all the investment coming into the EU, most of that coming from the United States. Its low levels of corporation tax are part of the explanation, but American and Japanese companies are also attracted to Britain because of the convenience of using English, which has become the international language of commerce. Concerns have been raised, though, about just how attractive Britain will remain as long as it opts to stay out of the euro zone (see below).

Britain traded with other parts of Europe centuries ago, and trade was at the heart of the development of the British Empire in the seventeenth century, when the first settlements were made in North America and the Caribbean, and the first trading stations opened in India. By 1700, Britain was already a dominating force in world manufactured trade, and in the commercial and financial services – and the non-financial services such as merchanting and brokering – that supported that trade. It imported primarily food and raw materials, and exported a select range of so-called export staples:

*Figure* 6.4    Britain's major imports and exports, 2000

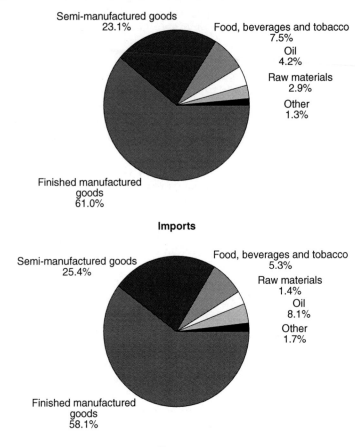

Semi-manufactured goods
23.1%

Food, beverages and tobacco
7.5%

Oil
4.2%

Raw materials
2.9%

Other
1.3%

Finished manufactured
goods
61.0%

**Imports**

Semi-manufactured goods
25.4%

Food, beverages and tobacco
5.3%

Raw materials
1.4%

Oil
8.1%

Other
1.7%

Finished manufactured
goods
58.1%

**Exports**

*Source*:    Office of National Statistics. Ranked by value.

machinery and transport equipment, cotton and wool textiles, iron and steel, and coal (Booth, 2001: 53). By 1900, Britain was the manager of the international financial and trading system, its corporations and manufactures dominated that system, and it had invested heavily in emerging overseas markets.

However, the early signs of Britain's eventual eclipse had already begun to emerge. The heavy reliance on food imports meant that insufficient investment was made in the industrial sector, US indus-

*Figure* 6.5 Britain's major goods trading partners, 2000

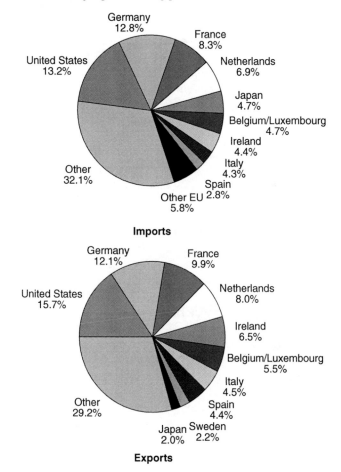

Germany
12.8%

France
8.3%

United States
13.2%

Netherlands
6.9%

Japan
4.7%

Belgium/Luxembourg
4.7%

Ireland
4.4%

Italy
4.3%

Other
32.1%

Spain

Other EU 2.8%
5.8%

**Imports**

Germany
12.1%

France
9.9%

United States
15.7%

Netherlands
8.0%

Ireland
6.5%

Belgium/Luxembourg
5.5%

Italy
4.5%

Other
29.2%

Spain
4.4%

Japan Sweden
2.0%   2.2%

**Exports**

*Source*:   Office of National Statistics.

try expanded rapidly during the late nineteenth century, and German
manufacturing power was on the rise. British industrial competitiveness fell dramatically during the First World War, and never fully
recovered, while demand for export staples grew only slowly, undermined by growing competitiveness from Japan and the USA, and
then hit by the market crash of 1929 and the depression that followed.
Furthermore, Britain had entered the war as a creditor nation but
emerged as a debtor (Booth, 2001: 59). From the early 1930s to the

late 1950s, British trade was heavily orientated towards the Empire, and the use of sterling for international transactions within this group created an informal sterling area.

The economic recovery of the 1930s, which allowed Britain once again to become a major creditor nation, was dealt another heavy blow by the Second World War. The wartime economy was good for manufacturing and agriculture, but Britain's overseas assets were quickly used up, exports were cut, and Britain had to borrow so much to conduct the war that it came out almost bankrupt. In 1944, the USA and Britain led an international conference at Bretton Woods in the United States at which plans were made for the postwar international economy. Agreement was reached on stable monetary relations, freely convertible currencies, expanded trade and economic growth, and the emergence of the dollar as the new international reserve currency.

At first the system seemed to work and Britain benefited from rapidly growing world trade, although its exports grew more slowly than those of other industrialized countries. Many different theories have been offered to explain this, including an excessive commitment to the sterling area, where markets were growing only slowly, and disproportionately high spending on defence in order to prove British independence and its continuing status as a world power (Booth, 2001: 74–5). Whatever the reasons, the British share of global exports was cut by two-thirds between 1950 and 1973, and there was a similar fall in the British share of world trade in services.

When six European countries launched an experiment in international integration in 1952 by merging their coal and steel industries, and then in 1958 by reaching agreement on the creation of a common market, Britain still saw its economic interests as lying primarily outside Europe. But political opinion soon changed and – after two false starts – Britain joined the European Economic Community in 1973, just 18 months after the United States took the dollar off the gold standard and thereby signalled the end of the Bretton Woods system. Britain now shifted its attention away from the sterling area and towards Europe. Although the hope for a new boost for British trade did not at first materialize, membership of the European Union has come to be the major influence on Britain's place in the global trading system, and has brought much change to the domestic economy.

**The Economic Implications of Europe**

Britain tried to rebuild its economy after the Second World War by concentrating on the sterling area, and trying to retain its status as a world power. It supported European economic integration, but did not see itself as part of the experiment. By the end of the 1950s, however, the government had begun to realize that it would be in British interests to join the European Economic Community; the six original members were enjoying fast growth and improved living standards, and their industrial strength was underpinned by growth in trade among themselves.

Once Britain joined the Community, Europe became the biggest influence on its economic and trade policy. Britain may have developed a reputation for being a 'reluctant' member of the EU, but it is a member nonetheless, and its economy is integrated with those of the other member states:

- Britain now does about half its trade with its EU partners, compared to about 15 per cent with the United States and 2–4 per cent with Japan.
- Many of the regulations that govern the behaviour of British industry come out of European law rather than domestic law.
- The EU has developed a common commercial policy under which all the key decisions affecting trade are taken collectively by the member states, which act as a unit in negotiations with the Americans or the Japanese.

Membership of the European Union has fundamentally redefined Britain's economic identity, as it has those of the 14 other member states. Instead of a group of independent national economies (to the extent that any economy can really be independent), there is now a federal economy in Western Europe, or one where the national and the European economies have separate and independent powers, but neither operates without the other. The most significant effect of European integration on economic activity has been the creation of a single European market in which is there is all but uncontrolled movement of people, money, goods and services, and where national frontiers are almost invisible. The basis of the single market is the Single European Act, an agreement signed by the EU member states in 1986, and which came into effect in 1987, under which a five-year timetable was set for the removal of all the remaining non-tariff barriers to free trade in Western Europe. The barriers took three main forms.

First, there were physical barriers such as customs and border checks, which allowed member states to control the movement of people, collect sales and excise taxes, enforce different health standards, control banned products, and prevent the spread of animal and plant diseases. Member states particularly wanted to control illegal immigration and the movement of terrorists and other undesirables. Under the Schengen Agreement, opened for signature in 1985, a computerized database of undesirables was developed, which helped address many political concerns. With effect from March 1995, virtually all border controls were finally eliminated by the signatories to Schengen, and the European Police Office (Europol) was created to help collect information and improve cooperation. Britain, citing its special concerns as an island state, has opted only into selected elements of Schengen, so its borders are not yet as open as those of other EU member states.

Second, there were fiscal barriers, the most important of which was different levels of indirect taxation (such as VAT), which caused distortion of competition and artificial price differences, thereby posing a handicap to trade. There were also different levels of excise duties, driven mostly by varying levels of concern about human health. In the 1980s, for example, Spanish smokers paid half as much on cigarettes as those in France, a quarter of the rate in Ireland, and one-sixth of the rate in Denmark. Agreement was reached in the 1990s on a minimum rate of 15 per cent VAT, and on working towards a single rate of VAT, or at least variations within a very narrow band. Much more controversial has been the suggestion that the EU harmonize tax rates in other areas, notably corporation tax or the setting of withholding tax on savings. Tax harmonization is seen by many as the first step towards the development of EU authority over the setting of income tax, a notion that has been opposed by the Blair administration.

Finally, there were technical barriers, notably the existence of different regulations and standards based on issues relating to personal safety, food safety, public health and environmental protection. Many of these regulations were in the interests of consumer safety, and were thus welcomed, but others amounted to a form of protectionism. The European Commission tried to develop EU standards and encouraged member states to conform, but this was a time-consuming and tedious task, and did little to discourage the common image of interfering Eurocrats. Several breakthroughs helped clear the political hurdles, notably a 1979 decision by the European Court of Justice that established that a member state could not block imports from another member state on the basis of local health regulations. Member states have since had to accept products from other states that meet domestic technical standards. Progress has been made on removing technical barriers to the single market in a wide variety of areas, from safety and operating standards for road vehicles to the content of processed food.

By addressing the problems created by these barriers, the Single European Act remains the most radical of all the steps taken in the process of European integration since it made its first halting steps in the 1950s. Completion of the single market not only accelerated the process of economic integration, but it has also changed the lives of every European, making economic integration more real even to British Eurosceptics. The changes it has brought include the following:

- With a few exceptions, residents of Britain can now live and work in any other EU member state, open a bank account, take out a mortgage, transfer unlimited amounts of capital, and even vote in local and European elections.
- The single market has helped remove many of the barriers that British corporations once faced, and has increased the number of consumers they can reach. Combined with privatization programmes in many countries and the general trend towards globalization, it has greatly increased the number of opportunities for acquisitions, joint ventures and corporate mergers, both within the EU and between European and non-European corporations. The European mergers and acquisitions market is now bigger than that of the United States, and – as noted earlier – Britain has the biggest such market in the EU.
- Because integrated infrastructure – such as transport, energy and communications networks – is an important element in the successful operation of markets, the EU has promoted the development of so-called Trans-European Networks (TENs). Helped by the enormous growth in European tourism (which has been particularly important to Britain, one of Europe's top-four tourist destinations), and by the revitalization of rail transport as a cost-efficient and environmentally friendly alternative to road and air transport, the EU has been developing a high-speed train network connecting

The Bank of England in London. Britain was one of only three European Union member states not to adopt the euro in 2002. The Bank of England remains a strong symbol of the desire by most Britons to retain the pound and stay out of the euro zone.

**Illustration 6.3   The Bank of England**

Europe's major cities. Key elements in this have been the opening of the Channel tunnel, and investment in British railway tracks to bring them up to the quality of those in France and Germany; for example, €13 billion is being spent on a high-speed train link between Paris, Brussels, Cologne, Amsterdam and London.
- A critical change spearheaded by Britain has been the loosening of regulations on air transport. Most European countries once had state-owned national carriers that had a national monopoly over most of the international routes they flew, so air transport was highly regulated, and expensive to consumers. When the Thatcher administration launched a liberalization programme in the

**Box 6.2   The euro: to be or not to be?**

In early 2002, after decades of anticipation and preparation, 12 of the 15 member states of the European Union undertook the single biggest currency conversion in history. Out went their national currencies – including francs, pesetas, lire, escudos, deutschemarks, and guilders – and in came the new single European currency, the euro. Talk of the need for a single currency had begun in the late 1960s when European leaders sought a response to the upheavals brought by the end of the Bretton Woods system, dominated by the US dollar. A feasibility plan was ordered in 1969 and a three-stage conversion was outlined, but then came the oil crises of the 1970s. An attempt was made in the 1980s to achieve exchange-rate stability as a prelude to monetary union, but it was not until the 1990s that there was sufficient political support to proceed.

When it came, the conversion involved preparing all coin- and banknote-operated machines in the EU to take the new currency, and the introduction into circulation of 50 billion new coins and more than 14 billion new euro banknotes. Despite concerns about shortages, and instances of unscrupulous vendors using the opportunity to hike their prices, the switch went remarkably smoothly, and by the end of February some 302 million people had made the switch. The euro also became a popular currency alongside national currencies in several eastern European countries, and in poorer non-European countries (such as Cuba) visited by significant numbers of vacationeers from the EU.

Even though it met the criteria needed to adopt the euro, Britain opted not to join, along with Denmark and Sweden. Public opinion remains deeply hostile to giving up the pound, with just over half of respondents in opinion polls against the idea, and less than one-third in favour. The debate over the euro has created some strange political bedfellows (Kelly, 1997: 292). There is no straight party division for or against, but rather there are supporters and opponents on both sides, using different logic to back up their case. Those opposed include old-style members of the Labour Party, concerned about the development of a 'Banker's Europe' and about the loss of devaluation as a tool of economic policy, and the right wing of the Conservative Party, who argue the need to protect national sovereignty, and criticize the concept of a 'fortress Europe'. Meanwhile, new-style members of Labour argue that joining the single currency could be a job creator, while more centrist Conservatives believe that joining would help control inflation, would promote the interests of the City of London and of the free market, and would undermine nationalism.

mid-1980s that led to the privatization of British Airways in 1987, and negotiated bilateral agreements with other EU member states, the lid was taken off the air transport market. Big carriers have taken over smaller ones, national carriers have created international alliances, new cut-price operators such as Ryanair and Virgin Express have taken off, and consumers now have greater choice and can fly much more cheaply than before.

While the single market has brought generally positive change to the British economy, the critical question now – as noted earlier – is whether and/or when Britain will adopt the euro (Box 6.2). The relationship between the pound sterling and attempts to set up the single currency has not always been a happy one. Britain initially opted to remain out of the exchange rate mechanism (ERM) that was set up in 1979 as a prelude to the creation of the single currency, and required that member governments take the action necessary to keep their currencies stable relative to each other. It then joined in October 1990 just as economic recession came to western Europe, and found that the high interest rates needed to keep the pound within the agreed range of exchange rates hurt exports and contributed to unemployment. On 16 September 1992 – otherwise known as Black Wednesday – Britain was forced out of the ERM. The economy began an almost immediate recovery, a fact which played into the hands of opponents of British membership of the single currency.

The Blair administration argued upon winning office in 1997 that it would not take Britain into the single currency without a positive vote in a national referendum, which would be held after the next election, should Labour win. Labour did indeed win the 2001 election, but it quickly became clear that Blair was reluctant to move too quickly, instead launching a campaign to convince British voters of the virtues of joining the euro. As noted in Box 6.2, the euro itself was introduced in January 2002, and – after a brief transitional phase – fully replaced the national currencies of 12 of the 15 EU member states in March 2002. Britain did not join, but Gordon Brown, the Chancellor of the Exchequer (Finance Minister), instead set five 'economic tests' for British membership of the euro:

- Are business cycles and economic structures compatible so that Britain and others could live permanently with euro interest rates?
- If problems emerge, is there sufficient flexibility to deal with them?

- Would adopting the euro create better conditions for businesses making long-term decisions to invest in Britain?
- What impact would adopting the euro have on the competitive position of the British financial services industry?
- Would adopting the euro promote higher growth, stability, and a lasting increase in jobs?

Those who thought that British public opinion might turn more in favour of the euro once it was adopted by other EU states, and once British travellers had become accustomed to using it, were disappointed by polls in mid-2002 that showed a hardening of opposition. Their arguments were undermined as the pound gained strength, as it became clear that the British economy was performing well outside the euro zone, and as a number of countries that had adopted the euro continued to experience poor numbers on inflation, unemployment and growth. The credibility of the euro was also being undermined by the 'growth and stability pact' agreed by European leaders prior to the launch of the euro, and designed to ensure investor confidence. Under the pact, member states agreed to control their budget deficits, limiting them to less than 3 per cent of GDP. However, several countries – including France, Germany and Portugal – experienced difficulties during 2002, and the President of the European Commission, Romano Prodi, was quoted in the French newspaper *Le Monde* as describing the pact as 'stupid', 'rigid' and 'imperfect'. Under the circumstances, it was unclear as this book went to press what would happen about the British referendum on the adoption of the euro.

# 7

# Culture and Lifestyle

Western culture in the new millennium has a strong American accent, but – as the birthplace of the English language, and a once aggressive colonizer – Britain has played a strong supporting role in the development of the art, literature and music associated with 'the West'. It is perhaps less well-known for the visual arts and classical music than for drama, literature and popular music.

- It has produced great painters such as Thomas Gainsborough, Joshua Reynolds, John Constable, J. M. W. Turner, Francis Bacon, Peter Blake and David Hockney, and has produced great sculptors such as Henry Moore and Barbara Hepworth, but its reputation is overwhelmed by the work of continental painters and sculptors.
- It has produced great architects such as Christopher Wren, Inigo Jones, Richard Rogers and Norman Foster, and great buildings are to be found in abundance in Britain, but the wealth of prewar architecture has been sullied by the frequent eyesores produced by bad postwar town planning.
- It has produced great classical composers and musicians, from Henry Purcell to Edward Elgar, Frederick Delius, Gustav Holt, Ralph Vaughan Williams and Benjamin Britten, but again has not achieved the same stature as most continental countries.

If anyone was to think about what best represented British culture at the global level, the figures that come to mind would be mainly writers – Chaucer, Shakespeare, Swift, Shelley, Austen, Wordsworth, Hardy, Tennyson, the Brontë sisters, Dickens, Shaw and Wilde provide just a sampling – and popular musicians – including the Beatles, the Rolling Stones, the Who, David Bowie, Eric Clapton,

Elton John, the Sex Pistols, Queen, the Police, the Spice Girls and Oasis. The impact of the former has been greater thanks to the spread of the English language, and of the latter thanks to the universal popularity of rock music. British cinema also plays an important supporting role to the popularity of American cinema, although just how the two are different any more is difficult to say. Nonetheless, the list of the most famous or influential names in British modern culture includes a strong contingent of actors, many of whom first made their names on the stage.

This chapter sets out to examine the features and the personality of British culture, beginning with a general outline of the definition of culture and of the dimensions and impact of the British version. It then provides an analysis of the meaning of 'Britishness', and the role this has had on understanding national identity and its links with culture, arguing that the multifaceted nature of English, Scottish, Welsh and Irish culture has been further diversified by the postwar arrival of ethnic minorities. Against this background, this chapter examines the state of the arts in Britain, with an emphasis on the theatre, film, television and popular music. It then looks at how the British spend their spare time, and finishes with an examination of the role of sports and religion in national life.


## Culture

For its size, Britain has had a remarkable influence on world culture, helped by the fact that English has become the global language (see Box 7.1). Even though the spread of English – particularly since the Second World War – has come largely out of the popularity of American culture and the power of American business, and even though many of the best writers in English today are not British (V. S. Naipaul, Nadine Gordimer and Derek Walcott come to mind), it was generations of British writers who developed the language and made it so portable and attractive in the first place. It has since been easier for the reputations of British writers and artists to be carried on the back of the spread of their language; there have been creative minds of equal stature in many other European countries, but – unlike painters, sculptors, photographers and musicians – their global status has been handicapped by the fact that few communicate in English.

Despite the global significance of British culture – and of icons such as the royal family, James Bond, the Beatles, Monty Python and

..y Potter – it is, like all cultures, ultimately the reflection of home-grown values and experiences, not all of which can be understood by foreigners. Seen from the broad view, British culture is the product of a long and complex history where politics, economics, religion, nationalism and the arts are all intertwined. The Second World War was a watershed, and the idea of Britain can be broadly divided into two eras: the imperial 'glories' of the prewar years (even though those glories were often anything but, and their retelling has been surrounded by myth and misconception), and the redefinition that has come with the postwar years, including the rise of the welfare state, the changing place of Britain in the world, the breakdown of the class system, and the increasingly multifaceted nature of British society.

During the 1930s, Britain's national leaders were individuals of global stature, its corporations reached all over the world, its products could be bought almost anywhere, and its music, literature and films were a central part of what was already being seen as an emerging Western culture. Then came the war, and although there are many who still hold that Winston Churchill correctly captured the feelings of an entire generation when he proclaimed in June 1940 that the fight against Nazism was Britain's 'finest hour', those few years were fundamentally to alter the view that Britons held of themselves.

The debacle at Suez in 1956 combined with the early successes of European integration to compel the British to think less from a global perspective and more from a European perspective, and even ulti-mately to open a discussion about the definition of the very identity of Britain itself: was it still a united kingdom, or was it an increas-ingly loose amalgam of England, Scotland, Wales and Northern Ireland? A post-imperial melancholy set in, characterized by inward contemplation, nostalgia, conformism and conflict over a variety of issues, ranging from Britain's place in the world to relations between management and workers, economic 'decline', the class system, race, the monarchy, and relations with America and Europe. The tensions came to be reflected in literature, theatre and films, which moved from a celebration of British exceptionalism to a self-conscious examination of everything that seemed to be going wrong with the country.

The contrast is exemplified by British films. In the late 1940s and early 1950s there were the Ealing comedies, which celebrated many of the hallmarks of being British, including simplicity, basic decency, and the ability not to take life too seriously. Then in the early 1960s there was the bleak realism of the British New Wave, and films such

**Box 7.1   English: the global language**

It is difficult to know for sure how many people speak English, but its stature as the dominating global language comes not so much from how *many* speak it as from *who* speaks it. There are many more people in the world who speak Mandarin (probably 800–900 million), but most of them live in China and are relatively poor. Estimates of the number of people who speak English range around 400–500 million, but these people can be found in many different countries, notably the United States, Britain, Canada, the Philippines, India, Australia, New Zealand, South Africa and Nigeria. English has also become the language of political and business elites around the world, the language of international communications, science, and education, and the most commonly used language for officials of both the United Nations and the European Union.

English is not only an official language in nearly 60 countries containing approximately one-third of the world's population, but English words and phrases have entered many other languages, so much so that in France there have been government-sponsored attempts for many years to develop French equivalents of words that have entered daily conversation. In non-white former British colonies, the use of English has been criticized as a symbol of the colonial past, but despite attempts to eliminate its use, for example in India, Malaysia, Nigeria and Kenya, it has persisted. Furthermore, it has been argued that many English words have now become virtually universal, and recognized almost all over the world; they include *airport, cigarette, hotel, OK, passport, stop, telephone* and *weekend*.

The status of English has been good for the British economy, most notably in the sale of English-language training programmes. It has been estimated that the teaching of English is one of Britain's largest sources of invisible earnings. It has also helped attract foreign students to British universities, seeking not just a British education but also the opportunity to learn or improve upon their English in an accent-free environment (which they would not find, for example, in the United States).

as *Saturday Night and Sunday Morning,* or *The Loneliness of the Long-Distance Runner,* which emphasized isolation and social dysfunction, and are often depressing to watch today. By the 1990s, British cinema had stopped being so self-conscious, and films were mining the rich seam of eighteenth- and nineteenth-century literature, were celebrating the pleasures of being middle class during a time of economic revival, were commenting on the new problems and inequalities brought by the free market, or had thrown social comment to the winds and were simply designed to make money.

A core element in the cultural changes taking place in the 1960s and 1970s was the changing class structure, and the greater willingness to question the assumptions long made by Britons about their appropriate 'place' in the social hierarchy. Nowhere was this process more obvious than in the use of satire, which gave rise to a famous string of shows on radio, television and the stage, in which poking fun at the class system was a central theme. A line can be drawn linking *The Goon Show* on BBC radio in the late 1950s and 1960s, to the stage show *Beyond the Fringe* in the early 1960s, to the cult television series *Monty Python's Flying Circus* (late 1960s and early 1970s). These were good examples of an emerging counter-cultural trend which in many ways helped the British deconstruct many of the stereotypes that had coloured the class-driven values of much popular culture until then.

Another element in the cultural changes was the increasing social diversity of Britain. As noted in Chapter 2, the non-white population grew steadily from the 1950s, and black and Asian culture became an increasingly important part of the national culture. White Britons had to redefine themselves according to their response to the issue of race, and ethnic culture made its mark on the growth of minority neighbourhoods in the bigger cities, the spreading popularity of Asian cuisine, the entrance of minority themes into literature and the cinema, and the growing religious diversity of Britain.

Today, it is only older and/or more conservative Britons who recall the war, the empire, the class system at its height, pre-European Britain, and the political, economic and social troubles of the 1960s and 1970s. The last decade has seen the emergence of a newly confident and reformed Britain, whose culture reflects not so much the problems of the past as the opportunities and realities of the present. Younger Britons do not remember the war or the empire, Britain has been a multicultural society and a member of the European Union as long as they have been alive, and most have enjoyed the benefits of an economy that has been growing rapidly. The change in attitude is caught nicely in two comments made by Americans. In 1962, then US Secretary of State Dean Acheson commented that Britain had lost an empire and not yet found a role. In 1999, a journalist for *The New York Times* commented that the British had 'finally stopped seeking a role and started getting a life' (quoted in *The Economist*, 6 November 1999).

## The Identity of Britain

The task of understanding British culture is complicated by debates over the meaning of 'Britishness'. Culture is closely tied to national identity, but as noted in Chapter 2, one of the characteristics of life in Britain is the strength of regionalism and nationalism. The idea of national identity in Britain is diluted by the superimposition – one on top of the other – of separate English, Scottish, Welsh and Northern Irish identities. That superimposition is symbolized by the national flag the 'Union Jack', which combines the cross of St George (for England) with those of St Andrew (for Scotland) and St Patrick (for Ireland). The concept of 'Britishness', which was always questionable, has come under increased scrutiny in recent years.

A 'nation' is usually defined as consisting of three components: a distinctive group of people with a common language and history; a specific territory occupied by those people; and a strong bond between the people and the territory (see discussion in Mohan, 1999: 28–33). There really is no British nation as such, because the people who make up the United Kingdom have separate (albeit overlapping) histories and cultures, and they lack a common bond to a common piece of territory. A number of developments in Britain since the Second World War have emphasized the contradictions that colour the concept of national identity and national culture, and have challenged the meanings of the symbols of Britishness:

- One of the forces that brought Britain together, and encouraged the four nations of the United Kingdom to think of themselves as British, was the empire, but that is now gone, and anyone who tries to revive it as a symbol of British identity is regarded as suspect.
- The second symbol of Britain, the monarchy, has lost much of its magic and some of its credibility, and is today regarded with less respect and reverence than perhaps at any time in its history. It does, however, remain as a symbol of the unity of Britain, and there is significance in the fact that the present royal family traces its ancestors to both Scotland and England, that the male heir to the throne is typically invested as the Prince of Wales, and that the royal family traditionally spends Christmas and much of the summer at the royal estate at Balmoral in Scotland. However, there is still much more about the royal family that is English rather than British.

**Illustration 7.1　The Queen Mother's Funeral**

The military band of the Welsh Guards parades outside Windsor Castle, west of London, before the funeral in 2002 of Queen Elizabeth the Queen Mother. The military and royal motifs in this scene include several potent symbols of British national identity.

- The third symbol of Britain – its resistance to the forces of extremism, nationalism or fascism on the continent – has been muddied by the effects of European integration. Eurosceptics have fought against integration by arguing in part that Britain is quite separate from Europe, and that British distinctiveness – as symbolized, for example, by imperial weights and measures, and the pound sterling – should be preserved as a means of protecting the identity of Britain. But a generational shift is taking place, with younger Britons being more enthusiastic about Europe than older Britons, and the distinctiveness of Britain is becoming less obvious.
- The arrival of immigrants from the New Commonwealth since the Second World War has brought a new social diversity that – rather than emphasizing the strength of British identity – has added to the divisions within British society. The political Right has often overtly or covertly identified 'Britishness' with 'whiteness', and

the far-right has aggressively adopted (and thereby demeaned) the symbol of the British flag in its protests against multiracialism.

The Wilson government in 1964 made much of the need to reinvent Britain, to move on from the 'decline of the wasted years', and to capitalize on the 'white heat' of new technology. It failed in its mission, and Britain was to go through many more troubled years before there was to be meaningful talk of revival. The Blair government of the late 1990s aggressively adopted the line, Blair himself talking of the need to 'repackage' or 'rebrand' Britain, to make Britain 'the creative powerhouse of the world', and to develop 'a clear identity and role for ourselves in the outside world'. Much was made of stories in the American press, talking of 'cool Britannia' and describing London as the cultural capital of the world.

Just what all this has meant in real terms has been debatable, but there may be something to be learned from the recent experience of British Airways (BA). After a generation of decorating its planes with various designs based on the Union Jack (the British national flag), its chief executive Bob Ayling decided in 1997 that it was time that BA stopped portraying itself purely as a British airline, and should instead package itself as a global airline. 'We are blending the best of traditional British values', Ayling said at the time, 'with the best of today's Britain – diverse, creative, friendly, youthful and cosmopolitan in its outlook, but open and responsive to change.' So BA planes were decorated with images from the countries to which the airline flew, including South African murals, Delft pottery, Chinese calligraphy and North American wood carvings. But then, in 2001, the airline announced that the idea had not been successful, and that the Union Jack design would be restored. The flag, said a BA spokesman, 'reinforces a core goal of Britishness in a more modern and less formal way'. The idea that BA should sell itself as a British-based global business was attractive to most Britons, but apparently not at the cost of watering down the visibility of one of the most visible exporters of Britain's identity.

Despite the doubts about how to define British culture, it is apparently not a problem for foreigners, because the tourist trade is one of the biggest long-term economic growth sectors in Britain, attracting growing numbers of people from continental Europe and North America. Travel and tourism were hurt by the fallout from the February 2001 outbreak of foot-and-mouth disease, which placed many rural areas out of bounds to visitors, and by the September 2001

*Figure* 7.1   World's top tourist destinations, 2001

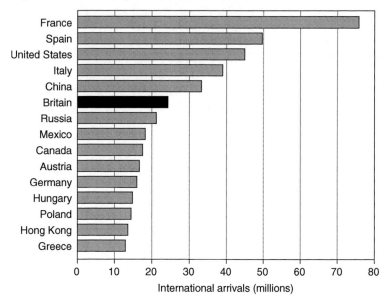

*Source*:   World Tourism Organization, http://www.world-tourism.org

terrorist attacks in the United States, which led many people to cancel holiday travel by air. However, trends in the 1980s and 1990s indicated that Britain was holding its position among the top-six tourist destinations, bringing in about 23–25 million overseas tourists each year (see Figure 7.1), and about €13 billion ($/€20 billion) in annual overseas earnings.

The major countries of origin of overseas visitors to Britain (in order) are the United States, France, Germany, Ireland and the Netherlands. The majority of overseas visitors come through London, where they often spend much or all of their time, attracted by its historical sights (such as the Tower of London, Westminster Abbey and Buckingham Palace), its museums and galleries (such as the British Museum, Madame Tussaud's, the National Gallery and the Natural History Museum), and its theatres and restaurants. Outside London, tourist attractions include cathedral towns (such as Canterbury, York and Chester), historic cities (such as Bath and Edinburgh) and royal castles and palaces (such as Windsor Castle and Hampton Court). Unfortunately, Britain is suffering

**Illustration 7.2   Stonehenge**

Stonehenge, the ruins of a druidic temple in southern England, built 3500–4000 years ago. A remarkable feat of engineering, it is an important historical link with the early inhabitants of the British Isles, and a popular tourist attraction.

the same effects from tourism as other European countries: overcrowding. Tourists everywhere tend to take their vacations at the same time, and to congregate in the same places, so that cities like London, Canterbury, Oxford, Cambridge and Bath have now become nightmares of congestion during the summer season, particularly August.

## The Arts

The British artistic heritage is both broad and deep, strongest in literature, film, modern music, theatre, poetry, painting and classical architecture, and perhaps weakest (but still considerable) in classical music and modern architecture. Britain is the birthplace of countless men and women who have become well known far beyond their national borders, and have contributed centrally to the development of the Western cultural tradition.

Britain has a particularly rich history of theatre, dating back hundreds of years. The Elizabethan era saw the first great flowering of British theatre, with the work of playwrights such as Christopher Marlowe and Ben Jonson, but it was dominated by William Shakespeare (1564–1616), without question the most inventive and influential playwright in the history of the English language. He was so creative that he added to the language itself, and is credited with having coined more than 2000 words, and many of the phrases still in daily use today (they include 'vanish into thin air', 'foul play', 'play fast and loose', and 'a tower of strength'). His plays are still routinely performed around the world in many languages, and have inspired modern interpretations in contemporary settings; for example the musical *West Side Story* was famously based on *Romeo and Juliet.*

The work of postwar British dramatists has often been compared to the golden age of the Elizabethan theatre. Their plays have fed off the complex social and political changes that have come to Britain since the war, ranging from the initial optimism and the prospects of the welfare state, to the dismay at continued austerity and the end of empire, and eventually running on through emerging nationalism, the sexual revolution, the conflict in Northern Ireland, Thatcherism and racism. The London theatre was given a reviving boost even before the war had ended by the Old Vic company, led by Laurence Olivier and Ralph Richardson. Then came the creation in 1946 of the Arts Council, which provided an important injection of state funding, and the emergence in the 1950s of the English Stage Company and the Theatre Workshop, both of which provided support for the work of new actors and playwrights.

The most influential of immediate postwar playwrights were Terrence Rattigan (*The Winslow Boy*, *The Browning Version*, *Separate Tables*) and J. B. Priestley (*An Inspector Calls*), some of whose work presaged the introduction of a different set of values to British theatre. In the mid-1950s, the complacency of British theatre was upset by the debut of works by Bertolt Brecht and Eugene Ionesco (whose play *The Lesson* was important in introducing absurdist theatre to London) and Samuel Beckett (whose *Waiting for Godot* raised controversial issues relating to censorship). In 1956, coincidentally the year of the Suez crisis, *Look Back in Anger* by John Osborne introduced a more radical tone into British theatre, representing a break with the past and a suggestion that the old world was over (Shellard, 1999: 53). The middle-class virtues of theatre were replaced by a new kind of drama that was more issue-based, and rooted more in the realities of daily life for most Britons. This period saw the birth of the Angry Young Men, a group of writers who were deeply critical of the conformity they saw around them.

In the early 1960s, two theatrical companies were created that were to have a lasting impact: the Royal Shakespeare Company in 1960, and the National Theatre (now the Royal National Theatre) in 1963. These inspired the development of new companies and the opening of new theatres in most of the major regional cities of Britain, such as Chichester, Sheffield, Nottingham and Edinburgh. The decade also saw the staging of such groundbreaking plays as *The Birthday Party* and *The Homecoming* by Harold Pinter, *A Day in the Death of Joe Egg* by Peter Nichols, *In Celebration* by David Storey, and *Entertaining Mr Sloan* and *Loot* by Joe Orton. It also saw the development of the reputations of a string of new playwrights, including Peter Shaffer, Tom Stoppard, Alan Ayckbourn and David Hare, and a growing crossover between stage and television drama, notably by writers such as Trevor Griffiths and Dennis Potter.

An important change came in the late 1960s, when censorship came to an end. One of the frustrations of the postwar years had been the role of the Lord Chamberlain, whose job had been to vet every new work and to decide what was permissible and what was not. Strong language and themes such as homosexuality, abortion and satire involving the royal family had all been considered legitimate targets. Social changes brought growing support for changes to the law, which eventually came with the Theatres Act of 1968. The rock musical *Hair* and the erotic review *Oh! Calcutta!* followed in short order, but the flood of permissiveness that supporters of censorship most feared never happened (Shellard, 1999: 147). Instead, a new spontaneity and sense of freedom was introduced to British theatre. This was followed by a greater prominence for political and avant-garde themes, and more plays being written by women and ethnic minorities.

Meanwhile, Britain continued to be well-represented in stage musicals, building on the tradition begun in the Victorian era by Gilbert and Sullivan. Many of the most commercially successful stage musicals of the last generation have been written or co-written by Andrew Lloyd Webber and Tim Rice; they include *Jesus Christ Superstar*, *Cats*, *Evita*, *Starlight Express*, and *Phantom of the Opera*. Some have achieved critical success, and have been credited with helping bring badly-needed tourist income into London, but questions have been raised about the extent to which they detract from the more serious goals of theatre.

Although it faced cuts in government subsidies during the Thatcher years, the theatre continued to prosper, and the West End of London continues to be one of the preeminent concentrations of drama in the world, with locals and tourists attending shows in increasing numbers, whether at the Adelphi, Aldwych, New Ambassadors, Royal Court, Young Vic or Theatre Royal. Nearly €250 million (€/$375 million) was invested in the building of new theatres and the restoration of old theatres in the period 1995–2002, and the Blair government has approved a substantial increase in the subsidy provided to theatre. Even regional theatres are mainly doing well, offering a variety of performances and attracting many of the leading actors of the day. There are more than 300 professional theatres in Britain, fed by a steady stream of world-class material ranging from Shakespeare through to modern playwrights such as Michael Frayn, Steven Berkoff and Caryl Churchill. Britain's many actors and actresses are among the best-known names on either the stage or the screen, counting among their number Kenneth Branagh, Simon Callow, Judi Dench, Ralph Fiennes, Ian Holm, Anthony Hopkins, Ben Kingsley, Ian McKellen, Alan Rickman, Maggie Smith and Emma Thompson.

There has been much crossover between theatre and film, and although the latter is another of the lynchpins of British culture, there is much less agreement about the health of British cinema. It has been argued by some that but for the intervention of the First World War, Britain – not the United States – might have become the dominating force in world cinema. Before the war, when cinema was in its infancy, British and other European directors were among the most innovative in the world, but after the war they lost their impetus, and the Americans not only better appreciated the commercial possibilities of cinema, but their technology was more advanced, and they quickly established the conventions and genres that established Hollywood as the lynchpin of cinema (Davies, 2000). The United States also attracted many of the most talented British directors and actors, including Charlie Chaplin, Stan Laurel, Alfred Hitchcock and Cary Grant. This drain of talent handicapped the British film industry before it had the chance to flower. British cinema never fully recovered, and while Britons today have a presence in world cinema that is second only to that of Americans, they have achieved this not through a home-grown industry but by hitching a ride on – and contributing to – the dominance of American cinema. As Street argues (1997: 197), 'it is more or less impossible to think of British cinema without reference to its relationship to Hollywood'.

The British film industry was moderately successful between the 1930s and the 1950s, helped by healthy cinema attendance figures, government subsidies, and a reduction in the number of films coming out of the United States during the war. Production companies such as Gaumont-British, London Films and the Rank Organization had many commercial successes, and the work of British directors like Michael Powell, David Lean and Emeric Pressburger, and of actors such as Alec Guinness, Noel Coward, Roger Livesey, Leslie Howard and Peter Sellers, had a large domestic following. During the war there were successful films with appropriate themes, such as *In Which We Serve* (1942, an ode to the Royal Navy), *The Way to the Stars* (1943, an ode to the Royal Air Force), and *Brief Encounter* (1945, about how the war impacted the relationship between characters played by Trevor Howard and Celia Johnson). After the war there were comedies and films with social comment, many of them produced by Michael Balcon and coming out of Ealing Studios in London, including *Passport to Pimlico* (1949), *Kind Hearts and Coronets* (1949), *The Lavender Hill Mob* (1951), and *The Ladykillers* (1955).

The government tried to sustain the industry after the war, but British cinema was still too class-ridden, while American cinema provided the escapism that cinemagoers in an austere postwar Britain sought. Then the advent of television led to a sharp drop in cinema attendance, which fell in the period 1955–63 alone by a remarkable two-thirds (Richards, 1997: 149). British production companies became unwilling to invest in making films, and only the big American producers, such as Paramount, 20th Century Fox and Universal, could afford to take the risks and sustain the losses.

Perhaps the last truly home-grown genre in British cinema came in the early 1960s with the British New Wave, a series of films which reflected the realities of postwar life in gritty detail, particularly for the working class; they included *Room At The Top* (1959), *Saturday Night and Sunday Morning* (1960), *A Kind of Loving* (1962) and *This Sporting Life* (1963) (Hutchings, 2001). They were all in black and white, and stood in stark contrast to the product coming out of the United States, all of it by then in colour, and increasingly using new technology such as Cinemascope. The only commercially successful films being made in Britain were catering to the mass market, and included the horror films produced by Hammer studios, and the *Carry On* series that were based on a particular brand of British humour that had little prospect of being exported.

In 1981, the British film *Chariots of Fire* unexpectedly won the Academy Awards for best picture and best screenplay, prompting its writer Colin Welland famously to declare that 'The British are coming'. The list of British films that have since had either commercial and/or critical success on both sides of the Atlantic has been impressive, to be sure, and includes *Another Country, A Passage to India, The Killing Fields* (all 1984), *My Beautiful Laundrette* (1985), *A Fish Called Wanda* (1988), *Howards End* (1992), *The Remains of the Day* (1993), *Four Weddings and a Funeral* (1994), *Trainspotting* (1995), *Secrets and Lies* (1996), *The Full Monty* (1997), *Shakespeare in Love*, and *Lock, Stock and Two Smoking Barrels* (both 1999).

Ultimately, though, it is difficult to be sure any longer what is really a *British* film, as distinct from a film using a story based in Britain and featuring British actors but financed and produced by Americans. The British film industry has been almost entirely absorbed by Hollywood, as evidenced by the fact that the Academy Awards make no distinctions between American and British nominees and winners, but treat almost everyone else, except perhaps Canadians and Australians, as foreigners. There are still independent British films, it is true, but the definition of that independence is suspect. As in many other countries, the bulk of programming in Britain is American, and even the most well-known 'British' films of recent decades, such as the James Bond series, any of the costume dramas based on Victorian novels, the Harry Potter series, and the *Lord of the Rings* trilogy, have been produced and financed by American film companies.

A related medium is television, where British directors, writers and actors have developed a long and productive history, but have largely failed to break in to the mass market outside Britain. The Scotsman John Logie Baird was one of the inventors of television, and the BBC in 1936 provided the world's first television service, yet until the 1950s it was very much subordinated to radio, and until relatively recently British television viewers had few choices available to them. The BBC had a monopoly on programming until the launch of Independent Television (ITV) in 1955, but there were still only two channels available until the launch of BBC2 in 1964, and then of the independent Channel 4 in 1982. British television has been a creative home for documentaries (such as *Civilization*, *The Ascent of Man*, and countless natural history programmes), for drama (notably historical series such as *Upstairs Downstairs*, *Brideshead Revisited* and *Jewel in the Crown*), for soap operas (such as *Coronation Street* and *East Enders*) and sitcoms (such as *Are You Being Served?*, *Fawlty Towers*, *Keeping Up Appearances*, *Only Fools and Horses* and *Absolutely Fabulous*), but few have broken into foreign markets. In the United States, for example, British television either spawns copies – such as the sitcom *Steptoe and Son* being turned into *Sanford and Son*, or the quiz shows *Who Wants to be a Millionaire?*, *Whose Line is it Anyway?* and *Weakest Link* being remade in American versions – or is restricted to non-commercial public television which has relatively few viewers.

The monopoly enjoyed by the BBC and ITV may have limited the viewing fare, but it arguably ensured a higher quality of output and more public affairs programming. As noted in Chapter 5, the television culture in Britain has been revolutionized in the last 10 years with the advent of cable, satellite and digital television, which may have expanded the choices available to viewers, but has also increased the competition for those viewers. The dangers of too much choice are very clear in the United States, where the number of channels available on cable has increased in the last 15 years from no more than a dozen to typically more than 100. There is still much fine programming on American television, but in their fight to win viewers and finite advertising revenue, American producers have often sought out the lowest common denominator in the viewing public. The result has been a decline in public affairs programming or high quality dramas, and a growth in the number of chat shows, sitcoms, and reality programming. British television is following a similar path, and in fact has led the way in recent years in the development of reality television and quiz shows.

While preeminent in theatre and film, Britain's most visible role in modern popular culture has been staked by rock music, one of the few art forms, for example, in which foreigners have really made any impact on American domestic culture. Until the late 1950s, Western popular music was dominated by Americans, whether through the big bands of the 1930s and 1940s or through the pioneers of rock and roll, such as Elvis Presley, Bill Haley and Buddy Holly. British singers of the 1950s – like Cliff Richard – either tried to ape their American counterparts, or developed their own home-grown form of music called skiffle. This all changed in 1963 when four young men from

Liverpool – John Lennon, Paul McCartney, George Harrison and Ringo Starr – developed a new and distinctive variation on rock which helped take Britain out of its postwar and post-imperial melancholy.

Representing an emphatic response to what was widely seen as the decline of British popular culture in the face of overwhelming American competition, the Beatles first took their home city by storm, then the country, then – in 1963–64 – the United States. The Beatles became the advance force of what was to become known as the British Invasion, opening the floodgates for a string of singers and bands from Britain to dominate popular music on both sides of the Atlantic. Not only has British popular music comprehensively broken into the American market, but it has also had an impact comparable to American music on the non-English-speaking world.

Rock music has produced some of Britain's biggest celebrities, who – alongside film actors – have been among the best-known

**Illustration 7.3   Sting**

Popular music has been Britain's most effective, visible and profitable cultural export since the 1960s. Among its many high-profile rock stars is Sting, formerly lead singer with Police, who has had a highly successful solo career since the early 1980s.

Britons globally, and have been a mainstay of British culture. Music has also been an important part of the British economy: in 2000, the British music industry as a whole was worth more than £4 billion (€/$6 billion), was worth £1.3 billion (nearly €/$2 billion) in exports, and employed about 120,000 people. There are signs, though, that British popular music may not be having as powerful an effect on global culture as it once did, certainly if its popularity in the United States is any indicator. Between the rise of the Beatles and the end of the 1980s, not a year went by without British artists featuring prominently in the American charts. Over the last 12–15 years, however, British artists have failed to make the charts in the United States, where the home-grown variety has dominated.

**Sports**

Britain is a sporting nation. Sport is one of the country's most popular leisure activities (see also Box 7.2), with about two-thirds of adults claiming to take part in some kind of activity, the most popular being walking, cycling, swimming and football. If they do not necessarily take part, the British are keen followers of sport, choosing from a wide variety of options. The stature of sport is exemplified by Britain's contributions to global sports, having been the birthplace (or nursery, at least) to football (the world's most popular sport), cricket, rugby, hockey, badminton, squash, golf, snooker, and the modern version of tennis. Other sports with a large following in Britain include boxing, equestrianism (particularly show jumping), horse racing, greyhound racing and sailing. Unique to Britain are the Highland Games pursued in Scotland (such as caber-tossing and hammer-throwing) and the Gaelic Games pursued in Northern Ireland.

If diversity is one of the hallmarks of sport in Britain, then the others are regionalism and the class basis of many sports (Holt and Mason, 2000: 168–72), two concepts which to some extent overlap. Cricket, for example, has always been primarily an English sport rather than a British one, and at least until the 1960s was closely associated with the upper class and the idea that playing the game was more important than winning, hence the famous put-down of ungentlemanly behaviour: 'It's just not cricket'. Equestrianism is associated with the landed gentry and the upper middle class, mainly because of its expense. Polo is often described as the sport of kings,

---

**Box 7.2   How the British spend their spare time**

The British are good at relaxing, although perhaps too good if recent studies are any indication. Where they would once leave the house regularly to visit sporting events, have a drink at the local pub, visit the theatre or an exhibition, or go for a walk in the country or a nearby park, they are becoming increasingly sedentary and staying at home. Discouraged by the increased cost of going out to restaurants, sporting events or the theatre by worsening traffic problems, and by the declining quality of public transport, and encouraged by the greater ease of finding entertainment at home, whether on television or the internet, and by a desire to invest in their homes by making improvements, more people are taking the easy option. Ironically, though, the amount of free time they have available has grown, and the British are spending twice as much of their income on leisure as they did 50 years ago.

The changes that have come to British society since the Second World War are nowhere more evident than in the matter of where people go on holiday. The economic and social changes that followed the war allowed the British to become more mobile, by giving them more disposable income and more leisure time. Until the late 1960s, the typical holiday was spent at a seaside resort town such as Blackpool, Torquay or Brighton, the average family staying in a hotel and not doing much more than exploiting the simple pleasures associated with resorts: sitting on the beach, swimming, walking, and perhaps going to a show. The advent of cheap, mass tourism in the late 1960s and early 1970s changed all this, and the British started becoming more adventurous, often holidaying in Spain, the Balearic Islands, the Canary Islands or the Greek islands. These still remain the destinations of choice for the majority of British package holidaymakers, but long-haul vacations to the United States (particularly Florida), the Caribbean, Australasia, Southeast Asia and southern and eastern Africa have become more popular, as has greater independence on the part of vacationers.

---

in large part because only the wealthy can afford to play it. The two different brands of rugby – rugby union and rugby league – are divided both by class and region. The more popular rugby union, which originated in the nineteenth century at Rugby School, an English private school, tends to have its greatest support within the middle class, while rugby league, a breakaway version, is concentrated in northern England and has long been seen as a working-man's sport. Horse racing straddles class divisions, with some of the premier events – including the annual Derby at Epsom, and the Royal

Ascot meeting every June – attracting aristocratic and upper middle-class interest, while routine weekly horse races will more often be supported by the lower middle and working class.

One of the great ironies about Britain is that despite the centrality of sport to British culture (see Table 7.1), it often does badly in almost all the sports it invented or nurtured. Consider the following:

- England has only won the football World Cup once (in 1966), and every four years the heroes of the winning team – including Bobby Moore, Geoff Hurst and Bobby Charlton – are pulled out of the closet as if to remind the British what none of their teams has been able to do since. Meanwhile, none of the British national teams – England, Scotland, Wales or Northern Ireland – has won the quadrennial European Football Championship since its inception in 1960.

- Cricket was exported with success to many former colonies, including India, Pakistan, Sri Lanka, Australia, New Zealand, South Africa and Zimbabwe, but the English national team is routinely defeated in international competition. One of the most famous rivalries in cricket is that between England and Australia. Following England's defeat by the upstart Australians in 1882, a joking obituary was written for the game of cricket, and a year later a cricket stump was burnt and its ashes placed in an urn. The two countries have since competed against each other for The Ashes. Despite the national pride that rides on an English victory, Australia won twice as many matches as England in the period 1980–2002.

- Rugby was also exported with success, but it has only been in recent years that the England rugby team has done well in the two major international competitions, the Rugby World Cup and the Six Nations Tournament (which includes Scotland, Wales, Ireland, France and Italy).

- Britain is home to some of the most hallowed golf courses in the world, such as St. Andrews, Muirfield, Turnberry, and Royal St George's. But while British players have performed much better over the last 30 years, with players such as Tony Jacklin, Nick Faldo, Sandy Lyle, Ian Woosnam and Colin Montgomerie winning an impressive number of tournaments, it is difficult not to conclude that Britain has often played below its potential.

- Formula One racing may not have been 'invented' in Britain, but most of its teams are based in Britain, and most of its cars are built with British technology and by British designers and engineers. Yet while British champions have not been uncommon (Jim Clark, Graham Hill, Jackie Stewart and Nigel Mansell to name a few), British drivers in recent years have often been outwitted by their Brazilian, German and Scandinavian competitors.

• Wimbledon is one of the four events in the international grand slam of tennis, yet Britain has not had a men's champion there since Fred Perry in 1936 or a women's champion since Virginia Wade in 1977.

The United Kingdom Sports Council, a government body which coordinates support to sports in which Britain competes internationally, claims that Britain is one of the five most successful sporting countries in the world. To be sure, there are plenty of examples to add to the occasional triumphs in rugby, golf and Formula One, notably Britain's presence in track and field sports, where world records and titles are often held by Britons, and where Britain's dismal record at the 1996 Atlanta Olympics (15 medals, including just one gold) was eclipsed by its excellent showing at Sydney in 2000 (28 medals, including 11 gold). But it is difficult not to conclude that Britain is punching below its weight, particularly when compared with the three other major European countries (Germany, France and Italy), all of which, for example, routinely outperform Britain at the summer Olympics.

*Table 7.1*   Britain's main sporting events

| Event | Sport | Venue |
| --- | --- | --- |
| All England Lawn Tennis Champs. | tennis | Wimbledon |
| Football Association Cup Final | football | Wembley |
| Open Championship | golf | various |
| The Derby | horse racing | Epsom |
| Grand National | horse racing | Aintree |
| Henley Regatta | rowing | Henley |
| Cowes Week | sailing | Isle of Wight |
| Formula One Grand Prix | motor racing | Silverstone |
| Isle of Man TT Races | motorcycling | Isle of Man |
| International matches | rugby | Twickenham; Murrayfield; Cardiff Arms Park |
| International test matches | cricket | Lord's; The Oval; Edgbaston |
| Badminton Horse Trials | equestrianism | Badminton |

What are we to make of all this? There are probably two major factors at work. First, the government in Britain has been notorious over the years for its unwillingness to provide much funding for sports, or to support the kinds of training and scholarship programmes that are available in many continental European countries. Second, British sportsmen and sportswomen often seem to lack the 'killer instinct' that makes them invest adequately in preparation, or go the extra mile in competition. For generations, the notion of good sportsmanship has meant that greater emphasis has been placed on taking part than on winning, and amateurism has been more greatly admired than professionalism.

Perhaps the greatest change that has come to British sport in the last two decades has been commercialism. Where once it was considered almost indecent to have a link between sports and corporate interests, the outfits of team members in cricket, football and rugby are now emblazoned with the names of their sponsors, mainly electronics companies, banks, brewers, and – until they were barred from advertising – tobacco companies. The injections of cash from sponsors has been joined by increased government spending, by greater sums being paid to the governing bodies of key sports for television rights, and by income from the National Lottery. Started in 1994, the lottery was set up on the condition that 28 per cent of its income should go to 'good causes', including sports. Swimming, football, cricket and tennis have since benefited from the injection of millions of pounds from lottery income.

## Religion

Religion plays only a small role in British national life. The majority of Britons – when asked – will claim one religious affiliation or another, but it is usually fairly weak. For most people, religious activity typically involves no more than occasional attendance at church; most Britons are still baptised and married in a church, and most funerals are held in a church, but regular weekly attendance at church is low. So while about 26 million Britons (nearly half the population) identify themselves with the Church of England, less than two million are active on a regular basis. Overall, fewer than one in five Britons participate in religious activity in any kind of sustained manner. The exception to the general rules can be found among Britain's newer religions, such as Islam, Hinduism and Sikhism; not only is support for these religions growing quickly, but their followers generally have a stronger sense of identity with the faith.

This restricted role for religion has not always been the case. Once Roman Catholicism had been accepted as the state religion in 664, all English kings maintained a close spiritual relationship with the Pope, and the hierarchy of the church was an important part of government, administration and law. However, the relationship changed forever in 1534 when King Henry VIII broke with the Roman Catholic church. The break was partly a result of a dispute over his attempt to divorce his wife Katharine of Aragon, but it was also an attempt to restrict the power of the church in public life. The ploy succeeded, and to this day the role of religion in public life is restricted to the monarchy: the British monarch remains the head of the Church of England (or Defender of the Faith, as she is formally known), which is regarded as the 'established' or national religion of England. (It is important to make a distinction between an established church and a state church; Anglicanism is regarded as the national religion, but the Church of England is not a state church, because it receives no financial aid from the government.) Meanwhile, the Church of Scotland is the national church there, but there are no established churches in Wales or Northern Ireland.

At first glance, the formal link between church and monarch would seem to compromise the idea of a separation of church and state, but it actually does the opposite, drawing attention away from any overlap between church and the elected government. The religious views of elected members of government, for example, are not usually a matter of public debate, and it is almost unheard of – in recent times at least – for the religion of a prime minister to be an issue of public debate; this has been true even of Tony Blair, who – unusually – has been open about his Christian beliefs. There are many reminders in the traditions of government about the links with religion, such as prayers in the House of Commons, but these are little more than symbolic gestures. In policy areas where religion might play a role – such as abortion, the teaching of religion in schools, or euthanasia (allowing a doctor to end a patient's life) – there is almost no overlap between religious values and government policy.

The Church of England is part of the international Communion of Anglican churches, which has 38 national members and claims to have a following of some 70 million people. It is divided into two provinces, one headed by the Archbishop of Canterbury and the other by the Archbishop of York. The former is regarded as the senior of the two, and has the title Primate of All England. The provinces are divided into dioceses overseen by 24 bishops, and these are subdivided into more than 13,000 parishes, each centred on a parish church overseen by a priest and (in larger parishes) assistants known as curates. The monarch appoints the leaders of the church on the advice of the prime minister, and those leaders have the right to sit in the upper chamber of Parliament, the House of Lords. Every 10 years, the Lambeth Conference brings together Anglican bishops from the different countries where Anglicanism is practiced, and it makes decisions on doctrine and important policy questions.

The Church has about 13,000 ordained ministers, of whom about 2100 are women. The ordination of women priests has only been allowed since 1994, and their advent has been symptomatic of a broader division within the Church of England (*The Economist*, 12 January 2002: 53.). On the one hand there are Anglo-Catholic traditionalists (otherwise known as high-church Anglicans) who are opposed to the idea of female and gay priests, many of whom left the church after 1994, leading to talk of a possible split. On the other hand, there are evangelicals who describe themselves as more progressive and more willing to accept change in the character and structure of the church. There has been an unspoken understanding over the years that the post of Archbishop of Canterbury should alternate between representatives of the two groups. However, when the evangelical George Carey retired in 2002 after 13 years in the post, he was replaced by another evangelical – Rowan Williams – who became the 104th Archbishop of Canterbury, and the first Welshman to hold the job in at least 1000 years. Regarded as a liberal, Williams supports the idea that the Church of England should lose its established status and have a standing equal with the Catholic church and other Christian churches in Britain. For many, his appointment represented the triumph of the progressive over the traditionalist element in the church.

While it has fewer overall members than the Church of England, the Catholic Church now has the largest active adult membership of any religion in Britain, with an average weekly attendance at mass of more than 1.2 million people. Where active participation among adults in the Church of England has fallen by nearly 45 per cent since 1970, participation in the Catholic Church has fallen more slowly, such that it is now the biggest church in the country. Organizationally, it is divided into eight provinces overseen by Bishops Conferences for England and Wales, and for Scotland. It is sub-divided into 30 dioceses, each with a bishop appointed by the Pope.

*Figure* 7.2   Religious activity in Britain

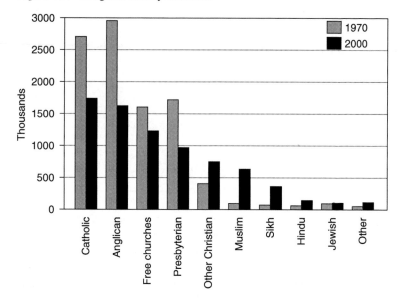

*Sources*:   Christian Research and Board of Deputies of British Jews, quoted in Office for National Statistics, *UK 2002* (London: The Stationery Office, 2001)

One of the most notable trends in British religion in recent years has been its growing diversity (Figure 7.2). For centuries, the British have been predominantly Christian, the only notable divisions being between the Churches of England and Scotland, and between Protestants and Catholics. But the arrival since the 1950s of immigrants from the Indian sub-continent has brought more Muslims, Sikhs and Hindus to Britain. While active adult participation in Christian religions has fallen by more than one-third since 1970, the number of Hindus has doubled, the number of Sikhs has quadrupled, and the number of Muslims has quintupled. There are now more than 1000 Muslim mosques in Britain, more than 200 Sikh temples, and more than 140 Hindu temples. Unfortunately, the diversity has brought social tensions, in part because these new religions are identified with ethnic minorities (and thus are an element in the racism that has become a feature of society in Britain), and in part because of the broader conflict between Muslims and the West.

# 8

# Britain and the World

Britain is no longer the dominating imperial power that it once was, but its influence is still widely felt, and it is still a major actor on the world stage. Variations of the British parliamentary model are used by almost every other liberal democracy, global culture is deeply permeated by British literature, drama and music, English is the most widely spoken language in the world and has become the standard for international commerce and communications (albeit thanks mainly to the United States), Britain is a leading member of all the key international organizations, its economy is the fourth biggest in the world, it is a nuclear power, and its military – while relatively small – is efficient and highly-respected.

Britain has long been an outward-looking society, interested and involved in events beyond its shores. As an island state, it might easily have followed the example of medieval Japan and cut itself off from the outside world. However, migrations from the continent meant that it was early influenced by events on the other side of the English Channel, the North Sea and the Irish Sea. The rule of monarchs with estates in France provided an additional link, as did the need both to intervene in, and protect itself from, military and political developments on the continent. Finally, the growth of industry demanded new sources of raw materials and new markets, which combined with the need to outwit its European competitors to encourage Britain to expand its political and economic interests into every continent.

As the builder of the biggest empire in world history, Britain has an important historical role in global affairs, and the political and cultural impact of that empire is still felt around the world today. Its contemporary role in international affairs continues to be unique, because Britain is the only country in the world that is a member of the UN Security Council, the European Union, NATO, G8, the OSCE, the Commonwealth, the OECD and the WTO. This gives it a critical role in bridging these different organizations, and in bridging the interests of different groups of countries. It takes its commitments to international agreements seriously, and has played a leading role in the development and implementation of most major international treaties.

This chapter looks at Britain's position in the world in political, economic and military terms. It focuses on key relationships, including those with the Commonwealth, within the Atlantic alliance, and with the United States. It assesses the significance of Britain's economic and military role in the world, and analyses the effects of European versus Atlanticist pressures on British foreign policy. It focuses in particular on an analysis of Britain's role in the European Union – why it joined late, the impact of membership, and an assessment of the nature of its troubled relationship with its European partners. It concludes that while Britain's place in the world has changed dramatically over the past two generations, it has established a new place for itself as a major actor on the global and European economic stage, and as a middle-sized but efficient military actor with influence on both sides of the Atlantic.

## The Changing British Role in the World

For much of the last millenium, Britain has been as much a part of the political and military conflicts that have divided Europe as any of its neighbours. It became one of the dominating actors early in the struggles that determined the continental balance of power, its territory being several times ruled by monarchs with interests in parts of France, occasionally fighting off threatened invasions by its competitors (notably the French and the Spanish) and frequently becoming involved in key European conflicts, from the Hundred Years' War (1337–1415) to the Seven Years' War (1756–63), the Napoleonic Wars (1799–1815), and the Crimean War (1853–56).

Britain first began to look further afield to pursue its economic and political interests during the reign of Elizabeth I, and eventually built an empire that would incorporate much of North America, the Indian subcontinent, parts of Southeast Asia, Australia and New Zealand, most of southern and eastern Africa, parts of west Africa, parts of the

Middle East, and islands in the Caribbean and in the Atlantic, Pacific and Indian Oceans. To maintain the empire required the development and protection of trade routes, and the commitment of soldiers and bureaucrats, both of which contributed to the expansion of its political and military influence.

By the nineteenth century, Britain was the dominating economic and military power in the world. Its factories were the engines of the global economic system, it traded with almost every part of the world, its troops were stationed on almost every continent, it took an active role in military operations in many parts of Europe, Asia and Africa, and it had a navy that dominated the world's oceans. The British Empire was the biggest the world had ever known, on which it was claimed that the sun never set. The world lived under the *Pax Britannica*, or the expectation that Britain would take a leading role in maintaining global peace (see Roberts and Roberts, 2002, chapter 25).

All this has changed in the last 60 years. Britain emerged from the Second World War with its economic resources stretched beyond their limit, with nationalist movements in many of its colonies agitating for independence, and unable to support a large and widespread military. The empire was dismantled in a relatively peaceful and orderly fashion, the military was withdrawn from many of its former fields of activity, and Britain became a supporting actor in the Cold War. Its aspirations are now much more modest than they once were, but it still plays an important role as a medium-sized military power and as one of the world's four biggest economies. Its impact is illustrated by its contribution to the work of six key international organizations:

- It was a founder member in 1945 of the United Nations, is one of the five permanent members of the Security Council with veto power (along with the United States, France, Russia and China), is the fifth largest contributor to the UN regular budget, and is a leading contributor to UN peacekeeping operations.
- It is the second-largest economy in the European Union after Germany, and while it was not a founder member of the EU, and has a reputation as a reluctant European (see later in this chapter), it nevertheless has considerable influence on the policy-making processes of the EU, and is clearly essential to the development of common European policies on trade, industry, defence and foreign policy.

- It was a founder member in 1949 of the North Atlantic Treaty Organization (NATO), and is second only to the United States in the extent of its influence over NATO policy and its contribution of military resources to the organization. Most Royal Navy ships are committed to NATO operations, and 55,000 British troops are committed to NATO's Rapid Reaction Forces. Britain is a champion of NATO interests in Europe, an issue over which it is often at odds with France.

- It is a member of the most exclusive international club in the world, the Group of 8 industrialized countries (G8), whose leaders meet at well-publicized and increasingly well-guarded annual summits, and where it plays a central role in the development of common economic and security policies.

- It is a member of the Organization for Security and Cooperation in Europe (OSCE), a regional security organization founded in 1994 that brings together 55 states to promote security, prevent conflicts developing, observe elections and provide post-conflict rehabilitation.

- It is the leading actor in the Commonwealth, a 54-nation voluntary association of mainly former British colonies and dominions that includes about one-third of the world's population.

Its most notable (and controversial) role at the high table of international affairs in the last 10–15 years has been the support it has provided to several US military and diplomatic ventures. There has often been a close relationship between Britain and the USA (see Box 8.1), a consequence of their common cultural heritage and the common positions they have usually (but not always) taken on security matters, but since 1990 there has been a repeated pattern of Britain being the leading supporter of US military operations abroad: during the Gulf War of 1990–91, Britain provided the second-largest military contingent after that of the USA; it was subsequently the only country to be militarily involved with the USA in enforcing no-fly zones over Iraq; it played the leading diplomatic and military role in support of the United States in NATO attacks on Serbia in 1999; and in 2002–03 Tony Blair was the most hawkish of leaders in support of US plans to attack Iraq in order to remove Saddam Hussein from power.

Despite its interest and role in international affairs, however, Britain is not the power it once was, and most of its influence now is exerted not unilaterally, but in concert with other groups of states. In

**Box 8.1  The special relationship**

Thanks mainly to a combination of their common histories and cultures, Britain and the United States have long had a 'special relationship', although the term is rarely used without being contained in quotation marks. Those marks are indicative of a degree of doubt about just how 'special' the relationship really is. There have been times when the two countries have had strong relations and a common purpose, but there have also been times when they have been at odds with each other.

Even the significance of the high-point of modern Anglo-American relations – the Second World War – is tinged with doubt. Both countries were united in their opposition to fascism, and Roosevelt and Churchill made many noble statements about their common principles and objectives. Yet the USA was reluctant to enter the war, and when it did it quickly took a dominant role that undermined Britain's leading position in conducting the war, and its influence in designing the postwar world. It is often charged that American pressure was a deciding factor in the end of the British Empire.

Its European neighbours – particularly the French – have often argued that Britain has been used by the United States as a conduit for its relations with the rest of Western Europe. Throughout the Cold War period (1945–90), the French were wary of US influence in European foreign and security policy, but Britain was an Atlanticist, promoting the idea of working with the United States and encouraging the USA to maintain a military presence in Western Europe. The special relationship was closest during the Roosevelt–Churchill years, cooled over the issue of Suez in 1956 and over Britain's refusal to commit troops to Vietnam, warmed again during the Reagan–Thatcher years when the two leaders had a common philosophy, cooled somewhat during the first Clinton administration, but then warmed again with the election of Tony Blair.

Blair was quick to come to the moral support of the United States following the September 2001 terrorist attacks, prompting President George W. Bush to proclaim (to the chagrin of Canadians) that 'America has no truer friend than Great Britain'. Blair made much of the 'pivotal' role that Britain could play in world affairs, with its twin loyalty to the USA and to the EU. The diplomatic importance of Britain was clear in 2002–03 when the Bush administration tried to build support for an attack on the Hussein regime in Iraq, and public and political opinion in the USA realized that international support – particularly from Britain – was important to the diplomatic success of an attack.

particular, its international interests focus today on three main arenas: the Commonwealth, the Atlantic alliance, and the European Union.

## The Commonwealth

Although it is the least important of the three arenas, and is perhaps more important for nostalgic cultural reasons than for hard political reasons, the Commonwealth nonetheless remains a factor in the way Britain defines its position in the world. An outgrowth of the British Empire, the Commonwealth is a loosely-structured and voluntary organization that consists of 54 countries, most of which were once British colonies or dominions (see Table 8.1). Members include Australia, Canada, New Zealand, many Caribbean states, India, and former British colonies in east, south and west Africa, such as Ghana, Kenya, Nigeria, South Africa and Zambia. Based originally around the old white dominions, the Commonwealth grew and became increasingly multiracial in the 1950s and 1960s as Britain's African, Caribbean and Asian colonies won their independence. It now has a collective population of 1.7 billion people (about 27 per cent of the world total), and has recently been joined by countries that were never colonized by Britain, such as Namibia (1990) and Mozambique (1995).

The Commonwealth Secretariat is based in London, its staff co-ordinating policy and operating the many funding, educational, economic assistance and cultural-exchange programmes run by the Commonwealth. It has an active policy of supporting sustainable economic development, and of developing regional investment funds to promote trade across and within the Commonwealth. Its economic interests are heavily influenced by the perspective of the relatively poor African and Asian states that make up the bulk of its membership; thus, its priorities tend to be driven by issues such as poverty, economic development, trade, and aid to underdeveloped countries.

There are biennial summits of the heads of government of the member states, and every four years the Commonwealth Games brings together athletes from the member states in a mini-Olympics (the most recent games were held in Manchester in 2002). The Queen is head of the Commonwealth, and *de jure* head of state in 15 member states (including Australia, Canada and several Caribbean states such as Grenada and Jamaica, where she is represented by a governor-general). The Commonwealth also has an important cultural role in

*Table* 8.1   Members of the Commonwealth

| | | |
|---|---|---|
| Antigua and Barbuda | Kenya | Seychelles |
| Australia | Kiribati | Sierra Leone |
| Bahamas | Lesotho | Singapore |
| Bangladesh | Malawi | Solomon Islands |
| Barbados | Malaysia | South Africa |
| Belize | Maldives | Sri Lanka |
| Botswana | Malta | Swaziland |
| Brunei | Mauritius | Tanzania |
| Cameroon | Mozambique | Tonga |
| Canada | Namibia | Trinidad and Tobago |
| Cyprus | Nauru | Tuvalu |
| Dominica | New Zealand | Uganda |
| Fiji | Nigeria | United Kingdom |
| Gambia | Pakistan | Vanuatu |
| Ghana | Papua New Guinea | Zambia |
| Grenada | St Kitts and Nevis | Zimbabwe |
| Guyana | St Lucia | |
| India | St Vincent and the Grenadines | |
| Jamaica | Samoa | |

world affairs, thanks in part to its use of English as the sole official language, and in part to the contribution it makes to the promotion of diplomatic ties among its member states.

However, while its members occasionally agree on common action, the Commonwealth has come to be defined more by what divides it than what unites it, and the interests of its richer white members and its poorer non-white members are often at odds. The inability of the Commonwealth always to speak with one voice has caused its diplomatic influence to decline in recent years (Jones and Kavanagh, 1998: 2). For example, while it may have expelled South Africa in 1961 because of its policies of apartheid (it rejoined in 1994), suspended Nigeria in 1994 because of the authoritarian policies of its military government, and suspended Pakistan and Fiji from its councils in 1999–2000 following military coups in those countries, the Thatcher government was unwilling to agree in the 1980s with Commonwealth arguments in favour of imposing sanctions on South Africa.

More recently, its claims to be a champion of democracy, good government, human rights, and the rule of law rang hollow in light of its prevarication on the issue of Zimbabwe. During 2001–02, Britain led attempts to punish the authoritarian regime of Zimbabwean president Robert Mugabe for its seizures of white-owned farmland, its intimidation of the judiciary, opposition political parties and journalists, and its manipulation of the 2002 presidential election. Although agreement was eventually reached in March 2002 to suspend Zimbabwe from the Commonwealth for one year – a move which was more symbolic than practical, and had little impact on the policies of the Mugabe regime – this came only after months of disagreement that saw white members falling out with black African members. While some felt that the decision over Zimbabwe would restore some credibility to the Commonwealth, others argued that the damage had already been done.

The Commonwealth has also meant less for Britain since it became part of the European Union. Prior to joining what was then the European Economic Community (EEC) in 1973, Britain had a number of preferential trading agreements with several Commonwealth states, that were either abandoned or significantly rewritten when Britain became a member of the Community (Clarke, 1996: 279, 343). Furthermore, as Canadian interests switch towards the economic integration of North America, Australian interests switch to Southeast Asia and the Pacific rim, and British interests switch to the European Union, the old cultural ties that defined the relationship between Britain and key members of the Commonwealth continue to weaken, raising questions about the value and the future direction of the organization.

Meanwhile, Britain has very few colonies left. From a time when the British Empire included a quarter of the world's population, it has shrunk to a microcosm of its former self. Following the return of Hong Kong and its seven million residents to Chinese control in 1997, there were just 15 Overseas Territories left, containing a total of 180,000 people: Anguilla, the British Virgin Islands, the Cayman Islands, Montserrat, and the Turks and Caicos Islands (all in the Caribbean), Bermuda, the Falkland Islands, St Helena, Ascension Island, Tristan da Cunha, South Georgia and the South Sandwich Islands (all in the Atlantic), Gibraltar on the coast of Spain, British Antarctic Territory, British Indian Ocean Territory, and four small islands in the Pacific, including Pitcairn.

Most have a high degree of self-government, locally elected legislatures being responsible for domestic affairs, and governors or commissioners appointed by the Queen being responsible for foreign affairs and security. None of the Territories has asked for independence, although the future of Gibraltar has been the subject of debate for many years. Under the 1969 constitution, Britain is committed to the principle that it will never pass the sovereignty of Gibraltar to another state (that is, Spain) without the support of its people. However, the Spanish have long made clear their desire to see Gibraltar returned to their control for the first time since 1713, and during 2002 there were controversial discussions about the possibility of a new relationship between the three actors.

## The Atlantic Alliance

Along with Canada, the United States and most other West European countries, Britain has been committed since April 1949 to the common defence policies of the North Atlantic Treaty Organization (NATO). NATO was created by the North Atlantic Treaty, signed against a background of threatening behaviour by the Soviet Union, notably its refusal to work with the Western powers on the administration of postwar Germany, and its institution of the Berlin blockade of 1948–49. Under the terms of the treaty, an armed attack on one member state was to be considered an attack on them all, and each member promised to take 'such action as it deems necessary . . . to restore and maintain the security of the North Atlantic area'. The treaty was signed by the United States, Canada, and 10 West European countries (excluding West Germany, which did not join until 1955).

With the end of the Cold War, and the collapse in December 1991 of the Soviet Union, the underlying rationale of NATO – to neutralize the threat posed by the USSR and its allies – was removed. Many new possibilities now emerged in the realm of foreign and security policy. In rallying support for the response to the Iraqi invasion of Kuwait in August 1990, President George Bush made a speech in which he argued that 'Out of these troubled times a new world order can emerge. A new era – freer from the threat of terror, stronger in the pursuit of justice and more secure in the quest for peace.' He never explained what he meant by 'new world order', and the world has been far from orderly since 1990, but the phrase seemed to draw a line in the sand between the old insecurities of the Cold War and the new insecurities of a world facing multiple new threats.

Britain joined actively in supporting the US-led coalition against Iraq following its invasion of Kuwait on 2 August 1990, and for a few months at least the Atlantic alliance seemed to be much stronger than

Prime Minister Tony Blair and US President George W. Bush at a press conference in 2002. Blair went against majority public opinion in Britain and within his own party in 2002–03 by backing Bush's attempts to build political support for the invasion of Iraq in March 2003.

**Illustration 8.1   Tony Blair and George Bush**

the European alliance. The Thatcher administration adopted the most hawkish stance among EU governments, and in her last few weeks in office Margaret Thatcher apparently played a key role in convincing US President George Bush of the merits of a rapid counterattack, and placed British troops under US operational command. Britain's commitment of 35,000 troops, 60 warplanes and 15 naval vessels was second only to that of the United States, was bigger than that of France (the next biggest EU member state, which committed 12,500 troops, 40 warplanes and 14 naval vessels), and stood in stark contrast to those member states that made much smaller contributions, and to Belgium (which refused to sell ammunition to Britain) or to Spain and Portugal (which allowed its naval vessels to be involved only in minesweeping or enforcing the blockade against Iraq).

Britain was also alone in participating in – and supporting – US efforts to enforce the no-fly zones over southern and northern Iraq after the war, played a key role in the UN regime imposed in 1991–99 to inspect sites within Iraq where weapons of mass destruction might have been under development, and played the leading role in providing political and military support for US efforts to pressure Iraq into removing obstacles to UN arms inspectors during 1998.

Britain was also a fully-fledged member of Operation Allied Force, the NATO attack on Serbia in March–April 1999 that came in response to the ethnic cleansing visited on the predominantly Albanian province of Kosovo by the regime of Slobodan Milosevic. European leaders were quick to condemn what was happening, and there was general support in the EU for the bombing war that took place in March–May, although levels of support varied. In the absence of American leadership, Tony Blair won a reputation as the leader most in favour of the attack, committed British air, sea and ground forces to the operation, and went so far as to suggest the commitment of ground troops before the bombing had ended. With the end of hostilities, the British military played a central role in reconstruction, making up one-third of the peacekeeping force sent in to Kosovo.

NATO was created against a background of Cold War tensions that are now largely gone; in a sense, NATO 'won' the war, and several former 'enemies' in Eastern Europe have been invited to join. Inevitably, questions are now being asked about NATO's purpose, about the US role in European defence, and about whether (and how) Britain and its EU partners can develop their own security capability independent of the Americans. Two other factors have helped show up some of the cracks in the Atlantic alliance:

- There is the new economic might of the EU, whose combined GDP almost equals that of the USA, whose population is one-third as big again as that of the USA, and whose share of world trade is half as big again as that of the USA. The Europeans have flexed their economic muscles in trade disputes with the USA over issues such as the US embargo on Cuba, the US imposition of tariffs on steel imports in 2001, and the question of subsidies to farmers.
- There have been many disagreements on policy between the USA and the EU. In addition to trade disputes, the Europeans have also

been at odds with the Americans on how to deal with the problems of Israel and Palestine, over what to do with the Hussein regime in Iraq, and over key international agreements, including attempts to deal with climate change, and the creation of an international criminal court.

In light of such disagreements, it seems logical to many that the Europeans should follow up their more independent and assertive role in international economic matters with greater independence in security and defence issues. European integrationists in particular want to see the EU developing a common foreign policy as a means of providing a counterbalance to US influence in the world. The problem, however, has been to encourage EU member states to build agreement as effectively as they have on international trade issues.

### Britain and the European Union

While the importance of the Commonwealth has waned, and the role of the Atlantic alliance is being redefined, there is no question any longer that the most important foreign policy arena for Britain today is the European Union (Map 8.1). In fact, it is so important that it is debatable to what extent Europe is any longer a foreign policy matter. Certainly it was initially approached as such by British political leaders, but EU membership has had important implications for domestic politics and policy. It has changed the structure of the British political system, has meant the introduction of a new tier of law that has demanded changes at the national level, and has introduced a new level of government with powers over domestic matters. The British still equivocate over the extent to which they are British and the extent to which they are European, but there is no question that British foreign policy – particularly on economic matters – is heavily driven by European policy.

When Europeans began building ties of economic cooperation among themselves in the 1950s and 1960s, they concentrated on reducing the barriers to trade and on building a single European market, with common external tariffs on goods coming into that market, and free movement of money, goods, services and people within its borders. European integration has since broadened and deepened significantly. There are few remaining barriers to internal trade, EU citizens can live and work in any of the member states (and

**Map 8.1   Political map of the European Union**

can even vote and run in local elections), intra-European investment has grown, as have corporate takeovers and mergers, internal transport networks are expanding, and the member states have brought domestic laws into line with European law in many different policy areas, including agriculture, transport, trade, competition, immigration and consumer policy (see Chapter 6).

The EU now has 15 member states, and the membership applications of 10 other (mainly Eastern European) countries have been accepted, with the first round expected to join as early as 2004: leading candidates include Poland, Hungary, the Czech Republic, Estonia, Slovenia and Cyprus. The member states among them negotiate common laws and policies through six major European institutions:

- A *European Commission*, responsible for proposing new European laws and policies, and for implementing them once they have been adopted. The Commission is a small (18,000-person) bureaucracy headquartered in Brussels, headed by a team of 20 Commissioners: two each from Britain, France, Germany, Italy and Spain, and one each from the remaining member states. The work and powers of the Commission are widely misunderstood – rather than having a life of its own, it cannot make final decisions on new laws and policies, and can only do what the treaties of the EU allow it to do.
- The *Council of Ministers*, the primary decision-making body of the EU, also headquartered in Brussels. The council has a rotating membership, so that depending upon the issue under discussion, the appropriate group of ministers from each of the member states is convened; hence, agriculture ministers will discuss agricultural matters, and environmental ministers will discuss environmental matters. Typically, ministers use either a simple majority to make decisions, or a qualified majority where each is given a different number of votes in rough proportion to the population size of each state. Thus, Britain has ten, Spain has eight, Sweden has four, and so on. (The numbers will change when new members join from 2004.)
- A 626-member *European Parliament*, which is directly elected by the voters of the EU for five-year terms, and divides its time between Strasbourg (France) and Brussels. Unlike conventional legislatures, it cannot develop new legislation, but instead shares responsibility with the Council of Ministers for voting on the adoption of legislative proposals developed by the Commission. Seats in the EP are distributed among the member states very loosely on the basis of population – Britain has 87 members, although that number will fall to 72 when new Eastern European states join the EU.
- Judicial matters are addressed by the *European Court of Justice*, based in Luxembourg. When a member state has a question about the application of EU law, or there is a dispute over the meaning or application of that law (involving EU institutions, member states,

individuals or corporations), a case may be heard before the Court, whose job is to provide clarity and consistency to the governing treaties of the EU. There are 15 judges on the Court, one from each member state.

- The *European Council* is a forum that brings the heads of government of the member states together for summit meetings at least twice each year. Until recently they met in the capital or a major regional city in one of the member states, but they now all meet in Brussels. The job of the Council is to make broad decisions regarding the future direction and priorities of the EU (for more details on EU institutions, see McCormick 2002, chapter 4).

- Decisions relating to the euro are taken by the *European Central Bank*, which is based in Frankfurt and is reponsible for overseeing monetary policy in the euro area, conducting foreign exchange operations, and managing the foreign reserves of euro member states. The national central banks of all the EU member states are members of the European System of Central Banks, but non-euro states such as Britain do not take part in decision-making.

Britain won a reputation from the outset of being a reluctant European (Box 8.2), and has developed an unfortunate habit of often being late to join its European partners in new ventures, and of being less than enthusiastic in engaging itself with Europe:

- It was late joining the Community (although this was not entirely its fault), and even then the Labour government held a referendum in 1975 on continued membership (the vote was 2 to 1 in favour).
- It was late joining the exchange rate mechanism that was to be a prelude to the single European currency, and is one of the three countries that has still not adopted the euro.
- Margaret Thatcher was strident in her demands in the early 1980s for a renegotiation of British budgetary contributions (although the Germans have since followed her example).
- The British have the lowest turnout at European Parliamentary elections, and opinion polls show low levels of enthusiasm among the British for membership of the EU.
- Segments of the British tabloid press persist in misleading and jingoistic attacks on the EU.
- Britain still has not lived up to its potential in efforts to develop a common European foreign policy (although this has changed with the Blair administration).

Eurosceptics see these characteristics as admirable caution, some even arguing that Britain should never have joined the Community in the first place, and that its key interests continue to lie outside Europe. For their part, Europhiles argue that Britain's laggardly attitude to European integration has prevented it from taking part in the critical planning stages of EU initiatives, thereby denying it the opportunity to mould that process more to its liking and its advantage.

The extent to which British public opinion is out of step with that in much (but not all) of the rest of the EU is reflected in the regular polls carried out by Eurobarometer, the EU polling service (see Figure 8.1). These reveal a low level of psychological attachment to the EU by most Britons, who are also less enthusiastic about the benefits of EU membership than the citizens of any other member state. Perhaps not surprisingly, the people who have the lowest regard for the European Union also admit to knowing less about it than the citizens of any other member state. There are several possible explanations for Britain's lukewarm approach to Europe:

- Britain's physical separation from the continent has helped make the British feel that they are somehow different from other Europeans, and indeed that they are not really European at all. Even today, many Britons still talk about Europe as something distinct from Britain.
- Where two world wars had discredited the idea of nationalism and the nation-state on the continent, they were vindicated in Britain by its independence and separation (Kavanagh, 2000: 70). Where European states concluded that only cooperation and integration could prevent future wars, it was its independence which – in the minds of many Britons – helped it avoid becoming caught up in the kinds of conflicts which had brought so many changes to the borders of continental European states.
- At the time that continental European leaders were planning the first steps in the process of integration, Britain still had many interests outside Europe: it had an empire, it had strong cultural links with its dominions and colonies (many of which still saw Britain as the mother country), and it had a strong relationship with the United States (in contrast to the distrust with which the French viewed – and continue to view – the USA).

The issue of Europe has been at the heart of policy debates within the major political parties, and indeed has become a cause for much

**Box 8.2   Britain: really such a bad European?**

It has become almost trite to describe Britain as the 'reluctant European', or the 'odd man out' in the EU, and to quote (as does this book) the many examples of its failure to go along with its EU partners, to drag its feet, or to insist on changing the rules of the game. Yet there may be reason for questioning the conventional wisdom:

- Britain tends to be visible in its Euroscepticism, in part because that scepticism has come to be expected, and in part because media and political attention tends to focus more on Britain than on other member states with similar leanings. For example, debates over the development of the euro tended to ignore low levels of public enthusiasm in other member states, such as Germany, Denmark and Sweden. Similarly, Britain has never voted against any of the European treaties, as did Denmark in 1992 or Ireland in 2001. Indeed, Denmark has developed a strong record of Euroscepticism, but is less visible in its actions.
- France arguably has done more to seriously disrupt the work of the EU. For example, it was France (or at least Charles de Gaulle) that twice vetoed the membership applications of Britain, Ireland and Denmark, and that set off the Community's most serious crisis in 1965 when it refused to take part in joint decision-making for six months. France is also out of step with most of its EU partners over policy on NATO, it stubbornly refuses to allow the chamber of the European Parliament to be moved to Brussels (with the farcical and expensive result that Parliament must move for one week per month to Strasbourg), and it engaged in an unseemly and nationalistic squabble in 1997–98 over who should be appointed first president of the European Central Bank.
- Britain is criticized for negotiating hard on the development of new EU laws and policies, but it is driven less by stubbornness or a wish to slow the process down than by a philosophy that it should not make any agreements that it cannot honour. Other member states, by contrast, will often say 'yes' and then find themselves unable to deliver on their promises. It is often forgotten that Britain has one of the best records in the Union on changing national law to fit with EU law.

division and disagreement. In the early 1980s, it was Labour Party policy to withdraw Britain altogether from the Community, a stance that helped bring about the breakaway of the Social Democratic Party, an event which in turn contributed to Labour's long spell in opposition. By the mid-1990s Labour had reversed that position, was arguing that withdrawal would be 'disastrous' for Britain, and was pushing for a more constructive role in the EU.

*Figure* 8.1   Public opinion on the European Union

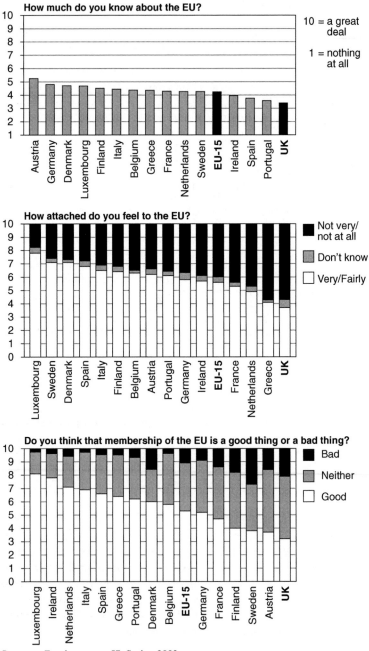

*Source*:   *Eurobarometer* 57, Spring 2002.

Meanwhile, the issue has been even more divisive for the Conservative party, which – under the leadership of Prime Minister Edward Heath – was the party that negotiated Britain's entry in 1973. Margaret Thatcher railed against what she saw as excessive bureaucratization and regulation by Europe, and argued that EU policies were undermining her attempts to free up the British marketplace. (This philosophy overlooked the fact that 'Europe' has few independent powers for making policy, and is still to a large extent the sum of its parts.) Her disagreements with pro-Europeans within her party contributed to her fall from power in 1990, the split continued to dog the Conservatives under the leadership of John Major, and it was a key factor in the 2001 party leadership election that saw pro-European candidates losing to the Eurosceptic Iain Duncan Smith.

Some Britons remain hostile to the 'federalist tendencies' of the EU, but many misunderstand the notion of federalism and fail to realize that it actually involves the retention of often substantial independent powers for the member states. At the same time, increasing numbers (particularly professionals and those in their twenties and thirties) are now arguing the benefits of membership. Perhaps nothing better symbolized Britain's new ties to its neighbours than the completion in 1994 – after many false starts – of a rail tunnel under the Channel between England and France. Despite its financial troubles, the tunnel is a key element in the high-speed rail network that is slowly linking all the major cities and regions of the EU.

One area in which the EU has made only mixed progress has been the development of a common foreign and security policy (Anderson, 1998; Holland, 1999). Backed by the vast size of the European market – which now accounts for nearly one-third of global economic production – the 15 member states have learned to work as one on global trade issues. They have also adopted common positions on a variety of headline international issues – such as the Israeli-Palestinian question and tensions between India and Pakistan over Kashmir – and have increasingly voted as a block in the United Nations General Assembly. However, they have so far lacked the political unity always to work together on the most critical security and defence issues. Several member states (such as Finland and Ireland) are neutral, Germany is not allowed by international law to commit its troops outside the NATO area, and the two major military powers – Britain and France – often have different policy priorities. Britain is a supporter of the NATO alliance and US leadership, but France tends towards a more independent European line on security issues.

These different sets of allegiances and priorities exemplify one of the persistent characteristics of European integration: the competing interests of member states that often pull the EU in contradictory directions, and as often undermine attempts to reach common policy positions. The Franco-German axis has long been the crux of European integration, a habit stemming from one of the underlying objectives of integration, viz. to make war between these two persistent enemies impossible. The French and the Germans have often reached their own bilateral understandings that have determined the direction of the EU. One of these has been the development of a European defence capability, something that has been on the EU agenda for many years, but towards which little of substance has been done until recently.

The key problem has been a difference of political opinion between France and Germany. In 1992, the two countries symbolically created the 50,000-strong Eurocorps, which was later joined by contingents from Belgium, Luxembourg and Spain. Since then, the 20,000-strong Rapid Deployment Force (EUROFOR) has been created for humanitarian and peacekeeping operations, along with a British-Dutch amphibious force and a non-permanent European Maritime Force. But the creation of these units means relatively little as long as opinion remains divided over the bigger question of whether the EU should keep its forces integrated within the NATO structure (the German preference), or should develop its own military capacity independent of the United States (the French preference).

Recent years have seen the Franco-German axis being replaced by a more complex set of bilateral and trilateral axes, with Britain – and specifically the Blair administration – sometimes playing the role of spoiler. For example, 1998–99 saw Britain and France taking the lead to develop agreement on the creation of a European rapid-reaction force. Where Britain had long opposed attempts to promote greater European military integration, Blair was sympathetic to the suggestion mooted in 1996 that the EU develop a defence and security 'identity' within NATO. The idea was that the Europeans would be able to to mount peacekeeping or monitoring operations without necessarily looking for the support of the United States or other NATO member states; interested countries would contribute military forces that would come together under a joint command system. In an unprecedented move, Blair met with French President Jacques Chirac at St Malo in France in December 1998 to discuss the terms of the arrangement, the French agreeing that the European Security and Defence Identity (ESDI) would not affect the EU's commitment to NATO. The ESDI was formally announced at the Nice summit of the European Council a few days later. It was agreed that the EU would not work towards the establishment of a European army, but would instead set up a rapid-reaction force that would only function where NATO as a whole was not involved. NATO, meanwhile, would remain the basis for the collective defence of Western Europe. The EU now committed itself to modernizing its armed forces so that it could develop the ability to commit 50–60,000 troops and supporting naval and air units for crisis management operations, as well as humanitarian and peacekeeping work. Britain's contribution could be up to 12,500 troops, 18 warships and 72 combat aircraft.

Blair argued that it was not a straight choice between an EU defence capability on the one hand and continued cooperation with the Americans on the other – he argued instead that both were possible. The political costs of this were dragged most obviously into the harsh light of day by the hawkish position taken during 2002–03 by the Blair administration on the question of plans by the United States to attack Iraq and remove Saddam Hussein from power. While there had been an outpouring of support and sympathy for the United States following the September 2001 terrorist attacks, the tide began to turn as the Bush administration shifted the spotlight of the 'war on terrorism' away from Afghanistan and towards Iraq. Bush claimed that Hussein was building weapons of mass destruction, and was supporting the al Qaeda terrorist network. Questions were raised about the lack of hard evidence, about the wisdom of setting a precedent of preemptive strikes, about how such an attack would fit with international law, about the extent to which such an attack would further destabilize an already unstable region, and about the real motives of the Bush administration.

As events unfolded in mid-2002, European leaders began withdrawing support from the Bush administration. The French equivocated, the Germans were positively hostile to American 'adventurism' (a position that was undoubtedly influenced by the closeness of the September 2002 German general election), while the conservative Berlusconi government in Italy gave its blessings. Meanwhile, the world was treated to the peculiar sight of Britain's Labour prime minister leading the chorus in support of a divisive policy pursued by a conservative American president. Forcefully arguing his case that Britain played a 'pivotal' role in world affairs,

Blair gave vocal support to the Bush administration, analysts suggesting that at least part of his thinking was that it was better to be involved – and thus to have influence – than not to be involved and thus to have little or no say in a policy that might end up damaging Britain's interests (*The Economist*, 9 March 2002: 60). Whatever Blair's motives, the contrast between his position and that of the two other major European powers – Germany and France – clearly indicated that the EU was some way from developing common philosophies and policies on security policy. The ESDI was intended to focus more on humanitarian operations than on defence or offence, but the different positions of the EU's three leading members raised questions about the practicality of this 'identity'.

## The Changing Role of the British Military

Britain once had the world's most powerful military forces, and counts within its military history some of the most effective soldiers and the most renowned of all military leaders. From those who won decisive victories over the French at the battles of Crecy in 1346 and Agincourt in 1415, to Sir Francis Drake and his defeat of the Spanish Armada in 1588, to the Duke of Marlborough who never lost a battle and defeated the French at Blenheim in 1704, to Lord Nelson and the Duke of Wellington who between them contributed so much to ending Napoleon's aspirations for European hegemony, to General Bernard Montgomery who inflicted the first major defeat on the Nazis at El Alamein in 1942, the list is impressive, and helps explain why Britain has not been invaded since 1066, and why it built the world's largest empire.

Following the Second World War, however, Britain began to withdraw from its military commitments around the world, and following the Suez crisis in 1956 was reduced to a second-rank power. It had played a leading role in the development of nuclear weapons during the closing years of the war, but was quicky overtaken by the United States, and while it still has an independent nuclear deterrent it is a relatively small one. From a time when British troops were committed all over the world to protect British interests and promote British policy, the British military in the 1970s was a shadow of its former self. Emphasizing its reduced condition, it came perilously close in 1982 to failing in a minor war against an inferior enemy.

On 20 April of that year, Argentina invaded the Falkland Islands, a British possession in the south Atlantic since 1834, inhabited by less than 2000 people. The Thatcher government responded by despatching a task-force of 100 ships and 25,000 soldiers and sailors, supported by a small number of aircraft carrier-based fighters. The troops fought bravely, but resources were spread so thinly that the task force had to commandeer commercial ferries and luxury cruisers to transport soldiers, the Royal Navy lived in danger of sustaining crippling losses from a handful of Exocet missiles fired by the Argentinian air force, and enough ships and helicopters were lost that the task force came close to losing the logistical support it needed to fight the war. The invasion of the Falklands ended with the surrender of Argentinian forces on 14 June.

In 1980, there were just over 320,000 personnel in the four branches of the regular forces: the Army, the Royal Air Force, the Royal Navy and the Royal Marines. The number went up slightly after the Falklands, but by 2001 had fallen to just under 211,000, a reduction of nearly one-third. Some of the slack was taken up by regular reserves, whose number increased over the same period by about one-third, to 282,000. At the same time, defence spending as a percentage of GDP was halved between 1985 and 2001, falling from 5.1 per cent to 2.5 per cent.

Soon after coming to power, the Blair administration developed the Strategic Defence Review (SDR), aimed at outlining Britain's options in the period until 2015. Published in 1998, it was the first such study in 17 years and the first to consider the needs and possibilities of the post-Cold War world (see Spear, 2000: 282–3). It concluded that there were no direct military threats to Britain, but that the end of the Cold War had introduced instability and uncertainty, and that there was a variety of new non-military threats faced by Britain, including the potential problem of the proliferation of nuclear, chemical and biological weapons, organized crime, and issues related to drugs, natural-resource issues and ethnic conflict. It argued that British forces would have to be ready to respond to a major crisis of a similar scale to the 1991 Gulf War, while being prepared for more extended commitments on a lesser scale, such as peacekeeping and relief operations. It also concluded that Britain should have the capacity to commit small and highly-trained groups of personnel into different situations at short notice. In support of the latter, the Blair administration gave its support to the development under EU auspices of a European rapid-deployment force.

**Illustration 8.2   The Royal Marines**

Royal Marine commandos during a live firing exercise in the Omani desert. The size of the British military has been reduced considerably in recent years, the new emphasis being on a small, efficient fighting force able to undertake many different roles.

Alongside its role in the conflicts in the Gulf, and in Serbia in 1999, the British military (Table 8.2) is a key element in NATO rapid-reaction forces, to which it has committed three aircraft carriers, 54 naval vessels, 12 nuclear-powered submarines, 55,000 troops and 140 aircraft. Meanwhile, it has been involved in UN peacekeeping operations in the Congo, Cyprus, East Timor and Georgia, international relief or evacuation operations in Angola, Eritrea, Mozambique, Rwanda and Somalia, as well as the following:

• After the breakdown of security in Sierra Leone in May 2000, and the taking hostage of UN peacekeepers by rebels, Britain deployed 600 troops to the war-torn country, and subsequently helped restore order and train a new army and police force.
• Britain contributes about 1700 troops to the Stabilization Force (SFOR) set up to help implement the 1995 peace accords in Bosnia and Herzegovina, as well as police officers taking part in the UN International Police Task Force. It also contributed about 10,000

*Table* 8.2   The British military, 2001

| Personnel: | 210,900 regular (114,000 Army, 54,000 Royal Air Force, 42,900 Royal Navy) and 282,000 reserves. Total: 492,900 |
|---|---|
| Nuclear warheads: | Less than 300, all sea-based, carried on four Trident submarines, no more than one of which is on patrol at any time with no more than 48 warheads |
| Aircraft: | 43 Jaguar fighters (scheduled to be replaced with the new Eurofighter), 48 Harrier fighters, nearly 200 Tornado fighter-bombers, more than 300 helicopters (including Apaches, Merlins, Pumas, Chinooks and Sea Kings) |
| Ships: | 3 aircraft carriers, 32 destroyers and frigates, 22 mine counter-measure ships, 10 Astute-class attack submarines armed with Tomahawk cruise missiles, 4 assault ships. Two new carriers on order, to enter service in 2012 |
| Defence spending: | 2.5 per cent of GDP |

*Source*:   Mainly Ministry of Defence, 2002, http://www.mod.uk.

troops to KFOR, deployed in Kosovo in 1999 to help restore peace following the NATO attack on Serbia.

● Following its small supporting military role in the attack on the Taliban regime in Afghanistan, launched by the United States following the September 2001 terrorist attacks in New York and Washington DC, Britain played the lead role in peacekeeping operations before handing over responsibility to Turkish forces in June 2002.

Ironically, the 1998 Strategic Defence Review was criticized for not dealing effectively with so-called 'asymmetric threats', such as terrorism and the threats posed by weapons of mass destruction, and also avoided the question of the development of a European defence identity. Yet these are the very issues which have now come to dominate discussions about the future of British defence policy.

The new role of terrorism in international affairs was most graphically illustrated by the September 2001 attacks. Among the more than 3000 victims of the destruction of the World Trade Center in New York were some 250 British citizens, making the event the biggest single loss of British lives in an attack of its kind. The Blair administration provided diplomatic and moral support to the new 'war on terrorism' declared by US President George W. Bush, and – as noted earlier – Tony Blair himself became the most visible and active of national leaders in support of US policies. It is still unclear, though, just how military forces are to be deployed in fighting a war against an unconventional enemy that is not tied to any one state.

# Conclusions

The major theme of this book has been change; it is the single concept that most completely defines the nature of contemporary Britain. Evidence of change can be found in almost every facet of national life, from the structure of the political system to the nature of society, from race and class relations to the links among the nations that make up Britain, from the definition of the family to the structure of the population, from the way people work to the way they play, and in almost every area of public policy, including the welfare system, education, health care, transportation, economic policy and foreign policy. It is ironic that a society with such deep roots in history, and that is so much a part of what is often described as the Old World, should be witnessing change at a pace far ahead of that found in most parts of the New World.

A key example of the nature of the changes can be found in Britain's political system. Its governing institutions – and the principles upon which its government is based – can be traced back more than 800 years, giving Britain a political continuity that is virtually unmatched in the world. Yet the role and the powers of the monarchy, of the office of prime minister, and of the two chambers of Parliament, and the relative roles of local, regional, national and European government have all undergone significant alteration even just in the past few years, with the promise of more to come.

Britain's economic record offers another example. From its status as the pre-eminent economic and trading power in the world, and the country that had the greatest single impact on the industrial revolution and on the development of capitalism, Britain first found itself building an extensive welfare state with a high level of government intervention in the marketplace, then undergoing rapid economic growth, then feeling the effects of retraction and crisis, then witnessing a sweeping withdrawal of government from the marketplace, then seeing both steady growth and rapid integration into the bigger European marketplace. The scale and the variety of change has

219

outpaced almost anything seen in the rest of Western Europe or North America.

The causes and the effects of all these changes have been examined in some detail in the preceding chapters. These conclusions will now try briefly to draw out some of the broader themes in the debate, underlining the forces that have had the most telling impact on the lives of Britons, and making some suggestions about where Britain may now be headed.

The most important influence on postwar Britain has been the re-definition of the meaning of 'Britain'. Externally, the British have had to adjust themselves to the idea that they are no longer a great power. From Suez to the collapse of the Berlin Wall, Britain was one of a group of middle-range powers that stood on the periphery of Cold War disputes between the superpowers. Today, it stands as one of a group of European powers that is undecided either over how to exert influence in the world or over how to influence the one remaining superpower, the United States. Fortunately, there are signs that the angst of post-imperial decline has finally been replaced by greater congruence between reality and aspiration. Instead of frustrating itself by trying to punch above its weight, Britain has finally reached the point where it is comfortable with its reduced role in the international system. The future will almost certainly see Britain acting more closely in concert with its European neighbours in its relationship with the rest of the world, and it will be defined less as a distinct political or economic entity, and more for its location within Europe.

Internally, the dominance of England over Scotland and Wales has declined. The last two generations have seen a newly assertive nationalism in both countries, more in the former than the latter, that has raised questions about the future health of the union. Although peace now reigns in the troubled province of Northern Ireland, it is a tenuous peace only, that regularly hovers on the brink of collapse as extremists on both sides of the divide reassert their objectives: continued union with Britain versus reunification with Ireland. Meanwhile, the definition of 'Britishness' continues to change as Britain becomes increasingly multicultural, and as Asian and Caribbean minorities are joined by waves of new arrivals from the continent, coming either as asylum-seekers or in the wake of the Europeanization of Britain. There is still much ground to be covered in the debate over the definition of 'Britain' and the 'United Kingdom', but it is unlikely that it will result in complete independence for Scotland.

The second important influence on postwar Britain has been the

European Union. Whether they like it or not, and many do not, the British are daily being further integrated into the networks that have pulled Western Europe closer together since the early 1950s. European law permeates British law, European policy plays a central role in areas as diverse as agriculture, consumer protection, the environment, fisheries, trade, transport and working conditions, and Britain makes its internal and external political and economic choices less in isolation and increasingly in concert with its European partners. While membership of the EU is voluntary, and Britain could theoretically leave if anti-European sentiment reached that level, even outside the EU it would be impossible for Britain to resist the gravitational pull of the continental European economic colossus. Eventual membership of the euro is all but inevitable, as are the creation of a European military force and the development of common European foreign and security policies. If for no other reason than to provide a counterbalance to the unilateralist tendencies of the United States in the world, it is important that Europe (with Britain) exerts its political, diplomatic and economic influence on the global stage.

The third important influence on postwar Britain has been the economic and social impact of Thatcherism. The prime minister herself left office in 1990, but her influence continues to be felt. While not all of her ideas may have been original, she – unlike some of her Conservative predecessors – was able to see those ideas implemented, and the combination of the changes made by her administration, some of them deliberate, some of them opportunistic, dramatically altered both the style of government and the economic and social character of Britain. Most notably, the government has stepped back from the marketplace. State monopolies have been replaced by competing private corporations, individuals have a greater direct role in the economy through ownership of shares and property, consumerism has grown, and British business now actually cares about what consumers want. Furthermore, instead of citizens expecting the state to provide, the state now asks citizens what they have done to merit that provision, and encourages greater self-reliance.

The changes that have come out of these three broad forces have been overwhelmingly positive. The British are healthier, wealthier and more self-sufficient than they were in 1945, they have rediscovered their competitive and entreprenurial spirit, greater emphasis is given than perhaps ever before to merit and social equality, and there is much greater general awareness of the problems that society faces and how they might be addressed. Many such problems remain, it is true, including poverty and social exclusion, racism, economic inequalities, inadequate public services, and crime. However, there is always a danger in focusing on short-term trends rather than the bigger picture, and there will always be a mixture of the good and the bad in those trends. Overall, Britain in the new millennium is a dynamic and forward-looking society with a global influence that is remarkable for a country of its size. It has undergone considerable change, and there is more to come as it both redefines itself, and redefines its place in the context both of Europe and the wider world.

# Recommended Reading

The literature on Britain is extensive and constantly changing, with literally thousands of new titles being published every year on the many different topics covered by this book. The selection that follows is very brief, emphasizes the most recent general introductions to each topic, and can do no more than help point readers in the right directions for further and more detailed study.

## 1  The Historical Context

Even though it focuses mainly on England and Wales, and is written for the American market, a general introductory survey to British history is the two-volume set by Roberts and Roberts (2002). A political and social history of Victorian Britain is offered by Rubinstein (1998), which can be followed up by two histories of the twentieth century, found in Clarke (1996) and Marwick (2000). There are numerous studies of developments in postwar British political history, including Coxall and Robins (1998) (which includes chapters on political parties and key policy issues) and Marsh *et al.* (1999). The literature on Thatcher and Thatcherism is extensive, but a good general survey is provided by Young (1990).

## 2  Land and People

Good introductory surveys to the geography of Britain include Johnston and Gardiner (1997) and Hardill *et al.* (2001). For books on the geology and natural resources of Britain, see Woodcock (2000) and Toghill (2002). Hawkes (1991) is a reprint of a book published in 1952 that is still regarded as an important study of the formation of the British landmass. Thomas (1996) offers a history of the changing relationship between people and nature in Britain, Hoskins (1999) provides a study of how the characteristic British landscape has evolved, and Garner (2000) looks at the environment as a political issue, and at key problems and responses. For a study of English national identity, see Kumar (2003) and for the equivalent on Scotland, see Pittock (2001). Adolino (1998) provides an assessment of the political context in which ethnic minorities find themselves.

## 3    The Social System

Two classic historical studies of class in England – which are still worth reading for context – are Engels (various) and Thompson (1966). A broader historical survey, assessing changes in the class system up to the Blair administration, is provided by Cannadine (2000), while Marshall *et al.* (1989) look at class structure and different conceptions of class. Singer (1999) has written a book that goes with the fascinating TV series *42 Up*, which looks at a group of Britons every seven years and watches how they change, providing insights into British society. McKay and Rowlingson (1999) offer a study of social security in Britain, while studies of health care and the National Health Service are offered by Baggott (1998), Ham (1999), Klein (2000) and Webster (2002). Much of the literature on education is critical or focused on making the case for reform, one example being Woodhead (2002). Croall (1998) looks at the links between crime and society, Davies *et al.* (1998) offer a guide to the criminal justice system in England and Wales, and Reiner (2000) has written a well-known text on the history and organization of the British police.

## 4    Politics and Government

There are numerous introductory surveys of British politics, including Kavanagh (2000), Jones *et al.* (2000) and Norton (2001), all of which cover all the key government institutions and political processes, but unfortunately have no chapters on public policies in Britain. Good edited collections offering recent analyses of key instititions and issues include Holliday *et al.* (1999), Budge *et al.* (2000) and Dunleavy *et al.* (2003). An edited collection of essays on public policy during the Blair administration can be found in Savage and Atkinson (2001). Smith (1999) writes a thought-provoking analysis of the 'core executive' in Britain, and Hennessy (2001) provides a survey of postwar prime ministers and their different governing styles.

## 5    Civil Society

Introductions to parties, elections, interest groups and the media can again be found in Kavanagh (2000) and Norton (2001). Leonard and Mortimore (2001) provide an introduction to the electoral system, while Baston and Henig (2002) have written a lengthy reference book with plenty of statistical data on the political characteristics of Britain. Butler and Kavanagh (2001) is the latest in the respected series of studies of general elections, and Worcester and Mortimore (2001) provide an analysis of Labour's victory at the polls in 2001. There are numerous studies of individual parties and their histories, but an overview is provided by Ingle (1999), while Giddens (2000) offers a defence of the logic behind the Third Way. Studies of the types and methods of pressure groups in Britain can be found in Grant (2000) and Coxall (2001), while the relationship between politics, the media and public relations is examined by Bartle and Griffiths (2001) and Davis (2002).

# 6 The Economy

Cairncross (1995) and Middleton (2000) provide assessments of British economic performance since 1945. A general survey of British economic policy is offered by Grant (2002), while a response to the idea of economic decline in Britain is offered by Booth (2001), which gives the broad view of the British economy during the twentieth century. There are numerous studies of the economic impact of Thatcherism, including Kavanagh (1987), Evans (1997) and Heffernan (2001) (the latter looks at the impact of her philosophy on Blair's Labour Party). Temperton (2001) looks at the pros and cons of Britain adopting the euro.

# 7 Culture and Lifestyle

Overall surveys of the state of British cultural studies – with an emphasis on the relationship between England, Scotland and Wales – are offered by Turner (1996), Bassnett (1997) and Morley and Robins (2001). A general assessment of theatre in Britain since 1945 is offered by Shellard (1999), a history of English literature can be found in Sanders (2000), and studies of British cinema are provided by Street (1997) and Murphy (2001). British pop culture is the subject of the book by Calcutt (2000), and the cultural and social impact of the Beatles is assessed by Inglis (2000). Two assessments of sport in Britain since 1945 are offered by Polley (1998) and Holt and Mason (2000).

# 8 Britain and the World

There are very few recent studies of the Commonwealth, but Kitchen (1996) provides a history, and Larby and Hannam (1993) provide a dated study of the organization. The few studies of Britain's place in NATO are now also dated, but the literature on NATO itself is extensive; examples include Sloan (2002) and Asmus (2002), while the Anglo–American special relationship is examined by Bull and Louis (1997) and Dumbrell (2001). The literature on the European Union is large and growing, with general surveys provided by Dinan (1999), Nugent (1999), Wallace and Wallace (2000) and McCormick (2002), and studies of Britain's relationship with the EU provided by Gowland and Turner (1999) and Pilkington (2001). Turner and Gowland (2000) offer a collection of key documents relating to Britain's relationship with the EU. For a study of the impact of EU policy on national defence policy, see Howorth and Menon (1997).

# Britain Online

In terms of the number of web sites available, and the number of people connected to the internet, Britain is second only to the United States. This means that there is a wealth of information that can be found electronically, and the list that follows barely scratches the surface. All these sites (and new ones as I find them) can be found on my webpage at http://mypage.iu.edu/ ~jmccormi.

## General

UKOnline: http://www.open.gov.uk
Office of National Statistics: http://www.statistics.gov.uk

## Society

National Health Service: http://www.nhs.uk
Department of Health: http://www.doh.gov.uk
Department of Education and Skills: http://www.dfes.gov.uk
Church of England: http://www.cofe.anglican.org
Church of Scotland: http://www.churchofscotland.org.uk
Commission for Racial Equality: http://www.cre.gov.uk
Law Society: http://www.lawsociety.org.uk
Home Office/British Crime Survey: http://www.homeoffice.gov.uk

## Government

British Monarchy: http://www.royal.gov.uk
Office of the Prime Minister: http://pm.gov.uk
Houses of Parliament: http://www.parliament.uk
Scottish Parliament: http://scottish.parliament.uk
National Assembly for Wales: http://wales.gov.uk
Northern Ireland Assembly: http://www.ni-assembly.gov.uk
Local Government Association: http://www.lga.gov.uk

## Civil society

Electoral Commission: http://www.electoralcommission.gov.uk
European Parliament: http://www.europarl.eu.int
Labour Party: http://www.labour.org.uk
Conservative Party: http://www.conservatives.com
Liberal Democrats: http://www.libdems.org.uk
Trades Union Congress: http://www.tuc.org.uk
Confederation of British Industry: http://www.cbi.org.uk
BBC: http://www.bbc.co.uk
ITV: http://www.itv.com
*The Times*: http://www.the-times.co.uk
Electronic Telegraph: http://www.telegraph.co.uk
*The Economist*: http://www.economist.com

## The Arts

Royal National Theatre: http://www.nationaltheatre.org.uk
Royal Shakespeare Company: http://www.rsc.org.uk
British Film Institute: http://www.bfi.org.uk
Britmovie: http://www.britmovie.co.uk

## Lifestyle

UK Sport: http://www.uksport.gov.uk
British Olympic Association: http://www.olympics.org.uk
Football Association: http://www.thefa.com
English Cricket Board: http://www.cricket.org/link_to_database/NATIONAL/
ENG
International Rugby Board: http://www.irb.com
UK and Ireland Tourist Boards: http://www.tourist-boards.com
British Tourist Authority: http://www.visitbritain.com

## International

Foreign and Commonwealth Office: http://www.fco.gov.uk
Ministry of Defence: http://www.mod.uk
Department of Trade and Industry: http://www.dti.gov.uk
The Commonwealth: http://www.thecommonwealth.org
European Union: http://www.europa.eu.int
North Atlantic Treaty Organization: http://www.nato.int

# Bibliography

Adolino, Jessica (1998) *Ethnic Minorities, Electoral Politics and Political Integration in Britain* (London: Pinter).

Adonis, Andrew and Stephen Pollard (1997) *A Class Act: The Myth of Britain's Classless Society* (London: Hamish Hamilton).

Alcock, Pete (2000) 'Welfare Policy', in Patrick Dunleavy, Andrew Gamble, Ian Holliday and Gillian Peele (eds), *Developments in British Politics 6* (Basingstoke: Palgrave).

Almond, Gabriel A. and Sidney Verba (eds) (1989) *The Civic Culture Revisited* (Newbury Park, CA: Sage Publications).

Anderson, Stephanie (1998) 'Problems and Possibilities: The Development of the CFSP from Maastricht to the 1996 IGC', in Pierre-Henri Laurent and Marc Maresceau (eds), *The State of the European Union Vol 4: Deepening and Widening* (Boulder: Lynne Rienner).

Asmus, Ronald (2002) *Opening NATO's Door* (New York: Columbia University Press).

Aughey, Arthur (2001) 'British Policy in Northern Ireland', in Stephen Savage and Rob Atkinson (eds) *Public Policy Under Blair* (Basingstoke: Palgrave).

Bagehot, Walter (1963) *The English Constitution* (Ithaca, NY: Cornell University Press).

Baggott, Rob (1998) *Health and Health Care in Britain* (Basingstoke: Macmillan, 1998).

Bartle, John and Dylan Griffiths (2001) *Political Communications Transformed: From Morrison to Mandelson* (Basingstoke: Palgrave).

Bassnett, Susan (ed.) (1997) *Studying British Cultures: An Introduction* (London: Routledge).

Baston, Lewis and Simon Henig (eds) (2002) *Political Map of Britain* (London: Politico's).

Booth, Alan (2001) *The British Economy in the Twentieth Century* (Basingstoke: Palgrave).

Budge, Ian, Ivor Crewe, David McKay and Ken Newton (2000) *The New British Politics*, 2nd edn (Harlow: Longman).

Bull, Hedley and William R. Louis (eds) (1997) *The Special Relationship: Anglo-American Relations Since 1945* (Oxford: Clarendon Press).

Buller, Jim (1999) 'Britain's Relations with the European Union in Historical

Perspective', in David Marsh *et al.* (eds), *Postwar British Politics in Perspective* (Cambridge: Polity Press).

Butler, David and Dennis Kavanagh (2001) *The British General Election of 2001* (Basingstoke: Palgrave).

Cairncross, Alec (1995) *The British Economy Since 1945: Economic Policy and Performance, 1945–1995*, 2nd edn (Oxford: Blackwell).

Calcutt, Andrew (2000) *Brit Cult: An A–Z of British Pop Culture* (London: Pion).

Cannadine, David (2000) *The Rise and Fall of Class in Britain* (New York: Columbia University Press).

Clarke, Peter (1996) *Hope and Glory: Britain 1900–1990* (London: Penguin).

Coxall, Bill (2001) *Pressure Groups in British Politics* (Harlow: Longman).

Coxall, Bill and Lynton Robins (1998) *British Politics Since the War* (Basingstoke: Macmillan).

Croall, Hazel (1998) *Crime and Society in Britain: An Introduction* (Harlow: Longman).

Davies, Alistair (2000) 'A Cinema In Between: Postwar British Cinema', in Alistair Davies and Alan Sinfield (eds), *British Culture of the Postwar* (London: Routledge).

Davies, Malcolm, Jane Tyver and Hazel Croall (1998) *Criminal Justice: An Introduction to the Criminal Justice System in England and Wales* (Harlow: Longman).

Davis, Aeron (2002) *Public Relations Democracy: Politics, Public Relations and the Mass Media in Britain* (Manchester: Manchester University Press).

Dinan, Desmond (1999) *Ever Closer Union: An Introduction to European Integration*, 2nd edn (Basingstoke: Macmillan, 1999).

Dumbrell, John (2001) *A Special Relationship: Anglo–American Relations in the Cold War and After* (Basingstoke: Palgrave Macmillan).

Dunleavy, Patrick (1997) 'Introduction: "New Times" in British Politics', in Patrick Dunleavy, Andrew Gamble, Ian Holliday and Gillian Peele (eds), *Developments in British Politics 5* (Basingstoke: Macmillan).

Dunleavy, Patrick (2000), 'Elections and Party Politics', in Patrick Dunleavy, Andrew Gamble, Ian Holliday and Gillian Peele (eds), *Developments in British Politics 6* (Basingstoke: Palgrave).

Dunleavy, Patrick, Andrew Gamble, Ian Holliday and Gillian Peele (eds) (2000) *Developments in British Politics 6* (Basingstoke: Palgrave).

Dunleavy, Patrick, Andrew Gamble, Richard Heffernan and Gillian Peele (eds) (2003) *Developments in British Politics 7* (Basingstoke: Palgrave Macmillan).

Engels, Friedrich (various years) *The Condition of the Working Class in England* (various publishers).

English, Richard and Michael Kenny (eds) (1999) *Rethinking British Decline* (Basingstoke: Macmillan).

Evans, Eric J. (1997) *Thatcher and Thatcherism*, 2nd edn (London: Routledge).

Fielding, Steven (2000) 'A New Politics?', in Patrick Dunleavy, Andrew Gamble, Ian Holliday and Gillian Peele (eds), *Developments in British Politics 6* (Basingstoke: Palgrave).

Finer, Catherine Jones (1997) 'Social Policy', in Patrick Dunleavy, Andrew Gamble, Ian Holliday and Gillian Peele (eds), *Developments in British Politics 5* (Basingstoke: Macmillan).

Gamble, Andrew (1999) 'State, Economy and Society', in Ian Holliday, Andrew Gamble and Geraint Parry (eds), *Fundamentals in British Politics* (Basingstoke: Macmillan).

Garner, Robert (2000) *Environmental Politics: Britain, Europe and the Global Environment*, 2nd edn (Basingstoke: Palgrave Macmillan).

George, Stephen (1992) *Britain and the European Community* (Oxford: Clarendon Press).

Giddens, Anthony (2000) *The Third Way And Its Critics* (Cambridge: Polity Press).

Gowland, David and Arthur Turner (1999) *Reluctant Europeans: Britain and European Integration, 1945–1998* (Harlow: Longman).

Grant, Wyn (1989) *Pressure Groups, Politics and Democracy in Britain* (London: Philip Allan).

Grant, Wyn (2000) *Pressure Groups and British Politics* (Basingstoke: Palgrave).

Grant, Wyn (2002) *Economic Policy in Britain* (Basingstoke: Palgrave Macmillan).

Hall, P. A. (1999) 'Social Capital in Britain', *British Journal of Political Science*, 29(3): 417–61.

Ham, Christopher (1999) *Health Policy in Britain* (Basingstoke: Macmillan).

Hardill, Irene, David Graham and Eleonore Kofman (eds) (2001) *Human Geography of the UK: An Introduction* (London: Routledge).

Hart, Vivien (1978) *Distrust and Democracy* (Cambridge: Cambridge University Press).

Hawkes, Jacquetta Hopkins (1991) *The Land* (Boston: Beacon).

Heffernan, Richard (2001) *New Labour and Thatcherism: Political Change in Britain* (Basingstoke: Palgrave Macmillan).

Hennessy, Peter (2001) *The Prime Minister: The Office and its Holders since 1945* (New York: Palgrave).

Hix, Simon (2000) 'Britain, the EU and the Euro', in Patrick Dunleavy, Andrew Gamble, Ian Holliday and Gillian Peele (eds), *Developments in British Politics 6* (Basingstoke: Palgrave).

Holland, Martin (1999) 'The Common Foreign and Security Policy', in Laura Cram, Desmond Dinan and Neill Nugent (eds), *Developments in the European Union* (Basingstoke: Macmillan).

Holliday, Ian, Andrew Gamble and Geraint Parry (eds) (1999) *Fundamentals in British Politics* (Basingstoke: Macmillan).

Holt, Richard and Tony Mason (2000) *Sport in Britain 1945–2000* (Oxford: Blackwell).

Hoskins, W. G. (1999) *The Making of the English Landscape* (London: Penguin).

Howorth, Jolyon and Anand Menon (1997) *The European Union and National Defence Policy* (London: Routledge).

Hutchings, Peter (2001) 'Beyond the New Wave: Realism in British Cinema, 1959–63', in Robert Murphy (ed.), *The British Cinema Book*, 2nd edn (London: British Film Institute).

Ingham, Geoffrey (1984) *Capitalism Divided? The City and Industry in British Social Development* (Basingstoke: Macmillan).

Ingle, Stephen (1999) *The British Party System* (London: Continuum International–Pinter).

Inglis, Ian (2000) *The Beatles, Popular Music and Society: A Thousand Voices* (Basingstoke: Macmillan).

Johnson, Nevil (1999) 'The Constitution', in Ian Holliday, Andrew Gamble and Geraint Parry (eds), *Fundamentals in British Politics* (New York: St Martin's Press).

Johnston, Ron and Vince Gardiner (1997) *The Changing Geography of the United Kingdom* (London: Routledge).

Jones, Bill and Dennis Kavanagh (1998) *British Politics Today*, 6th edn (Washington, DC: CQ Press).

Jones, Bill, Dennis Kavanagh, Philip Norton and Michael Moran (2000) *Politics UK*, 4th edn (Harlow: Longman).

Kaletsky, Anatole (2002) 'Sour Noises, but What a Sweet Taste', in *The World in 2003* (London: *The Economist*).

Kavanagh, Dennis (1987), *Thatcherism and British Politics: The End of Consensus?* (Oxford: Oxford University Press).

Kavanagh, Dennis (2000) *British Politics: Continuities and Change*, 4th edn (Oxford: Oxford University Press).

Kelly, Gavin (1997) 'Economic Policy', in Patrick Dunleavy, Andrew Gamble, Ian Holliday and Gillian Peele (eds), *Developments in British Politics 5* (Basingstoke: Macmillan).

Kendall, Ian and David Holloway (2001) 'Education Policy', in Stephen Savage and Rob Atkinson (eds), *Public Policy Under Blair* (Basingstoke: Palgrave).

Kerr, Peter (1999) 'The Postwar Consensus: A Woozle that Wasn't?', in David Marsh *et al.* (eds), *Postwar British Politics in Perspective* (Cambridge: Polity Press).

Kitchen, Martin (1996) *The British Empire and Commonwealth: A Short History* (Basingstoke: Macmillan).

Klein, Rudolf (2000) *New Politics of the National Health Service* (Harlow: Prentice Hall Thorne).

Kumar, Krishan (2003) *The Making of English National Identity* (Cambridge: Cambridge University Press).

Larby, Patricia and Harry Hannam (1993) *The Commonwealth* (Piscataway, NJ: Transaction Publishers).

Leonard, Dick and Roger Mortimore (2001) *Elections in Britain: A Voter's Guide* (Basingstoke: Palgrave).

Lowe, Philip and Jane Goyder (1983) *Environmental Groups in Politics* (London: Allen & Unwin).

Louis, William Roger and Roger Owens (eds) (1989) *Suez 1956: The Crisis and its Consequences* (Oxford: Clarendon Press).

Margetts, Helen (2000) 'Political Participation and Protest', in Patrick Dunleavy, Andrew Gamble, Ian Holliday and Gillian Peele (eds), *Developments in British Politics 6* (Basingstoke: Palgrave).

Marquand, David (1988) 'The Paradoxes of Thatcherism', in Robert Skidelsky (ed.), *Thatcherism* (London: Chatto & Windus).

Marsh, David, Jim Buller, Colin Hay, Jim Johnston, Peter Kerr, Stuart McAnulla and Matthew Watson (1999) *Postwar British Politics in Perspective* (Cambridge: Polity Press).

Marshall, Gordon, David Rose, Howard Newby and Carolyn Vogler (1989) *Social Class in Modern Britain* (London: Routledge).

Marwick, Arthur (2000) *A History of the Modern British Isles, 1914–99* (Oxford: Blackwell).

McCormick, John (2001) *Environmental Policy in the European Union* (Basingstoke: Palgrave).

McCormick, John (2002) *Understanding the European Union,* 2nd edn (Basingstoke: Palgrave).

McKay, Stephen and Karen Rowlingson (eds) (1999) *Social Security in Britain* (Basingstoke: Palgrave Macmillan).

Meehan, Elizabeth (1999) 'Citizenship and Identity', in Ian Holliday, Andrew Gamble and Geraint Parry (eds), *Fundamentals in British Politics* (New York: St Martin's Press).

Middleton, Roger (2000) *The British Economy Since 1945* (Basingstoke: Macmillan).

Mohan, John (1999) *A United Kingdom? Economic, Social and Political Geographies* (London: Arnold).

Morley, David and Kevin Robins (eds) (2001) *British Cultural Studies: Geography, Nationality and Identity* (New York: Oxford University Press).

Murphy, Robert (ed.) (2001) *The British Cinema Book,* 2nd edn (London: British Film Institute).

New Policy Institute/Joseph Rowntree Foundation (2002) *Monitoring Poverty and Social Exclusion,* <http://www.poverty.org.uk/intro/index.htm>

## 234    Bibliography

Norton, Philip (2001) *The British Polity*, 4th edn (New York: Longman).

Nugent, Neill (1999) *The Government and Politics of the European Union*, 4th edn (Basingstoke: Macmillan).

Obelkevich, James and Peter Catterall (1994) 'Understanding British Society', in James Obelkevich and Peter Catterall (eds), *Understanding Post-War British Society* (London: Routledge).

Pierre, Jon and Gerry Stoker (2000) 'Towards Multi-Level Governance', in Patrick Dunleavy, Andrew Gamble, Ian Holliday and Gillian Peele (eds), *Developments in British Politics 6* (Basingstoke: Palgrave).

Pilkington, Colin (2001) *Britain in the European Union Today*, 2nd edn (Manchester: Manchester University Press).

Pittock, Murray (2001) *Scottish Nationality* (Basingstoke: Palgrave Macmillan).

Polley, Martin (1998) *Moving the Goalposts: A History of Sport and Society since 1945* (London: Routledge).

Reiner, Robert (1999) 'Order and Discipline', in Ian Holliday, Andrew Gamble and Geraint Parry (eds), *Fundamentals in British Politics* (New York: St Martin's Press).

Reiner, Robert (2000) *The Politics of the Police*, 3rd edn (Oxford: Oxford University Press).

Richards, Jeffrey (1997) *Films and British National Identity: From Dickens to Dad's Army* (Manchester: Manchester University Press).

Riddell, Peter (1989) *The Thatcher Decade* (Oxford: Basil Blackwell).

Robbins, Keith (1998) *Great Britain: Identities, Institutions and the Idea of Britishness* (London: Longman).

Roberts, Clayton and David Roberts (2002) *A History of England, 1688 to the Present*, 4th edn (Englewood Cliffs, NJ: Prentice Hall).

Royal Society for the Protection of Birds (2002) <http://www.rspb.org>

Rubinstein, W. D. (1998) *Britain's Century: A Political and Social History 1815–1905* (London: Arnold).

Sanders, Andrew (2000) *The Short Oxford History of English Literature* (Oxford: Oxford University Press).

Sanders, David (1997) 'Voting and the Electorate', in Patrick Dunleavy, Andrew Gamble, Ian Holliday and Gillian Peele (eds), *Developments in British Politics 5* (Basingstoke: Macmillan).

Savage, Stephen and Rob Atkinson (eds) (2001) *Public Policy Under Blair* (Basingstoke: Palgrave).

Scammell, Margaret (2000) 'New Media, New Politics', in Patrick Dunleavy, Andrew Gamble, Ian Holliday and Gillian Peele (eds), *Developments in British Politics 6* (Basingstoke: Palgrave).

Shellard, Dominic (1999) *British Theatre Since the War* (New Haven: Yale University Press).

Shoard, Marion (1980) *The Theft of the Countryside* (London: Temple Smith).

Singer, Bennett (1999) *42 Up* (New York: New Press).

Sloan, Stanley R. (2002) *NATO, the European Union, and the Atlantic Community: The Transatlantic Bargain Reconsidered* (Lanham, MD: Rowman & Littlefield).

Smith, Adam (1976) *An Inquiry into the Nature and Causes of the Wealth of Nations* (Oxford: Clarendon Press).

Smith, Martin J. (1999) *The Core Executive in Britain* (Basingstoke: Macmillan).

Spear, Joanna (2000) 'Foreign and Defence Policy', in Patrick Dunleavy, Andrew Gamble, Ian Holliday and Gillian Peele (eds), *Developments in British Politics 6* (Basingstoke: Palgrave).

Street, Sarah (1997) *British National Cinema* (London: Routledge).

Temperton, Paul (2001) *The UK and the Euro* (London: John Wiley).

Thomas, Keith (1996) *Man and the Natural World: Changing Attitudes in England 1500–1800* (Oxford: Oxford University Press).

Thomas, Robert (1999) 'Law and Politics', in Ian Holliday, Andrew Gamble and Geraint Parry (eds), *Fundamentals in British Politics* (New York: St Martin's Press).

Thompson, Edward (1966) *Making of the English Working Class* (London: Random House).

Toghill, Peter (2002) *The Geology of Britain* (Shrewsbury: Airlife Publications Ltd).

Turner, Arthur and D. A. Gowland (eds) (2000) *Britain and European Integration: Primary Sources Since 1945* (London: Routledge).

Turner, Graeme (1996) *British Cultural Studies: An Introduction,* 2nd edn (London: Routledge).

Wallace, Helen and William Wallace (eds) (2000) *Policy-Making in the European Union,* 4th edn (Oxford: Oxford University Press).

Wallace, Michael and J. Craig Jenkins (1995) 'The New Class, Postindustrialism and Neocorporatism: Three Images of Social Protest in the Western Democracies', in J. Craig Jenkins and Bert Klandermans (eds), *The Politics of Social Protest: Comparative Perceptions on States and Social Movements* (London: University College London Press).

Webster, Charles (2002) *The National Health Service: A Political History* (Oxford: Oxford University Press).

Woodcock, Nigel (2000) *Geology and Environment in Britain and Ireland* (London: Taylor & Francis).

Woodhead, Chris (2002) *Class War: The State of British Education* (London: Little, Brown).

Worcester, Robert and Roger Mortimore (2001) *Explaining Labour's Second Landslide: Polls, Politics and Principles* (London: Politico's).

Young, Hugo (1990) *One of Us* (London: Pan Books).

Zurcher, Arnold J. (1958) *The Struggle to Unite Europe 1940–58* (New York: New York University Press).

*Note*:   Unless otherwise indicated, most statistics used in this book come from the Office of National Statistics (2001) *UK 2002: The Official Yearbook of Great Britain and Northern Ireland* (London: The Stationery Office), from the webpage of the ONS at <http://www.statistics.gov.uk>, or from Office of National Statistics (2002), *Social Trends 32* (London: Office of National Statistics).

# Index

238  *Index*